THE PLEASURES OF DEATH

THE PLEASURES OF DEATH

KURT COBAIN's Masochistic and Melancholic Persona

ARTHUR FLANNIGAN SAINT-AUBIN

Louisiana State University Press   Baton Rouge

Published by Louisiana State University Press
www.lsupress.org

Designer: Barbara Neely Bourgoyne
Typefaces: Sentinel, text; Gotham and Veneer Clean, display

Jacket image: *Cobain Death Mask,* 2020, by Hector Oman Hernandez

Illustration from *Journals* by Kurt Cobain, copyright © 2002, 2003, by The End of
Music, LLC. Used by permission of Riverhead, an imprint of Penguin Publishing Group,
a division of Penguin Random House LLC. All rights reserved.

Library of Congress Cataloging-in-Publication Data
Names: Saint-Aubin, Arthur Flannigan, author.
Title: The pleasures of death : Kurt Cobain's masochistic and melancholic persona /
    Arthur Flannigan Saint-Aubin.
Description: Baton Rouge : Louisiana State University Press, [2020] | Includes bibliographical
    references and index.
Identifiers: LCCN 2020018194 (print) | LCCN 2020018195 (ebook) | ISBN 978-0-8071-7349-7
    (cloth) | ISBN 978-0-8071-7468-5 (pdf) | ISBN 978-0-8071-7469-2 (epub)
Subjects: LCSH: Cobain, Kurt, 1967–1994—Criticism and interpretation. | Cobain, Kurt,
    1967–1994—Diaries—History and criticism. | Grunge music—History and criticism. |
    Masculinity. | Masochism. | Melancholy.
Classification: LCC ML420.C59 S23 2020 (print) | LCC ML420.C59 (ebook) | DDC
    782.42166092 [B]—dc23
LC record available at https://lccn.loc.gov/2020018194
LC ebook record available at https://lccn.loc.gov/2020018195

CONTENTS

ACKNOWLEDGMENTS

I am indebted to several friends who have encouraged and facilitated, in various ways, the researching and the writing of this book. I thank, first, Scott Hartstein, Michael Levy, and Gregory Toth for reading and commenting on initial drafts of some of these chapters. Next, I thank David Blank, mathematician at Grant High School in Van Nuys, California, for his generosity in sharing his incredible music collection, one that includes every genre and tens of thousands of twentieth- and twenty-first-century recordings, from the very obscure to the internationally famous. In addition, it was a distinctive joy to observe artist Hector Oman Hernandez create the cover image for the book. Finally, I thank William Poundstone, not only for his assistance in preparing the manuscript for this book, but for all the ways in which he enriches my life.

THE PLEASURES OF DEATH

READING KURT COBAIN
Consolation for the Disconsolate

Kurt Cobain was adept at creating complex, engaging lyrical and narrative texts. He was equally skilled at inventing captivating but unnerving characters that resemble him. *The Pleasures of Death,* at its most fundamental level, identifies and analyzes the persona that Cobain creates in his lyrics and journals. It interrogates the aesthetics and the politics of the first-person narrators and the other protagonists he creates in these literary texts. In undertaking a close reading of what Cobain writes, this book examines his signifying practice, that is, his narrative and lyrical strategies, and the ways in which his lyrics and journals "make sense." And what Cobain writes would seem to make particular sense for the bereft fan, for the disconsolate reader.

Although my reading of Cobain draws from previous studies of popular music culture that pose sociological questions and that speak to historical processes, it is also informed and shaped by theory, in particular by cultural studies, as this discipline has itself been informed by psychoanalytic aesthetics and by feminist, queer, and antiracist scholarship. Through an analysis of Cobain's writings, this study demonstrates how his creative texts operate to illuminate and, simultaneously, to complicate psychoanalytic paradigms of masochism, melancholy, and the death drive. To this end, the following chapters recursively pose a determinative question: How does Cobain succeed so uncannily in creating the persona of a young, white, heterosexual man who seeks self-destruction as the ultimate act of pleasure? In other words, how do gender, sexuality, and race appear conceptually and rhetorically within Cobain's creative writings? How does he conceive of these identity categories and what language and images does he use to convey them?

This defining query leads to the posing of two additional, interrelated questions. First, how does the white male body—as it appears within Cobain's lyrics and journals as a symbolic, gendered, and racialized construct—function as a defining theme within his writings? Second, how do his lyrics and journals function as a creative space, one in which memory and phantasy, real events and imaginary ones, interweave to produce fictions of an ideal, masculine self?[1]

Scholars and journalists have written hundreds of articles about Nirvana's front man, as well as several books that include some discussions of his life and music. Yet there is no book-length critical study that examines his creative writings exclusively and comprehensively. Most of what has been written about Cobain the person and the performer, both general-interest and scholarly publications, has been produced by writers who are also devotees of Nirvana and avid admirers of Cobain as a songwriter and musician. I did not, however, begin this present study of his lyrics and journals as a Nirvana fan, in the usual understanding of fandom. I did know, from interacting with hundreds of fans principally via social media, that the group's music possesses the capacity to profoundly move many listeners. And although I have come to appreciate Nirvana's music, I have been especially touched in specific ways by all of Cobain's published writings and by some of his visual art, as found in the drawings and sketches in his journals and on album covers.

Cobain's texts elicit powerful sensations and sentiments. They inspire me to think critically about notions of subjectivity and agency within the context of contemporary North American culture and politics. By "subjectivity," I mean the psychical structures and functions, like masochism and melancholy, that lead a person to a sense of self (an identity) and that, simultaneously, result from that sense of self. By "agency," I mean the comportments and actions that reinforce and crystallize one's identity for oneself and for other people.

In addition to prompting me to think discerningly about subjectivity and agency, some of Cobain's writings, like some of his visual art, call into account my material interests and implicate my sense of corporeality. I find certain of his lyrics, journal entries, and illustrations to be profoundly disquieting. I discover buried in them something disheartening about how the creative process functions, even though I do not discern in any single song, journal entry, or illustration some heretofore unknown truth about the *historical* Kurt Cobain. Rather, just as critical attempts to uncover the so-called truth about any artist can produce unanticipated results (McDayter, 133), what I also discover buried in Cobain's written texts—in a song like "I Hate Myself and Want to Die" or in a journal entry like "A Leonard Cohen Afterworld"—is a spectral embodiment of my own fear and desire.

While teaching a course in the mid-2000s (at a liberal arts college in Los Angeles) on the nineteenth-century French poet Arthur Rimbaud (1854–1891), I received an essay in which the student made a brief reference to the "parallels" between Cobain's lyrics and Rimbaud's poetry. His comparison first sparked my interest in Cobain and Nirvana. To be sure, there is indeed congruence between the Romantic traditions in general and Cobain. The very notion of a connection between authentic art and the premature death of the young artist—a notion that has come to encapsulate the popular image of Cobain and his music—traces back to the nineteenth century. The Romantic hero emerged as a rebel who valued authenticity and who resisted the way society was structured and functioned.

Over the past four decades, several scholars have explored "the historically grounded reasons for defining rock musicians as Romantics" (Rovira, *Introduction: Rock and Romanticism*, xv). Lexington Books publishes a series, titled appropriately "Rock and Romanticism," devoted to exploring this relationship. Books in the series examine the ways in which twentieth- and twenty-first-century rock musicians are inspired by and continue the traditions associated with the British Romantic poets, in particular Blake, Keats, and Wordsworth.[2] As Jennifer Otter Bickerdike summarizes:

> The bedrock of rock-and-roll mythology—youth, death, and authenticity—is clearly based on...Romantic traditions. The Romantic artist as hero embodying these traits provides the prototype for the later canonised rock singer. Rock and roll inherits the mythology of Romanticism, casting a new set of members in the roles of tragic icon, allowing familiar stories from the 19th century to be rehashed by a myriad of fashionable updates (1960s/1970s Bohemia, 1970s/1980s post-punk, 1980s/1990s grunge). (44)

My initial sampling of Nirvana's sound was not altogether positive. Although I found the music on the group's first album, *Bleach,* exhilarating, like many other listeners, I could barely decipher some of the lyrics. So I put the album aside with no intention of relistening. It was not until several years later, during a class discussion, when another student (in a survey course on French

Romanticism) began to insist on the comparisons between Cobain and the Romantics, that I decided to revisit Nirvana's music. On that occasion, I listened to the group's second and third studio albums, *Nevermind* and *In Utero*. More significantly for the evolution of my interest in Cobain, I researched the lyrics to some of these songs. Just as Warren Zanes in "A Fan's Notes" finds himself more interested in "image experiences than in music experiences" (293) when engaging with popular music culture, I found myself, as I listened to these two albums, more attuned to Cobain's words than to Nirvana's music.

Although the very sound of Cobain's voice certainly captivated me, the words he was singing, mumbling, and screaming—including the wordplay, the alliteration, and the unusual syntax—especially drew my attention and preoccupied me. Further, my specific teaching, research, and personal interests have informed my reading and interpretation of Cobain's lyrics, as well as my assessment of the significance of the writings and illustrations in his journals. These interests include French feminist and critical theories, francophone literature, and literary representations of the intersections of race and masculinity. As a result, my readings of Cobain's creative writings are necessarily "founded upon acts of appreciation and judgment within definite social [and cultural] relations" (Pickering, 44). As I shall underscore throughout this study, my approach to Cobain's works represents just one way, among others, of engaging with these texts.

There are musicological studies of grunge, and of alternative rock more broadly, that include analyses of Nirvana's songs.[3] But it is beyond the scope of this book to offer more than a passing, parenthetical observation on Nirvana's musical sound. Therefore, except for a few remarks that I specify, when I write about "music," I mean Cobain's lyrics. Like other students of literature, I concede that as a particular kind of literary and cultural critic, I am predisposed to analyze the written word. I am fully aware, however, that citing lyrics alone does not entirely get at all of the distinctive features that define about one-fourth of the written texts analyzed in this book. I realize that noise, rhythm, and "the grain of the voice"—to appropriate Roland Barthes's expression—are essential to the affective import and impact of Cobain's songs and his signifying practice.[4] As Catherine Strong writes, "looking only at lyrics misses important aspects of Cobain's delivery—such as ironic tone of voice—that affect the meaning of the words and the sound of the music itself" (9).[5]

Nevertheless, this study focuses primarily on Cobain's lyrical and narrative strategies in his songs and in his journals. It explores how his written texts emerge from within, engage with, and challenge a particular patriarchal social order. For the kind of reading of Cobain's texts undertaken here, I exploit some innovative scholarship in cultural studies that intersects with psychoanalysis as the theory has been critiqued and reformulated by politically progressive scholars and activists. Psychoanalytic aesthetics provide especially heuristic insights. They offer an incisive, critical language for examining Cobain's works because of the way psychoanalysis constitutes a theory of the content and structure of the psyche, a theory that allows for an understanding of how phantasy works. More decisively for my analysis of Cobain's creative output, psychoanalysis describes and then theorizes how the psyche interrelates with the body as a gendered and racialized construct. And Cobain's creative texts reveal themselves to be fatefully undergirded by the representation of a profound and irrepressible sense of corporeal vulnerability, including an unremitting disquiet because of the body's whiteness.

THE STRUCTURE AND CONTENT OF *THE PLEASURES OF DEATH*

It is manifestly as a classic literary analysis and as a cultural commentary that this book enters into a dialogue with the scholarship on Cobain, with popular culture scholarship more broadly, and with contemporary studies on gender, sexuality, and race. To this end, the book is divided into three interrelated parts: *Contexts, Texts,* and *Theories.* Part I begins with chapter 1, "From Punk to Nirvana: Toward a Profeminist, Gay-Affirmative Cultural Practice." This first chapter summarizes the roots and the constituent musical components of grunge. It also briefly outlines the genre's ideological and cultural effects. A summary account like the one presented here necessarily omits certain details and nuances. But even if this chapter did not present an abridged account, it could not provide a definitive history of grunge's birth and evolution, in part because the various observers and participants in the scene have different memories and conflicting opinions about this cultural phenomenon.

Since grunge's inception, a fair amount of revisionist history, oral and written, has taken place. It is precisely this revision and how the passage of time has altered certain fans' memory of their experiences that Catherine Strong investigates.[6] Some readers of my account of the history and cultural effects of grunge will surely balk at the nature and the extent of what I, too, have omitted or misinterpreted. As incomplete as this summary account might be, it is necessary, in part I of this study—subtitled *Music Histories and Masculinities*—to provide a historical framework with which to contextualize the specific details of the literary, cultural, and theoretical analyses that follow in parts II and III.

Part I continues with chapter 2, "The Cobain Persona, the White Male Body, and the Creation of an Ideal Masculine Self." This chapter has two objectives. It serves as an introduction to the literary analysis of Cobain's writings that follow immediately in the next two chapters, and it also lays the groundwork for the theorizing of the Cobain persona and for the cultural commentary that constitute the subjects of the final two chapters of the book. The second chapter reveals why representations of a white male body emerge as a symbol and as a symptom in Cobain's creative writings of all the iniquities that plague contemporary society. This chapter demonstrates why, therefore, an analysis of masculinity, whiteness, and heterosexuality occupies the very center of this study.

Further, chapter 2 also reveals why Freud's writings on masochism and melancholy and Melanie Klein's theories of "unconscious phantasy"—as well as her revision of Freud's theory of melancholy—are particularly expositive for understanding the persona that Cobain so meticulously creates in his lyrics and journals. At the same time, the chapter establishes why this book, although it draws upon the explicative potential of psychoanalytic theory, does not attempt to "psychoanalyze" the historical Kurt Cobain. Chapter 2 reveals why Cobain, even in his personal journals and in what appear to be autobiographical references in his lyrics, succeeds principally in writing pure fiction. Or, more precisely, he writes fiction as if it were his autobiography.

Part II of this book (*Texts: Lyrics and Journals*) begins with chapter 3, "Kurt Cobain's Lyrics: The Anxiety of Living as Male and Straight in a Misogynist and Heterosexist Culture." This chapter advances the current, limited scholarship on Cobain's lyrics. As Nick Soulsby indicates in *Dark Slivers,* previous studies generally fail to give full attention to how Cobain structures his songs. Therefore, chapter 3 examines these texts to the extent that they constitute, separately and collectively, a semiotic system and function as *representations*. It explores how signs and symbols in Cobain's lyrics operate to represent a certain kind of man and a particular mode of masculine comportment, thinking, and feeling. In examining the precise manner in which Cobain composes his songs, the chapter spotlights the literary techniques and modes of composition that he employs. In various ways, chapter 3 responds to the following questions: How do Cobain's narrative songs go about telling a story and creating characters? How do his lyrical songs go about generating and ascribing value to certain notions like masculinity? And how do specific subject matters, such as the male body, function as topics of reflection and as organizing themes within his lyrics?

Chapter 3, therefore, builds on previous studies of Cobain's lyrics but goes a step further. It demonstrates how the most conspicuous themes in his songs (contemptible masculine behavior, debilitated male corporeality, a desire for castration) constitute arresting representations of masculinity as a problematic subjectivity, as an identity, as I indicate, that is masochistic and melancholic. The chapter reveals, further, how specific Cobain lyrics posit death as the only possible means to recover a lost, ideal self. It also explores how and why phantasies of death, dying, and self-murder function within Cobain's lyrics in a coherent way. Most importantly, the chapter demonstrates how these phantasies operate in a way that does not depend on interpreting these songs in relation to Cobain's biography. It reveals how all of Cobain's songs, even when they might seem manifestly nonsensical, possess their own internal logic that does not depend on anything outside of this collection of texts—except an attentive, engaged reader—to produce meaning and make sense. Rather than referring to Cobain's biography, chapter 3 explores how different songs dialogue and intersect with each other to function as an ensemble. As a result, Cobain's overall lyrical production, I argue, possesses a certain consistency and an overarching cogency. His songs exhibit a defining logic and consonance that are present in his journals as well.

Part II of this book, which constitutes an in-depth literary analysis, continues with chapter 4, "The Pages of Kurt Cobain's Journals 'Smell Like Semen': Writing (with) the Male Body." This chapter comprises two sections. The first draws upon the writings of Melanie Klein in which the analyst establishes that phantasied experiences, or the workings of our inner world, do not have to be identified or interpreted according to their relationship to the events, objects, and people that exist in our real, outer world. Klein's writings inspire me to analyze Cobain's journals as an independent text, one that stands alone. Therefore, similar to my analysis of Cobain's lyrics, chapter 4 explores how his journal writing displays its own thesis and internal disputation, independently of his biography. When examined in this manner, the structure and content of Cobain's journals allow readers to discern the dynamics of the creative process in general, in other words, how a literary text comes into existence.

In the second section of chapter 4, I read Cobain's journals as a text that dialogues with and complements his lyrics. The chapter demonstrates how the text employs some of the same literary techniques as Cobain's lyrics and how his journals provide a rehearsal space for his songwriting. In one crucial way, however, Cobain's journals constitute the antithesis of his lyrics. Whereas his songs are devoid of any explicit mention of race or racial politics per se, racial difference undergirds some of the entries and illustrations in this fragmented text. That is, the text encodes the Cobain persona indelibly as white. The fragments that make up Cobain's journals establish, in ways that are both implicit and explicit, that hegemonic masculinity, as a social construct, cannot be extricated from whiteness.

In the second section of chapter 4, therefore, I read Cobain's journals as a *racialized* space. The text functions as a creative space in which the iniquity of racist acts and attitudes are cleverly exposed. Cobain's handwritten journals constitute a racialized space also to the extent that the writing is haunted, along with the text's other impressionistic narratives and surreal images, by a captivating but elusive "blackness." This part of the chapter demonstrate how and why the ghost of songwriter, musician, and performer Huddie William Ledbetter, aka Lead Belly (1889–1949), comes to loom over Cobain's personal writings. It also explores what Lead Belly's presence suggests about the relation between white and black masculinities, and their relationship to music performance, in the phantasy universe Cobain creates.

Part III of the book (*Theories: Masochism and Melancholy*), which presents a theoretical exploration and a cultural analysis, opens with chapter 5: "Power, Pleasure, and Pain: Creating a Masochistic Persona." The chapter begins by underscoring why the concept of masochism offers an effective, interpretive tool for analyzing Cobain's literary texts. Understood as a site where bodies, gender identities, and cultural norms converge, masochism allows me to examine the specific ways in which Cobain's lyrics and journals represent the white male body, caught within the throes of agony and ecstasy, as symbolic of hegemonic power.

The chapter presents, then, a concise assessment of the three principal texts in which Freud describes and theorizes masochism: *Three Essays on the Theory of Sexuality* (1905), "A Child Is Being Beaten" (1919), and "The Economic Problem of Masochism" (1925). Freud's understanding of the different degrees and the varying manifestations of masochism provides insights into how Cobain's creative writings represent the relationship, not only between masculinity and femininity, but also the relationship between hegemonic masculinity and nonhegemonic and queer masculinities. Both Freud and Cobain reveal, in similar ways, masculinity to be an extremely fraught, never-ending process, rather than a fixed, stable identity. In addition, it is in understanding Freud's theories that readers can appreciate how other theorists and scholars—like Gilles Deleuze, Kaja Silverman, and Judith Butler—have challenged Freudian theory in ways that facilitate an even deeper understanding of Cobain's creative process. These challenges illuminate the manner in which his texts represent masculinity as a particular way of experiencing cultural power wherein male subjects seek pleasure in physical pain and humiliation.

Chapter 5 proceeds to illustrate how Cobain's lyrics and journals confirm and, at the same time, contest the principal thesis of two seminal studies of masochism and the so-called masochist text: Kent L. Brintnall's "Masculinity, Masochism, and the Crucifixion: The Male-Body-in-Pain as Redemptive Figure" and David Savran's *Taking It Like a Man: White Masculinity, Masochism, and Contemporary American Culture*. Brintnall's reading of the masochist text and figure in literature, film, painting, and photography has inspired my reading of Cobain's creative output as representations of the male body as diseased and debilitated, as an object that is incomplete and constantly in the process of coming further undone.

For his part, Savran historicizes the relationship between masculine subjectivity and masochism in a way that authorizes my reading of Cobain's works within the broader context of certain American literary texts published throughout the second half of the twentieth century. Through this analysis, the chapter explores how Cobain's creative writings help to unravel the enigma that masochism poses for the overall coherence of psychoanalytic theory (and for the pleasure principle specifically): What is the exact origin of the male masochist's pleasure, his desire for pain and punishment? Cobain's writings also help to shed light on another question that has flummoxed some theorists and practitioners: What is the precise nature of the fault for which the male masochist finds ecstasy in being "whipped"?

Chapter 6, "The Pleasures of Death: Creating a Melancholic Persona," continues the cultural analysis and theoretical discussion begun in chapter 5. After briefly outlining the limitation of Freud's theory of mourning to make sense of the melancholic persona Cobain creates in his writings, this chapter draws from Melanie Klein's theories and from the work of more contemporary scholars like Ester Sáchez-Pado and Leo Bersani. These scholars address, among other topics, the politics of melancholy and the reasons why melancholy has traditionally been described as a *masculine* form of expression. Further, in exploring the notion of the "gender of melancholy," this chapter analyzes Cobain's suicide letter as a narcissistic performance of a doomed masculinity.

Chapter 6 then proceeds to demonstrate how recent historicist and theoretical writings (by Jennifer Radden, Julia Kristeva, Hélène Cixous) facilitate an understanding of Cobain's texts in two significant ways. On the one hand, these writings bring into sharper focus how Cobain's texts establish a relationship between the grieving of an insufferable loss and sexuality. On the other hand, these writings illuminate how Cobain's lyrics and journals establish a relationship between grieving and creativity. Further, Kristeva's literary analysis of the nineteenth-century poet Gérard de Nerval helps to expose even further the deep parallels that exist between Cobainian grunge, as a literary genre, and French Romantic aesthetics. This chapter posits that Cobain and Nerval are part of a continuing literary tradition, one that speaks to the commensurability of creativity, madness, and the compulsion to commit suicide.

As with masochism, Cobain's lyrics and journals both illuminate and complicate psychoanalytic understandings of melancholy. His creative texts provide a possible response to a question that remains unsatisfactorily answered within psychoanalytic theory concerning the origins and the effects of melancholy: Under what precise circumstances and for what kind of subject does the normal process of mourning turn into clinical depression and the madness of melancholy? Although Cobain's writings certainly do not put forth a simple or definitive answer to this complex question, they do point us in a productive direction.

Finally, the concluding chapter in this book ties together the arguments developed throughout the three sections. It reveals the specific and sometimes surprising ways in which Cobain's lyrics and journals buttress the notion that there exists a relationship between madness and literary genius. The chapter demonstrates the uncanny way Cobain's melancholy lyrics and journal fragments, like the most affecting verse by the Romantic poets, do more than simply allow readers to revel in the creative universe he brings into existence. His inventive texts, even as they put forth death as the ultimate act of pleasure for someone in utter despair, do more than point to suicide as ineluctable on the part of the dispossessed and the bereft. Cobain's most poignant lyrics and journal fragments suggest the ways in which both writing and *reading* about melancholy can be life-affirming, can provide a means to self-knowledge and a self-transformation. Thus, as the forthcoming chapters implicitly reveal, reading and actively engaging with Cobain's creative writings can provide some consolation, even for the irremediably disconsolate.

CONTEXTS
MUSIC HISTORIES AND MASCULINITIES

1

FROM PUNK TO NIRVANA
Toward a Profeminist, Gay-Affirmative Cultural Practice

In his 1993 book *From the Velvets to the Voidoids,* English critic Clinton Heylin wrote that the 1970s New York punk bands had "set out to reform rock music, believing in an immutable alliance between pop and rock." The early Seattle Punks had pursued pretty much the same goal, with perhaps a slight digression during the early Sub Pop years. Nirvana's *Nevermind* was a slickly packaged CD whose superficially simple sound masked a wide array of influences, from the Sex Pistols to the Pixies. The band turned the rage of classic punk into a pure, crystalline entity. It turned *despair* into defiance, *depression* into urgency. Its ugliness was beautiful.
   —CLARK HUMPHREY, *Loser: The Real Seattle Music Story* (169; emphasis added)

The persona that Kurt Cobain adopts in his written texts is represented as a young man immersed in a painful process of self-discovery, a process profoundly marked by experiences of despair and depression. He presents himself explicitly as oppositional to the cultural hegemony. A resistance to the aesthetics and politics of mainstream rock music symbolizes this opposition, as Cobain takes on the persona of a songwriter and performer dedicated to music as art, as opposed to the commercial product distributed by the music industry. He is also a young man who brandishes his profeminist, gay-affirmative politics. But as the Cobain persona emerges in individual texts like the song "In Bloom" or like the central entry in his published journals, he displays a complex and contradictory identity. Though loudly professing his punk ethics, he also reveals his mainstream inclinations; and though embracing a progressive stance in regards to women and to black and gay men, he simultaneously reaffirms his white-male, heterosexual privilege. As the portrait of this conflicted persona comes into partial focus from one Cobain text to the next, it confirms that identity itself is always a fraught process that is subject to failure (Seshadri-Crooks, 358). The persona in which Kurt Cobain is so invested is represented, ultimately, as aspirational but never completely achieved. Like every instance of identification according to Judith Butler, this persona can only be a phantasy, the result of desperate but doomed efforts to align the real and the imaginary, body and psyche, the physical and the emotional (*Bodies That Matter,* 105).

If Clark Humphrey, as cited in the above epigraph, is correct, then the album *Nevermind* might be seen as emblematic of the complexity and the contradiction that define the persona that Cobain inhabits. To the surprise of some record executives, the album began its ascent to the top position on the American charts late in 1991. Since that time, critics, musicians, and audiences have debated what constitute the precise sonic components and the evolution of the so-called Seattle sound. In particular, as I shall have occasion to highlight below, journalists and academics continue to debate two related questions: Which band was the first to adopt the distinctive, dirty guitar sound that has come to be identified as grunge? And which bands have performed the music in its purest, original form?[1] One can attribute this polemic to the fact that there are varying definitions of grunge, which, as a music subgenre, constitutes a hybridized sound that emerged and evolved during the 1980s and 1990s. Grunge is also a sound that various musicians have produced in different ways.

The objective of this chapter is simple. As indicated in the introduction, it provides the historical context within which readers can situate the literary, cultural, and theory-based analyses of Cobain's lyrics and journals that constitute parts II and III of this study. By suggesting how grunge, and specifically Nirvana's sound and image, emerged within a punk aesthetic, the chapter locates Cobain's music within the larger U.S. alternative rock scenes and subcultures.[2] Alternative rock was nourished in particular by the music practices of hardcore and heavy metal. I summarize specifically the relationship between these genres, on the one hand, and experiences of the male body and performances of white masculinity, on the other, as a prelude to my examination of representations of gender, sexuality, and race in Cobain's written texts.

Although the sound and images of grunge constitute a distinct subgenre, this sound and these images are indeed diverse. This diversity of sound allows for the mainstream success of some musicians and the marginalization of others. In examining the cultural significance of grunge, one should distinguish between three variations of the genre. Early grunge (proto-grunge) must be differentiated from commercial grunge, which in turn must not be conflated with the "post-grunge aftershocks" (Henderson, 3). These aftershocks have continued to influence bands enjoying commercial success during the 2000s (such as Creed and Nickelback). Postgrunge sounds have also influenced other twenty-first-century music movements such as emo and stoner rock in particular (Strong, 20). It is important to point out that early on in the development of the subgenre, practitioners and observers of the scene rejected the term "grunge" as it came to be used within the music industry and within the popular press.

As a rock subgenre, grunge can be located, as the epigraph to this chapter suggests, within a specific historical period. The history of the United States in the 1980s and 1990s, and the social and cultural changes that characterize this period, are crucial for a thorough understanding of the music that Kurt Cobain produced and consumed. Nevertheless, there are theoretical and practical implications of attempting to confine any popular music genre to an exact chronological period. Therefore, even as I sketch a brief history of grunge, and of alternative guitar rock more broadly, as an introduction to my analysis of Cobain's written texts, I call into question the very notion that these genres have followed a linear development from their inception to their seeming decline or disappearance.[3] Popular music genres do exist within particular groups of individuals at particular historical moments, but the borders that define popular genres are never fixed or uncontested. On the contrary, they are porous, shifting, and often challenged.

In this sense, I subscribe to Keith Negus's approach to popular music history, an approach that examines this history as a continuing process. During this process, new musical forms are created as the result of how these emerging forms draw from and refashion those that preceded them. In this sense also, although I concentrate in chapter 3 on Cobain's songs as discrete texts that together form an eclectic ensemble, I realize that his lyrics entertain a relationship not only with the lyrical productions of other musicians during the 1980s and the 1990s, but also with rock songs from previous generations.

In addition, as suggested in the introduction, we must understand the content and the structuring of Cobain's songs as existing within even broader historical and cultural traditions. These traditions include not only the lyrics of other rock musicians; they encompass, in addition to nineteenth-century Romantic poetry, other cultural productions like postmodern art and literature, and other sociological phenomena such as the civil rights, women's, and gay movements.

In analyzing Cobain's written texts, I construct my argument upon the premise that grunge is not only, or even primarily, a music genre defined by its sonic components. I posit grunge, as the term applies specifically to Cobain's lyrics and journals, as a subject-position. Grunge designates a specific social and cultural identity, a particular way of viewing the world and one's relationship to it. As Negus reminds readers, it is Will Straw who underscores that alternative rock, along with dance music, are the two most conspicuous genres for the way they create race, gender, and age boundaries and, simultaneously, for the way they respond to already existing divisions (23).

Even though I argue that grunge constitutes more than a music expression, I begin by summarizing and contextualizing the discussions that center on its sonic features. I also summarize and put into context some of the extramusical practices involved in the making of and listening to the music, such as dancing and the particular way musicians talk about their participation in the subculture. As I explore how Cobain's texts are structured and how they produce meaning, these discussions have informed my overall understanding of Cobain's version of grunge as one sign of a social and psychical crisis of masculinity. The debate concerning the sonic features of grunge has also informed my understanding of grunge as a *performance* of affect (melancholy) and as the expression of a particular relation to social and cultural power (masochism).

When grunge is isolated as a subgenre within contemporary rock, the relatively unknown Seattle band Coffin Break were among the first to produce what has come to be known as the Seattle sound.[4] In addition, because of the group's extensive touring, some participants in the scene consider these musicians to have been the first to "spread Seattle rock gospel along a developing grunge trail" (Humphrey, 114). Further, there seems to be little dispute that the group Mudhoney also played a determinant role in coalescing and popularizing the Seattle subculture and its music. Mudhoney constituted the showpiece of Sub Pop Records, the independent label closely associated with the creation of the mythology surrounding grunge. For some observers, Mudhoney were the musicians who "spearheaded the Seattle grunge explosion, [and] who blazed a trail for Nirvana" (Azerrad, *Our Band,* 411). Sub Pop helped to nurture the Northwest alternative subculture, and the label's owners succeeded in selling the myth of the subculture internationally.

Most popular music historians and most fans see Nirvana as the group that epitomizes Seattle grunge. They consider Cobain, as the group's front man and songwriter, the poster boy of grunge ethics and aesthetics. In the simplest of terms, grunge, even as it morphed and molted as an alternative rock subgenre, continued to be characterized by its powerful riffs, its distortion and feedback, and its heavy drumming. In this respect, grunge, as Cobain wrote and performed it, represents principally a marriage between hardcore punk and heavy metal, as Perry Grossman has documented in "The Dialectics . . . of Grunge."

Within the overall history of grunge and alternative music (or independent rock), Cobain does occupy a singular position. Like other practitioners of the music, he drew from the practices of hardcore punk, heavy metal, and other genres. He did so, however, in a particular way. While engaging with the sounds, words, and images of the emerging grunge subgenre, he synthesized these elements in a distinctive manner that resulted in the creation of a music style and, most importantly, the forging of a persona that showcased his creative talent and that appealed to many listeners. As Negus concludes about a certain category of exceptional performers, Cobain succeeded in producing new music, words, and images by "working at the fuzzy boundaries where [the] generic codes and stylistic conventions" (146) of hardcore, heavy metal, new wave, and elements from other subgenres fuse and interconnect.

Given Cobain's influences and his method of composing music and lyrics, it is necessary to explore, first, why certain musicians like him appropriated and then reinflected a version of punk rock known as hardcore together with heavy metal into the music practice of grunge. Next, it is necessary to explore why grunge, seemingly conceived in part as an antidote to corporate, mainstream music, would appeal to young white men in general and, for my present purposes, to the persona that Cobain was cultivating in particular. A brief examination of these two questions allows me to explore more precisely how Cobain's words and images produce meaning. At the same time, I am able to speak to the overall cultural significance of his creative writings.

PUNK: THE GENESIS OF COBAIN'S AESTHETIC IDEAL AND PRACTICE

When Cobain proclaims himself and his music, in his journals specifically, to be "punk," he means what many other musicians, like the Minutemen, for example, meant during the 1980s by the term. He was professing a connection to a particular community and a method of creative production and self-expression, more so than affirming a preference for a narrowly defined sound (R. Moore, 73). First-wave punk developed between 1974 and 1976 initially in the anglophone countries of the United Kingdom, the United States, and Australia. As Ryan Moore specifies, punk emerged during a period of social and economic change:

> With the benefit of historical distance, we can . . . see that punk emerged in a pivotal moment of transition in the global political economy, as social democracy of [the postwar economy] gave way to a more unforgiving brand of unfettered capitalism. The story of punk's ignition therefore takes on further significance as a harbinger of the descent into a callous society devoid of alternatives. Punk should be seen as the final stage in the collapse of Sixties utopianism and the broader conditions of economic affluence and cultural idealism that nurtured it. (36–37)

Like Cobain's cohort, earlier musicians and audiences had also used the term punk more frequently to designate a particular attitude and sensibility (having to do with personal style and a method of music production) than to designate a specific music sound or style. Musicians who adopted this attitude and who exhibited this sensibility—from the Ramones to Blondie—also produced a diversity of sounds.

As Moore also confirms, punk emerged as a response to what musicians, audiences, and observers considered the decline of rock in wake of the ineffectiveness of 1960s' utopianism. According to this view, the rebellion of rock music and the demands for social change that defined the counterculture had ceased to play a significant role in contemporary society. Rock had devolved into a pure commodity consumed by a duped audience. Because of their disdain for rock as a music expression deemed socially irrelevant and responsible for separating performers from fans via stadium concerts, first-wave punk rockers, in the name of authenticity, prized a direct connection to their audiences.[5] In addition to putting a premium on access to the means of music production, musicians also valued the do-it-yourself (DYI) ethic when it came to touring, recording, advertising, and distributing their music. All these practices were designed to distinguish punk rockers from what was seen as the excessive, self-indulgent touring and recording demands of the most commercially successful rock bands at the time (for example, The Who and Styx). Such demands, according to practitioners of punk, played a crucial role in the emergence of an inferior, commercial product.

Dick Hebdige has linked punk's resistance to the radical aesthetic practices of the post-World War I artistic movements (the Dadaists and the Surrealists). He links punk to these movements because of the way the punk subculture created different modes of dress and language in addition to different preferences in music (Hebdige, 106). All these differences defied in some way the conventions of the larger culture. Historians also link punk to the avant-garde artists, thinkers, and political theorists and activists of the mid-twentieth century (the Situationist International). In this sense, punk impulses constitute concerted efforts to de-center and subvert the conventions of bourgeois society.

It is in this sense precisely that Cobain's aesthetic ideal and practice can be considered punk. His lyrics and journals function, in part, to resist conventional norms of gender and sexuality, and, implicitly at least, practices of racial injustice as well. His creative writings put forth a symbolic defiance of these conventions, rather than a resistance with a clearly articulated, coherent political objective. Defiance is manifest in the way his lyrics and journal writing are meant to be verbally and visually provocative. This provocation, nevertheless, does have a certain political resonance, even if it is devoid of an actual political aim or effect.

Cobain's Aesthetic Dichotomy: The Allure and Repulsion of Hardcore and Heavy Metal

By the end of the 1970s, punk was experiencing both a musical and a cultural division. On the one hand, some musicians, marketed as "new wave," modulated the harshness of their music and even achieved some commercial success. Among this cohort, certain performers continued to eschew commercial acceptance and instead chose to innovate and experiment, both lyrically and musically, in ways that precluded their mainstream viability. On the other hand, practitioners of hardcore, a faster and more aggressive form of punk, came to dominate the different scenes. The hardcore sound is exemplified by the expression "Loud Fast Rules," which is the title of a single by a little-written-about New York band, the Stimulators, and the name of a Minneapolis band (aka Soul Asylum). Hardcore musicians aligned themselves with local underground scenes in ways that produced a variety of punk hybrid sounds, scenes, and subcultures. The underground scenes in the state of Washington would come to influence Cobain and he would leave his imprint on them.[6]

Because rock is an evolving music form that intersects with, draws from, and transforms both current and past forms, it is not surprising that during a span of time in the 1970s in the United States, some journalists, fans, and musicians used the terms "punk" and "hardcore" together and interchangeably. In effect, some groups, like the Dead Kennedys, began by recording first-wave punk music but then transitioned to a hardcore style with their later recordings. Only during the late '70s did the term "hardcore" begin to designate more consistently a mode of music that was stylistically and sonically different from original punk. Whether one labels this mode "hardcore punk" or, more frequently, simply as "hardcore," one of the subgenres that drew Cobain's attention is indeed played at a faster pace; it is more abrasive and assaultive to the ears.

In addition, hardcore vocalists frequently do not sing; rather they distinguish themselves in part by screaming, growling, and talking. There was a variety of sounds, looks, and styles within the different hardcore scenes, too. All of them, as a general rule, accentuated the male-dominated center of gravity and the masculinist orientation already present, though not always dominant, in original punk. This center and this orientation are evident also in the entirety of the rock movement since its very inception.[7] Within hardcore, as within other rock subcultures, it was a particular form of dancing and a particular group dynamic during live performances that came to signal the masculinist orientation and the centrality of the male body within the hardcore scenes.

Initially, hardcore participants were generally younger than the original punk rockers and, judging from the songwriting and some of the nonmusical antics of musicians and their audiences during live performances (fighting and excessive drinking in addition to dancing), they seemed more frustrated and angrier as well. Hardcore shows, for example, would devolve typically into violent interactions between young men often misbehaving. As some musicians and critics ask, either explicitly or implicitly, should we conclude that it was because hardcore shows would often degenerate into violent interactions that some women chose not to attend? Or would it be more accurate to argue that it is because more women did not attend that hardcore shows became, so predictably, violent showcases?[8]

Whatever the reason, some hardcore performances came increasingly to attract younger and more easily provoked groups of young, predominantly white men who seemed bent on acting on, and acting out, their individual and collective frustrations and phantasies. In this way, hardcore differed from original punk. Though exhibiting a soupçon of masculine rebellion and male strutting, punk celebrated self-expression and self-empowerment in other nonmacho ways that did not automatically marginalize or exclude altogether women practitioners. Cobain, explicitly in his journals and implicitly in some of his lyrics, resists the masculinist impulses of hardcore by claiming femininity as an integral part of the persona he was cultivating. He also resists by recognizing and celebrating the contributions of women, not only to music but to the arts in general and to humanity overall.

In some of their initial attempts to theorize the relation between rock music and experiences of gender and sexuality, sociologists postulated that the music functioned in part to *express* and to *police* heterosexual masculinity (Frith and McRobbie, "Rock and Sexuality"). Rock musicians and their audiences, however, deliberately engage in musical and extra-musical practices and strategies that do more than express and police gender and sexuality. These practices actively construct dominant versions of masculinity and heterosexuality. In other words, the masculinist orientation of the alternative scenes was part of a process that Robert Walser, in *Running With the Devil*, calls "identity work." Cobain's lyrics and journals confirm—just as Negus concludes about popular music in general—that the practices of hardcore, rather than merely reflecting the gender identity of bands and fans, "are caught within, arise out of, and refer to a web of unequal social relations and power struggles" that exist within the culture at large (70).

Cobain's creative writings, I argue, lead us to conclude more specifically that a particular mode of white-masculine heterosexuality, or what Mimi Nguyen refers to as the "whitestraightboy hegemony," mediates the creation and reception of hardcore (Duncombe and Tremblay, 12). The genre, in turn, operates to facilitate the ways musicians and audiences construct their gender, sexual, and racial identities. In addition, the hardcore that Cobain inherits, just like the heavy metal he absorbs, has come to be constructed as masculine and heterosexual in a specific manner that makes it difficult, but not impossible, for the codes and conventions of these two genres to accommodate antisexist and gay-affirmative sentiments and practices. As I shall explore, Cobain's lyrics and journals succeed, in distinctive ways, in taking on the challenge that these countervailing generic codes and conventions pose for the persona he was espousing and the cultural politics that this specific persona implied.

Heavy Metal, Experiences of the Male Body, and the Construction of White Masculinities

What is it about heavy metal that would appeal to the sensibilities of the persona Cobain was so consistently projecting during his media appearances and that he was inscribing implicitly in his lyrics and explicitly in his journals? As with other rock labels, the meaning of "heavy metal" depends on the date to which one is referring and on who is using the term. Many critics and journalists—during a period in the 1970s in particular—have used the labels "heavy metal" and "hard rock" (not to be confused with hardcore) to describe music that is very similar but not precisely identical. The music of Aerosmith, for example, is designated in the 1983 *Rolling Stone Encyclopedia of Rock & Roll* as both heavy metal and hard rock. Many other bands during the early period of heavy metal, like Blue Oyster Cult (1977) and Kiss (1974), could have been tagged with either or both labels. Take, for instance, AC/DC's debut album *High Voltage.* Whereas rock historian Clinton Walker maintains that AC/DC was never truly heavy metal, the editors of the *Rolling Stone Encyclopedia* describe the music as an example of very good Australian heavy metal.[9]

Heavy metal as a distinctive sound can be traced back to the late 1960s and early 1970s in the United Kingdom first and then in the United States. Inspired in heavy metal's earliest manifestations by both blues-inspired rock and psychedelic rock, heavy metal musicians favored a sound that resorted to amplified distortion and indulgent solos by guitarists. Metal's overall sound is usually described, appropriately, as "heavy" and "massive." "Heavy metal picked up the loudest and gloomiest sounds to emerge from blues-inflected rock at the end of the 1960s. As a style, it merged the hippie counterculture with the hypermasculine, proletarian image of the motorcycle gang" (R. Moore, 9). U.K. bands like Black Sabbath, Led Zeppelin, and Deep Purple count among the musicians who pioneered the sound and whose recordings would influence Cobain and other alternative musicians in the United States during the 1980s and 1990s.

Lyrically, and in terms of stage performance, heavy metal operates in a dialectical relationship with a particular notion of masculinity that is shamelessly macho and aggressive. Critics contribute the genre's appeal and longevity, in large part, to the exclusionary masculinity that the subculture absorbs, reconstructs, and projects. Most critics, especially academics, dismiss heavy metal because of its reliance on visual spectacle and its blatant pursuit of the trappings of commercial success. Critics also consider metal's music to be formulaic and stylized and its typical lyrics to be vacuous, insipid, or asinine.[10] Yet there is a lyrical tradition in metal that Cobain adopts, though he does so more often in his journals than in his actual lyrics. In the tradition of Black Sabbath, for example, the stereotypical metal lyrics are somber and depressing narratives of death, phantasy, and escapism. These same kinds of dark narratives do appear in a few of Cobain's journal entries.

Overall, heavy metal, like hardcore, would appear to be anathema to the ideals and sensibilities of the persona that Cobain so skillfully constructs, as represented especially in many of his journal entries. The typical metal fan, as Ryan Moore persuasively argues, is a young, white, working-class man who identifies, at least symbolically, with the image that he has of a rebellious Hell's Angels–type man, an iconic figure of an earlier working-class subculture. This enduring prototype is characterized by a militaristic hypermasculinity and by a deep suspicion of—and sometimes open hostility—toward racial, gender, and sexual differences.

Influenced by earlier theorists of punk, Moore begins his own incisive study of the subculture with the premise that there are "points of intersection between music and youth culture, on the one hand, and the transformation of political economy and social structure, on the other" (5). He puts forth a method of understanding popular music as a reflection and a corollary of social and economic structures and changes. He does so in a way that can help explain the specific manner in which Cobain's written texts represent race, gender, and generational differences. Moore's analysis demonstrates precisely how music production and consumption during Cobain's lifetime can be linked to twentieth-century historical developments in American society (specifically, the ascension of right-wing politics during the Reagan and Bush administrations).

The typical U.S. metal enthusiast may not be able to articulate the exact cause of his alienation. Nevertheless, according to critics who adopt a materialist approach in studying music subcultures, he feels disempowered because of the social and political changes brought on in particular by the civil rights and women's movements and by changes in the economy of the period. These changes were accompanied by a decline in the standard of living for many white, working-class families. Rather than finding recourse in political activism or social mobilization and thereby confronting *real* power, though, fans and musicians turned to metal and the phantasy worlds that the genre provides. Within the metal subculture, these men symbolically empower themselves, assume roles of domination, and indulge their rebellious instincts within metal's mythological and supernatural narratives. Metal's volume and noise provide a vicarious and creative way for certain white, working-class youth to express their anxiety and aggravation in light of their declining economic, political, and social fortunes. The volume of heavy metal, as evident in early bands like Blue Cheer, owe a debt to Jimi Hendrix, Cream, and The Who. Hendrix, along with other U.S. and U.K. guitarists, forged a template that seemed forever to have associated a spectacular style of guitar playing and stage performance with suggestions of male power and explicit displays of normative male sexuality.

From the perspective of the materialist account that Moore and other critics undertake, they propose that Cobain's particular vocal style of mumbling, the sarcasm and irony of his lyrics, and the ostensible indifference and sometimes lethargy of his on-stage persona can illuminate the broader social conditions within which grunge came into being. This approach has unquestionable merit when it comes to understanding Cobain's creative output. I propose, however, that we can also understand Cobain's vocal style, as well as the content and structuring of his lyrics and journals, in ways other than their relation to the social and economic transformations of the final decades of the twentieth century. Further, as I explore in part II of this study, one phenomenon that Cobain's creative writings frequently make explicit is that social and cultural forces often reveal themselves as bodily manifestations. In alternative rock, these social and cultural forces cannot be divorced from the ways musicians and audiences frequently display their bodies when engaging with the music.

Like the enthusiasts of hardcore, the young men attending heavy metal concerts seem to experience their bodies and they therefore dance in a specific manner because of the structure of the music itself. As Deena Weinstein suggests, these young men also display, and undoubtedly experience, their bodies in a particular manner because of the sexist and heterosexist penchants (if not overt ideology) of the musicians and their audiences (130). Dancing consists of two principal movements: a rhythmic thrusting of the arm upward to signal pleasure and group solidarity, and "headbanging," or marking the rhythm of the music with forceful back-and-forth movements of the head. Metal concerts are also usually characterized by stage diving and crowd surfing and by a kind of disorganized group interaction called "moshing." The tradition of stage diving, crowd surfing, and moshing will continue with grunge and with certain Nirvana performances specifically.

Jon Savage's description of a 1993 Nirvana performance at the Roseland Ballroom in New York City encapsulates the essence of moshing as a collective experience, one for which the male body provides the generative dynamic. During this ritual, the male body constitutes an instrument of pleasure, and it provides the glue that bonds these young men. But the body also functions as a weapon with the potential to incur self-damage as well as to cause injury to others:

> The dance floor is a war zone: A simulated war to be sure, but still not for the faint-hearted. Hundreds of young men ricochet off each other at high speed in the "moshpit," creating flows and eddies that take on a life of their own. And then, by a combination of individual effort and group will, one of them will crest on the surf of this human tide, splaying his body out in pure abandonment before disappearing again. It's a communal, physical release. (63)

Though the moshpit evolved from punk pogo dancing, moshing in general, and metal moshing expressly, is decidedly more uncontrolled, aggressive, and violent in a way that seems to appeal in particular to certain young men. Punk dancing had constituted more of a collective rite that was not quite as uninviting to women; it did not render female bodies as utterly vulnerable as the heavy metal version. Even though Jonathan Gruzelier presents his own personal experience of moshing as expressions of "subcultural solidarity" and near "brotherly love" (66), moshing writ large, though communal, constitutes more of an individual competition than it does a tribal rite of male bonding.

Heavy metal did have an enormous hold on Cobain's phantasy world, even though certain aspects of the genre and its subculture, again like certain features of hardcore, contradict the aesthetics and politics of the persona he was cultivating. As I underscore in my analysis of certain of his journal writings, in professing his punk credentials, Cobain is separating himself specifically from the codes and conventions of heavy metal. He expresses, for example, a disdain for virtuosic guitar playing. And, in proclaiming his prowoman, pro-feminist, and gay-positive sensibilities, he denounces what emerges in the written entries and the visual art in his journals—as in some of his lyrics—as the toxicity of the modes of masculinity and sexuality that metal both reflects and constructs.[11]

When I explore in detail the content and the dynamics within Cobain's written works, I implicitly pose the following two questions: How does the persona that Cobain takes on embrace the music codes and practices of heavy metal and hardcore while also rejecting the ideology of these genres? And what are the consequences of this conflict between his aesthetics and his politics? I argue that the male body comes to be represented in his lyrics and in his illustrated notebooks as the very locus of this conflict. That is, the male body emerges as primordial in Cobain's writings. He structures his most compelling lyrics and journal entries around a representation of corporeality, the form, functions, and experiences of a body represented as male. His written texts and his illustrations represent the male body as a problematic presence in the world, as debilitated, diseased, and poised to contaminate the whole of society.

Heavy Metal + Hardcore Punk

The heavy metal and the punk subcultures of the 1970s were antagonistic, even if they were not completely antithetical, in their music practices and their cultural and social values. Not without reason, punks viewed the typical metalhead as politically clueless. Metal enthusiasts suspected that the typical punk was unnecessarily arrogant. During the 1980s, however, and by the time Cobain was beginning to emerge as a musician and songwriter, one began to see a crossover between the metal and hardcore subcultures. Hardcore bands like Motörhead and especially Black Flag succeeded in mixing punk and metal in an innovative manner. They combined punk's quintessential speed with metal's defining volume. Some thrash musicians like Metallica, Slayer, and Anthrax also succeeded in combining elements of the two genres in ways that appealed to many listeners, including the members of Nirvana.

To a greater degree than in some other locales, heavy metal and punk intermixed in Seattle because the two subcultures were very small; participants often found themselves, by necessity, in close personal contact. They frequently found themselves sharing venues and thus often listening to the same music. As a result, the particular sonic mixture that emerged in Seattle was not precisely the same as in other cities.[12] The state of Washington in the late 1970s and the 1980s had already seen the merging of hardcore and heavy metal, as well as psychedelia, in bands like TKO, Culprit, and Alice in Chains. By the early 1990s, many of the alternative bands in cities in other American states also began to take on the sounds not only of heavy metal but also of pop and rap. By the 1990s, "hardcore" itself was a broad term that included several subgenres, including mathcore, emocore, rapcore, and melodic hardcore.

Bands that would eventually catch the ear and the fancy of Cobain and his bandmates, including Hüsker Dü, Minutemen, and the Meat Puppets, though still inspired by hardcore, exposed their metal influences by attenuating the music's speed and volume. It was northern West Coast bands in particular, including Melvins (a group formed in Montesano, Washington, that Cobain canonizes in his journals), Seattle's Green River (whose Mark Arm would later perform in Mudhoney), and San Francisco's Flipper, that developed a sound invariably described as "sludgy" and "aggressive." Cobain absorbed this sound. While maintaining the intensity and passion of hardcore, these northern West Coast bands, too, like their counterparts in other locales, adopted heavy metal's more moderate tempo. Other U.S. and British bands inflected heavy metal in this manner, including Led Zeppelin, a group Cobain cites as an influence and as a foil for his own music. It is in part this evolving sound that would come to be referred to as "alternative rock," within which grunge would emerge as a distinct subgenre.

There is a particular way of reading the history of post-1970 popular music that sees alternative, underground music as a genre that came into its own in the 1980s and that modulated in a specific way in the 1990s when alternative music emerged as the dominant genre both underground and in the mainstream. Indeed, the alternative rock subcultures existed long before *Nevermind* reached the top of the charts. Henry Rollins, for example, had joined Black Flag and had emerged as a seminal figure in the alternative subculture a decade before Cobain. As Azerrad specifies, "Black Flag was more than just the flagship band of Southern California. They were required listening for anyone who was interested in underground music" (*Our Band,* 14). Because they toured extensively across the country, the group inspired many bands with varying sounds, including Nirvana. In addition, Black Flag's guitarist, Greg Ginn, created the independent SST Records (1978) that served as a model for small labels in other U.S. cities, including Seattle's Sub Pop (1986).

Each independent label created its own identity not only with the musicians it chose to record and promote, but also by circulating their catalogs and distinctive covert art for singles and LPs. It is because alternative rock musicians subscribed to the punk ethic that they intended to make a statement not merely with the sound of their music but also with the way they recorded and distributed it. As indicated at the beginning of this chapter, a rejection of the major labels—companies deemed principally responsible for the demise of authentic rock and the emergence of a bland, corporate product—can be seen as a "metaphor for rebelling against the system in general" (Azerrad, *Our Band,* 9). As I shall explore, it is in Cobain's journals that this metaphor finds one of its most sustained and entertaining expressions.

In the history of alternative scenes in the state of Washington, observers make a distinction between the scene as it emerged in Seattle (as represented by the Sub Pop's philosophy) and the scene in Olympia (as represented by K Records).[13] Humphrey writes, for example, "In Seattle, it was OK to seek commercial success as long as you did not act like a rock star. In Olympia you weren't even supposed to think of music as a career" (154). Everett True echoes this same distinction when he attempts to account for the constituent features of Cobain's music practice. Whereas masculine posturing, male bonding, and a certain potential for violence tended to characterize the Seattle scene, macho posturing did not undergird the Olympia scene in the same way. Thus the scene in Olympia was more disposed to embrace and showcase women performers. For example, Beat Happening, a group that featured Heather Lewis on drums, guitar, and vocals, recorded with K Records. The label also produced solo musician/writer Lois Maffeo as well as groups such as The Go Team (with Tobi Vail) and the all-women Fifth Column. Cobain, as a lyricist, drew inspiration from the Olympia aesthetic and cultural vibe.

A particular connection existed between the musicians and facilitators (concert promoters, organizers, record store owners) in Olympia and those in Washington D.C. because they expressed the same attitude and adhered to a similar philosophy.[14] The presence in both Olympia and Washington D.C. of musicians like Dave Grohl, Nirvana's drummer, and the group Bikini Kill (Kathleen Hanna, Tobi Vail, Kathi Wilcox, Billy Karren) attests to the points of convergence between the scenes in these two cities located a continent apart.

Tobi Vail and Kurt Cobain became a couple for a brief period. In his journals, he intimates that his interactions with Vail and her bandmates prompted him to think through and to articulate his woman-positive, profeminist perspective. There is no doubt that Bikini Kill's riot grrrl feminism inspired Cobain to compose particular lyrics as well as certain liner notes and cover art for Nirvana's albums.[15]

In part II of this study, I return to the implicit and explicit cultural politics of Cobain's lyrics, liner notes, and cover art. But the members of Nirvana, in spite of their apparent politics and sensibilities, were not immune to the same masculine "virus," as Cobain writes in his journals, that afflicted the self-indulgent, aggressive male rocker. For example, Nirvana on occasion decimated their instruments on stage just like the stereotypical rockers that Cobain often disclaims or ridicules. Nor were members of the group beyond falling into the mode of young-white-men-behaving-badly, for example, by provoking confrontations with some of the men attending their performances. In his creative writings, though, Cobain represents certain instances of such bad behavior as a "good" solution to an intractable problem. He creates a persona represented as a young man who engages in certain bad behavior, ironically, in order to call attention to (what his lyrics and journals condemn as) the incurable malignancy of conventional masculinity: the legacy of sexism and homophobia.

DIVERSITY AND COHERENCE WITHIN THE ALTERNATIVE SCENES: THE SOUNDS AND IMAGES OF COBAIN'S VERSION OF GRUNGE

From the beginning of the 1980s, as indicated earlier, the alternative subculture was far from monolithic. Across the United States, there were many different scenes with different-sounding and different-looking bands and fans. No single unifying sound or fashion connected these scenes. Rather, it was the way musicians interacted with their audiences and the role played by facilitators and arbiters of taste that lent the sense of a collective objective and common experience for participants within the different scenes. Because *young* men dominated the different alternative scenes, critics have paid special attention to the ways manifestations of youth culture drove these scenes. Several writers have also underscored the ways race and gender have shaped youth culture in general and popular music culture specifically (Bannister; R. Moore). These writers, however, have generally paid less attention to the manner, and especially the degree to which, particular experiences of the male body and of heterosexuality (as an imperative) intersect with whiteness and youth culture phenomena to undergird the alternative music subculture during Cobain's lifetime.

I examine Cobain's creative writings precisely as one way to explore how gender, sexuality, and race coalesce in ways that reveal and simultaneously conceal how the individual white male body exerts actual power in specific circumstances and how it functions as an emblem of cultural authority overall. His lyrics and journals speak to the workings of real and symbolic power in our culture. I am not suggesting that Cobain, in the construction of a specific white, masculine, straight persona, was typical of the young men in his cohort. In creating such a persona, he was, nonetheless, responding to the same social, cultural, and political forces that shaped members of Generation X during the final decades of the twentieth century.[16]

The persona that Cobain constructs comes across as a young man who experiments with gender identity, sexual expression, and, to a lesser extent, with racial identity. As Rupa Huq explains in *Beyond Subculture,* the inclination of the young to experiment with their identity is not unusual. Within Western cultures, youth is defined as a holding-pattern period of life, a time during which the absence of responsibilities of adulthood allows the young to put on and take off different identities with a relative degree of impunity. At the same time that popular music culture offers Cobain a way to think about, modify, or reinvent his identity by taking on a persona, the culture also allows him to reinforce aspects of his existing gender, sexual, class, and racial identity. I am calling this amalgamation his *grunge identity.* As I shall explore, this identity has both counterhegemonic and hegemonic components.

The noun "grunge," according the *Oxford English Dictionary (OED),* as a slang term used in a general sense to mean "dirt, filth, something repugnant, odious, unpleasant," first emerged in the mid-1960s in the United States. Many observers believe that musician Mark Arm was the first person to employ the term to refer specifically to Seattle music. In a 1981 letter Arm wrote to Humphrey's fanzine *Desperate Times,* he describes the music of his then group (Mr. Epps and the Calculations) as "'Pure grunge! Pure noise! Pure Shit'" (cited in Henderson, 21). Later, as a member of Green River, Arm produced a commercially viable sound that combined punk, glam metal, and hardcore in a mixture that drew from Black Sabbath, the Stooges, and Aerosmith. As most commentators have also pointed out, it was only after the success of commercial grunge that the label became a generalized term used indiscriminately by marketers and some critics to designate proto-grunge, grunge, and some postgrunge sounds.

By 1986, a Seattle bar called Squid Row was hosting bands advertised variously as barf rock, punk rock, noise rock, and grunge; therefore, it was not always easy to recognize the ostensible borders between the subgenres. For some observers, it is Mudhoney's music that might best represent the essence of the sound that came eventually to command the attention of the mainstream in the 1990s. Their single "Touch Me I'm Sick," released by Sub Pop in 1988, is deemed "the first and purest evocation of the sludge-punk ethos" (Humphrey, 127). The song's sludge-punk ethos would mutate into the grunge that popular music historiography has consecrated. We can, however, put this sound in parentheses. More importantly for my analysis of Cobain's creative writings, the song's lyrics provide one key to understanding a principal theme in his journals as well as in his lyrics. "Touch Me I'm Sick" explicitly posits the male body as the locus of a contagion ("I'm full of rot") that represents a menace to others ("Gonna give you, girl, what I got"). The song also communicates a psychical malaise ("I feel bad, and I've felt worse") that finds echoes in and ricochets throughout Cobain's creative writings and in some of his visual art as well.

Sub Pop gained exposure on College Radio and a national profile because of Mudhoney. "The image of the group that emerged initially in the Seattle press suggested that they were worthy of attention precisely because they were not rock stars, but merely self-despising, long-haired," grungy white boys producing a form of white noise for predominantly white listeners (Humphrey, 139; citing the *Seattle Times*). This image certainly corresponds to the persona that emerges in Cobain's journals. Bruce Pavitt, who launched Sub Pop in 1986, had been music critic for the alternative music monthly *The Rocket,* and he had begun the fanzine *Subterranean Pop* in the early '80s. Jonathan Poneman, a musician himself as well as a show promoter and a DJ at the University of Washington's radio station (KCMU), became Pavitt's partner. He would assume responsibility for overseeing the business dealings of the label.[17]

Notwithstanding the lip service that Pavitt and Poneman paid to the notion of local music production and consumption in defiance of corporately distributed music, the two men were, ultimately, self-interested businessmen with a keen sense of their product and their desired market. As a result, they created a specific identity for Sub Pop: a punk-inspired sound and ethic adopted by working-class youth who took on a lifestyle commensurate with their class. They also "devised a distinct image for the label: Long hair, flailing heads, slam dancing and stage diving, beer, cynicism, male bonding, feedback, ear damage, smoke, no politics, no intellectualism, no fashion, no sincerity, no R&B, no women in sight" (Humphrey, 140). Sub Pop not only promoted an identity but, like other local labels, it also facilitated a sense of community through the comments and descriptions of the music and musicians in its catalogue and liner notes. The label sold T-shirts, adorned with the smart-alecky tag "Loser," that further contributed to the image of an alternative, so-called slacker community. Although in his lyrics and journals, Cobain repudiates certain features of the image that Sub Pop was helping to fashion, it is easy to see why the persona that he adopts would, nonetheless, fit right into this community.

Writers and critics have tended to describe Cobain and Nirvana as epitomizing the angst and alienation of an entire American youthful generation that found itself, seemingly, in an untenable position, caught between a miserable past (childhood) and a dismal future (adulthood). Many observers, like Dick Dahl (writing in *Utne Reader* in 1992) and like Clark Humphrey (as cited in the epigraph to this chapter), understand the essence of Cobain's lyrics as oscillating either between defiance and resignation or between anger and depression. Dahl and Humphrey see Nirvana's music as symptomatic of this fluctuation between emotional and psychical states. They describe the group's music as alternating between choruses characterized by fast, loud-noise power riffs, and verses that are slower, quieter, and melodic. Dahl concludes that Nirvana, like other grunge groups, "describes a world of youthful alienation. Sometimes the music broods; sometimes it swaggers. But it does so in a dark intellectual valley walled on one end by mindless adolescence and on the other by the empty, spirit-killing world of adulthood" (42–43; also cited by Kahn).

In chapters 3 and 4, I drill down and add specificity to what critics characterize in general terms as "mindless adolescence" and "the empty, spirit-killing world of adulthood." I demonstrate how we can best understand these emotional and psychical states in terms of a feminist and Romantic-inspired understanding of melancholy. As a result of this analysis, I demonstrate the extent to which Cobain's creative writings problematize not only masculinity but also heterosexuality in a specific way. In these two chapters, I also examine the implications of the presumptive whiteness of the punk subcultural resistance that Cobain represents. In his imaginative writings, Cobain creates, and he attempts to embody, a persona represented as a *white* man experiencing a problematic relation to his own body. He is also a young man enamored with the idea of his own demise.

From Grunge to Emo and Back Again

If the practitioners of heavy metal and hardcore punk constitute Cobain's progenitors, then the young, predominantly white men who make up the emo subculture constitute some of his progeny. The masochistic and melancholic persona Cobain creates would be squarely within his element in twenty-first-century emo chat rooms, spaces in which participants express finding pleasure in pain and in their condition of seemingly unending suffering. This cohort is also known for habitual self-cutting and anorexia (emorexia). But the definition of emo, like hardcore and grunge, is not always precise because, like other alternative genres and subgenres, it is not a monolith.

Originally known as emocore, the aesthetics of the subgenre has been reshaped over the years of its existence, though emo persists in presenting itself as fundamentally apolitical. Some historians date the music from the mid-1980s with bands like Rites of Spring (1984–1986), though the style came into its own in the early to mid-1990s with an admixture of music influences with bands like Jimmy Eat World (1993–present) and Weezer (1992–1998). By the 2000s, some of the music and the extra-music features of the subculture—including the fashion, attitudes, and actions of participants—stirred a backlash when bands like My Chemical Romance (2001–2013) became popular seemingly overnight. Presently, it is critics and fans who label bands or themselves as "emo." Bands rarely, if ever, use the label themselves. "This interesting refusal of bands to be labelled 'emo' is a curious case, yet it is understandable due to the pejorative connotation of the word" (Träger, 183).[18]

Lyrically and musically, emo shares characteristics with Cobain's version of grunge. The names of bands as well as the titles of songs seem to have been lifted from his personal notebooks. As Träger points out, bands include, along with My Chemical Romance, a group named All Time Low, while song titles include "Our Lady of Sorrow," "Kids in the Dark," "Bulimia," as well as "Death of Seasons" (184). Like Cobain's version of grunge, emo also has a hardcore punk, indie-guitar-rock sound; but emo "makes use of minor chords and major nines, which tend to create a somber, pensive mood rather than an adrenaline rush" (Anastasi, 313). Typically, prevailing emo themes constitute expressions of sadness, despair, or discomfort, the same motifs that Cobain rehearses.[19]

In the manner of the persona that Cobain takes on in his lyrics and journals, the emo subculture facilitates nonhegemonic performances of masculinity by these predominantly heterosexual men. But, as parts II and III of this study show, the Cobain persona, just like members of the emo subculture, ultimately succeeds in reproducing a form of conventional, heterosexual masculinity. There are, of course, very visible and vocal "emo gay boys" (Peters, 129). But whether straight or gay, these young white men present themselves personally in various ways as victims, a role they relish. As I shall also explore later, the Cobain persona, again like emo men, constructs masculinity "through the appropriation of normatively feminine characteristics [such as emotional earnestness and physical vulnerability] . . . and through the appropriation of characteristics of homosexuality (e.g., same-sex kissing)" (Ryalls, 84).

Reconstructing the Image of Grunge as Irreducibly Male

There is an ostensible difference between Sub Pop's version of the grunge subculture during the late '80s and early '90s and the emo subculture of the '90s and beyond. Whereas in the emo subculture young men do dominate as lead singers and lyricists, young women are also active. As for grunge, Charles Peterson's at times blurred, black-and-white photographs of live Seattle performances, sometimes used as cover art for recordings, produce a visual to match the identity that Sub Pop was promoting. His photographs created an image subtended by a youthful and distinctively *masculine* dynamic. Peterson captures, for example, Cobain's facial expression and body while smashing his guitar in a manner that resembles an intense moment of boyish glee, with only a hint of macho rage. His photographs, taken as a whole, reveal "Marvels of controlled chaos . . . the same quality that makes the best live rock music exciting—the riveting tension between its sturdy basic structure and the very . . . possibility that it may all fly apart at any moment" (*Screaming Life*).[20] As Humphrey remarks, just as the fuzzbox alters the audio signal of the electric guitar, Peterson's technique produces a visual effect that is often grainy and evokes a degree of tension, aggression, and force. He possesses a distinct technique, the methods of a photographer who adores his subjects. In addition, his typically out-of-focus shots suggest the kind of sensory distortion produced during a state of inebriation.

This image, as developed and permanently "fixed" in Peterson's film-based photographs, is very misleading because of the way women are typically absent from it. The image is, nonetheless, alluring and powerful. It is problematic, however, precisely because it reinforces the overarching gendered relations of power in American culture. In exploring how the passage of time has distorted fans' memory of grunge, Catherine Strong demonstrates how women, even though they played crucial roles in the development of grunge, were marginalized in the commercialization of the genre. After grunge's heyday, the fans Strong interviews had largely forgotten these women. She writes:

> The [one] woman . . . most often remembered, Courtney Love, is used to re-inscribe traditional gender relations through a condemnation of her rejection of [these relations]. The other women musicians from the time of grunge and the challenge they made to gender stereotypes . . . have been either forgotten or re-labelled as "Riot Grrrls." This re-labeling allows the threat being posed [by these women] to patriarchal relations to be compartmentalized and contained, while the "grunge" label is re-inscribed as a form of "masculine" rock. (105)

In this sense, Peterson's images do not so much capture a reality as they help to construct and reinforce one. In addition to erasing two specific women who are cast in Cobain's journals as special friends and confidants (Tobi Vail and Kathleen Hanna), Peterson's images that have been the most copied and shared on social media such as Pinterest also strategically leave out the region's other women rockers. These musicians include Mia Zapata (the Gits), Elizabeth Davis (Seven Year Bitch), and Carrie Akre (Hammerbox). The absence of women is especially noticeable in retrospect because women would come to be more visible and vocal during the early '90s, the time of Nirvana's moment in the national and international spotlight. In light of this marginalization, if not complete erasure of women, Cobain's lyrics and journals reveal the extent to which he was creating the persona of a young man who both resists and reproduces the image of grunge as a masculine expression.

The contributions of women notwithstanding, male bonding and homoeroticism were part and parcel of the Seattle underground scene. Peterson claims to have "gotten shit" for photos that drew attention to this aspect of the scene, as captured in shots depicting the pleasure that is evident on the faces of groups of sweaty, often shirtless young men smashing their bodies into each other, participating in stage diving, or groping at the body of their on-stage idol. Peterson reports that he was criticized also for circulating unposed photos of musicians like Chris Cornell (Soundgarden) and John Robinson (The Fluid) revealing their alluring, sexy physiques to their adoring, mostly male audiences. The photographer remained undeterred by these negative comments. He was intent, he insists, on evoking the homoerotics of the scene because of the central, even if unacknowledged, role that eroticized male bonding played in the genesis and the perpetuation of the subculture.

It is no coincidence, perhaps, that the names of two iconic bands refer to the male anatomy or sexual function. Andrew Wood, lead singer of Mother Love Bone, revealed that in attempting to name the group, he simply made a list of the words he enjoyed saying and hearing, pairing then in various combinations. "Love bone," however, is slang for penis. When paired with "mother," the expression has been taken by some fans to mean "the mother of all love bones," or a spectacular erection. And, on social media, one of the most accepted meanings of Pearl Jam is "the production and emission of semen" during the production of music.[21] It is also no coincidence that Cobain himself chose "The Stiff Woodies" for the name of one of his pre-Nirvana groups. All these names suggest the content and the jocular tenor considered typical among some young men in certain all-male contexts, such as locker rooms, fraternity houses, or rehearsal spaces for aspiring rock bands. This content and this tenor, however, are the very ones that Cobain's creative writings succeed in calling into question. He indicts in particular macho, phallic masculinity and he transforms semen into a weapon deployed against certain men he demonizes in his journals as "dickheads."

Sub Pop described Nirvana, even if the label did not aggressively promote them, as young men of a particular type: "The whole real working-class . . . *white trash*—something not contrived . . . [with] a pre-grassroots or popular feel" (Azerrad, *Come As You Are*, 71, citing Peterson, Azerrad, and Pavitt). I put aside for the moment what some observers of the alternative rock subculture have identified as the racist implications of the term "white trash." Mimi Schippers suggests, for example, that since the slur assumes that "nonwhite people are always already trash" (127), the qualifier "white" must be added to distinguish this specific category from natural trash.[22] Whether or not the identity that Sub Pop promoted was accurate, the record company did succeed in allowing some young, creative white men to articulate and to share with others their angst and alienation in music form.

With the assistance of Peterson's images, the label also created a marketable mythology about the entire Seattle alternative scene.[23] The myth of grunge as a masculine expression continues to persist in written accounts of the genre. Published in 1995, *Screaming Life: A Chronicle of the Seattle Music Scene* constitutes just one example, even if an extreme one, of an engaging, nonacademic account that is problematic. The book is problematic in the same way and for the same reason that Strong calls into question fans' memory of the subgenre. Bruce Pavitt writes the book's foreword, Michael Azerrad composes the introduction, and Charles Peterson provides the photographs.

The three men subscribe to the masculinist "myth of origins" of the music when they contend that grunge, at its inception, grew out of the shared experiences of a group of adolescent boys who were considered by their high school peers as creepy outcasts. These outcasts, the men contend further, heroically sought and found refuge in punk rock. Pavitt, Azerrad, and Peterson demonstrate a pronounced nostalgia for a romanticized, lost male adolescence. Further, as owner of Sub Pop, Nirvana biographer, and scene photographer respectively, they have a professed business interest as well as a personal connection to the music, to individual musicians, and to the alternative subculture overall. Notwithstanding their intention with the publication of *Screaming Life,* they actively engage in the packaging and selling of grunge as a masculine art.

In spite of the way Cobain's journals in particular denounce the masculinist orientation of rock music in general, the image of the alternative rocker that his written entries and illustrations bring into focus corresponds to the image that emerges from *Screaming Life.* At the same time, however, Cobain's creative texts suggest how the shared male experience, the homosocial bonding that shores up the alternative scene, does not exist in opposition to homosexual relations. Rather, his lyrics and journals suggest, ever so whimsically, that this version of male bonding exists on an erotic continuum with same-sex physical relations. His texts, then, help readers to understand the extent to which the experiences of these young men emerge from and exist within a heterosexist and homophobic social order.

When contrasted with the image crafted by Sub Pop, some of Peterson's photographs do suggest the degree to which a heroin aesthetic, if not actual heroin use itself, was emerging as a signifier within grunge's inner circle. A heroin aesthetic includes the valorizing of listlessness and an inattention to hygiene and to one's outer appearance in general. Prior to Cobain's death in April 1994, Jim Norris had died of a heroin overdose in 1988. He had been a member of two bands, Crisis Party and Young Boys Gone Bad (YBGB), both of which critics have labeled punk-thrash bands rather than grunge proper. In addition, Andrew Wood died of an overdose in 1990. After Cobain's suicide, Stefanie Sargent of Seven Year Bitch and Kristen Pfaff, bassist for Hole, died of overdoses in 1992 and 1994 respectively. Tragedies resulting from heroin overdoses continued into the 2000s with the deaths of two members of Alice in Chains: Lane Staley in 2002 and Mike Starr in 2011. Many of the songs on this band's 1992 album, *Dirt,* constitute lamenting descriptions of the insidiousness of heroin addiction. The album captures these themes in a manner that underscores the drug's valence within the underground scene.[24]

In addition to specific entries in Cobain's journals that address the physiological and emotional challenges of addiction, one of the narrative techniques he employs, both in his lyrics and in his journals, produces a style of writing that appears to mimic the effects of intoxication and addiction. As I shall explore, these texts typically display a confused and confusing narrative perspective. They shift between the first, second, and third persons, seemingly without rhyme or reason. At times, certain stories appear as a succession of narrative fragments strung together, it would seem, by a series of invisible ellipses that operate to create gaps in the story Cobain is telling. At other times, his opaque stories are circular and repetitive and display no linear development at all. Compared to his would-be narrative texts, Cobain's lyrical texts, whether in the form of songs or journal entries, frequently put forth a collage of disparate, surreal images that can be captivating yet disorienting and discomfiting for readers.

Cobain's Aesthetic Practice: Merging Art and Commerce

Although it may indeed be impossible for music historians to identify the first group to produce a distinctive, dirty guitar sound or to declare which group was the grungiest, some writers, like Stephen Tow, consider John Leighton Beezer's band, the Thrown Ups, to constitute the grunge group *par excellence.* The Thrown Ups, asserts Tow without equivocation, "embodied the aesthetic of grunge more than anyone else in Seattle. And I mean *real grunge*—the organic version that existed in Seattle in the late '80s, not the mass-marketed phenomenon of the '90s" ("Interviewing ... Beezer"). Tow's remarks attest to another persistent myth: grunge emerged organically and spontaneously. According to this myth:

> [T]he grunge scene in Seattle, before it hit internationally, was the last bastion of independent, regional rock-and-roll in America ... the last time and place where a bunch of people could get together and make a lively, creative community without it being packaged and sold back [to them and the masses] by profiteers, cool hunters, and corporate drones ... intent on finding the next new thing and figuring out how to sell it. (Henderson, 9)

Azerrad's *Our Band* offers a compelling, quasi-historicist account of alternative music post-Nirvana. He suggests that some alternative musicians "sold out" by signing with major companies. In doing so, these musicians, he regrets, abandoned the defining imperative of the underground subculture, which was to revive and rescue rock music. Musicians should have accomplished this imperative, the argument goes, by refusing to allow the major labels, and the corporate culture they epitomize, to determine the fate of rock music. It was the responsibility of the makers of the music to disallow corporate control of its production and distribution. Within this logic, journalists and critics like Azerrad make known their contention that the future of rock should remain the exclusive province of the practitioners themselves, a sentiment that Cobain reiterates explicitly in his journals and implicitly in some of his lyrics. In spite of their anticorporate stance, some of the Seattle musicians, including Nirvana, of course, did eventually sign with a major label. Therefore, they did participate in the commodification of their music by business executives, the same executives Cobain excoriates in his journals as "corporate dickheads."

In addition to musicians themselves, music critics and journalists also typically establish an opposition between the independent record labels and the majors, specifying that the independents are more knowledgeable of and can appreciate sounds that are new and challenging. As a result, independent labels are believed to be more inclined to give priority to music as a creative production over music as a commercial product. This opposition, if one uses Cobain as the example, does not fully withstand scrutiny. In addition, writers like Simon Frith in the essay "The Good" have long pointed out that creativity and commerce are not necessarily antithetical. According to Ryan Moore, for instance,

> [A]lternative music became absorbed into . . . [postwar] forms of capitalism in which culture has a crucial economic role in promoting commercialized forms of individuality, creativity, and diversity. The ideological opposition between art and commerce . . . collapsed in this new age of capitalism where markets absorb new trends faster than ever before and the consumer culture thrives on expressions of difference, novelty, and authenticity. (11)

Capitalism, in other words, and as Moore continually reminds readers, adapts; markets recognize and co-opt new trends. They co-opt especially youthful rebellion, and they do so with deliberate speed and facility. Consumer culture, in other words, takes what is different, unusual, and creative, repackages it, and, as Henderson observes, then sells it back to the very people who created it. This process is what transpired with grunge, confirming that the border separating the artistic and the commercial can indeed become fluid and permeable.

Corporate record companies did begin aggressively and misleadingly using the label "alternative" as a marketing tool to sell music to their targeted demographic. In spite of corporate incursions, however, alternative rock continued to thrive in part because many of the participants in the alternative scenes were not taken in by the corporate strategy. In addition to rejecting outright the grunge label, they came to mock and to resent the music industry's embrace of alternative subgenres in general (Cohen and Krugman). Therefore, just because Cobain's music was recorded and distributed under the auspices of a major label does not mean that the industry controlled how fans listened to and used this music. Put simply, production does not ineluctably determine consumption.

It does not necessarily follow that in appropriating the sound and energy of Cobain's music and lyrics, corporate culture completely co-opts and nullifies the social critique and the cultural resistance that inspire his creativity and that sustain the subculture to which he belongs. In addition, even on Sub Pop, Nirvana's music was always already a commodity, as the efforts by its executives to market its products clearly confirm. It is easy to debunk the myth of the antithetical relationship between art and commerce by pointing out how and why grunge, even before the mainstream discovered it, had already been commodified. As a recording artist on the Sub Pop label, Cobain's music and lyrics, as Negus writes about the distribution of popular music in general, was necessarily "mediated by a series of technological, cultural, historical, geographical, and political factors" (65).

Therefore, I too conclude that a strict opposition between art and commerce is untenable in an analysis of popular music as it was evolving during Cobain's lifetime. Nevertheless, the very notion of such an antithesis, as my reading in particular of Cobain's journals will reveal, provides the songwriter and the putative autobiographer with a precise and rigorous way to think about his aesthetic ideal and practice, about the state of the music industry, and about his relation to it. By way of his lyrics and journals, Cobain represents a premier example of the force and resilience of youthful subcultures that persist in spite of, and perhaps even because of, mainstream incursions and appropriation.

2 THE COBAIN PERSONA, THE WHITE MALE BODY, AND THE CREATION OF AN IDEAL MASCULINE SELF

I turn my attention now to the concepts of corporeality, gender, and race that underpin Cobain's creative works. I address the specific way Cobain, by taking on the persona of a white, straight, masculine subject, succeeds in creating a particular kind of phantasy, even though he may appear to be writing autobiographical fragments. In addition, this chapter reveals the way psychoanalytic theory, in spite of its blind spots, can be used to map out the logic of Cobain's literary aesthetic and cultural practice. Thus, to complement the historicizing of grunge presented in chapter 1, aimed at providing a broader context for my reading of Cobain's creative texts, this chapter lays the *theoretical* groundwork for the literary analysis and cultural commentary presented in the remainder of the book.

Cobain's creative writings, in spite of their surface "noise" and their seeming inscrutability, succeed foremost in calling into question the patriarchal social order in general and the masculinist ideology of independent rock specifically. Therefore, an interrogation of masculinity figures at the very center of this chapter and the remainder of the book. That is, an analysis of gender perceptions, experiences, and politics constitutes the fundamental, interpretive tool that allows readers to make sense of Cobain's frequently opaque writings. But masculinity, as it is conceived, experienced, and represented within contemporary U.S. culture, is a vexed term that ultimately has no meaning when divorced from conceptions, experiences, and representations of race, class, and sexuality. Accordingly, the masculinity that is the object of my examination of

Cobain's writings is demonstrably white and middle-class and presumptively heterosexual.

Nevertheless, as will become clear, I do not take an essentialist position in regards to gender, sexuality, or race. I take none of these categories perforce to be natural, self-evident, or permanently fixed. Nor do I assume that Cobain's lyrics and journals necessarily reveal his real cultural identity, or even the identity of the complex persona that he assumes on stage, during interviews, or in his creative writings. The inconstancy and unpredictability of the persona that Cobain embraces, just like the events in the life of the historical Kurt Cobain, are too varied and intricate for his lyrics and journals to reflect accurately or in any way that is not manifestly problematic. His creative productions, in other words, do not function as mirrors. In fact, "no music can be a mirror . . . [that captures] events or activities in its melodies, rhythms, and voices. The world, a society, an individual life, or even a particular incident is far too complex for any cultural product (book, film, or song) to be able to capture and spontaneously 'reflect'" (Negus, 4).

Music's inability to function as a mirror applies also to the most inauspicious of circumstances and incidents, such as Cobain's heroin addiction and suicide. Nevertheless, biographers and music journalists have persisted in declaring that a desire for self-destruction constitutes the ultimate meaning embedded within Cobain's music. They often do so without presenting concrete evidence; moreover, they do so in an uncritical manner that confuses biographic details with literary artifacts. From an examination of a few of Cobain's lyrics, Duane Fish in "Serving the Servants," for example, concludes that the young musician did not succeed in creating an art form that was uniquely his own. Fish surmises that Cobain, in spite of his aesthetic ideals, ended up becoming so irretrievably co-opted by the corporate mainstream that he saw suicide as the only way to extricate and redeem himself. Most readers of Cobain's suicide letter reach this same conclusion, after no more than a superficial reading of this remarkably nuanced text.

The persona that Cobain takes on, in his suicide letter as well as in his lyrics and journals, possesses a specific psychical and emotional profile: He is masochistic and melancholic. It is a profile that psychoanalytic theory can help readers to unravel more easily. Further, as indicated in the introduction, the persona that Cobain takes on in his writings is that of a young man who experiences a profound and irrepressible sense of corporeal vulnerability. In addition, because he presents himself as uncomfortable in his own skin, again whether in his suicide letter or in his lyrics and journals, all of Cobain's writings are structured around representations of specific experiences of a body not merely represented, but also incessantly *elegized,* as male.

Therefore, when reading Cobain, "it is quite logical . . . to make critical links between the body, musical sound [and lyrics], and the construction of identity; [these links] are relevant to a serious appraisal of the ways in which popular music performance helps to shape ideas around gender and race in general and masculinity [and whiteness] in particular" (White, 6). Because psycho-analysis describes how the psyche interrelates with the body as a gendered and racialized construct, the theory provides critical insights for an analysis of Cobain's writings. As David Savran points out in *Taking It Like a Man,* inasmuch as psychoanalysis constitutes "a science" that studies phantasy, desire, and sexual difference, it does provide a pertinent language and a persuasive theory for analyzing the construction of any and all gendered and racialized identifications (10). Since these identifications are steeped in phantasms and since they emerge from experiences of desire and perceptions of self and other, they lend themselves to a specific kind of interpretation.

As will become clear in the forthcoming chapters, I am making a simple distinction between "identification" and "identity" that bypasses the extensive scholarship on the meaning of these two terms in various disciplines including sociology, psychology, and psychoanalysis. I use "identification" to signal an act or an instance of identifying, and I use "identity" to mean a primary sense of who one is or who others consider one to be. In this sense, I write, on the one hand, of the underlying masculine *identity* of the persona that Cobain creates and, on the other, I examine specific lyrics and journal fragments that reveal the feminine *identification* of this alter ego.

Still, I do not take on psychoanalytic aesthetics as a set of theories and con-cepts to be applied to a reading of Cobain's texts. Most crucially, rather than psychoanalyzing the historical Kurt Cobain, I make use of the psychoanalytic paradigm less as a theory designed to provide a roadmap to meaning than as a practice of interpretation. This practice is equipped to call into question what the text does not or cannot say. I use psychoanalytic aesthetics as a method-ology to connect the dots, both the ones within an individual song or journal entry that assure the text's coherence, as well as those that allow these indi-vidual songs and entries to cohere into an eclectic ensemble. As I redeploy the psychoanalytic model, it constitutes a strategy that is poised to give voice to the silences within a particular Cobain text and thus to identify the gaps within it. The model allows me to make explicit what Cobain's writings merely suggest about the interrelation between masculinity, heterosexuality, and whiteness.

It is from this perspective that the final chapters of this book engage with Freud's writings on masochism and melancholy and with Melanie Klein's theories on "unconscious phantasy," as well as with her writings on melancholy and the death drive. But it takes on the theories of these two analysts by way of the critical reinterpretations put forth by contemporary theorists and cultural critics such as Julia Kristeva, Judith Butler, and Leo Bersani. All these critics use feminist and queer theories to challenge and expand traditional psychoanalysis in specific ways. My reading of Cobain also draws upon the theories of more recent scholars who are not necessarily within the psychoanalytic tradition, including José Muños and Tavia Nyng'o. Their works provide, nevertheless, insights into Cobain's creative process and, specifically, the logic of his representations of gender, sexuality, and punk performance.

Just as my reading of Cobain is informed by scholars who contest but enlarge upon psychoanalytic theory, it also engages, in an indirect and implicit manner, with the theories of Freud and Klein as they have been challenged and "corrected" by antiracist scholarship, in particular, the writings of Christopher Lane, Kalpana Seshadri-Crooks, and Badia Sahar Ahad. As with all the theorists from whom I draw insights, I remain skeptical about the empirical validity of what Freud in particular writes. Nevertheless, I make use of some of his descriptions and insights specifically to interrogate and to explain the logic of patriarchal culture as it appears within the phantasy universe that Cobain creates. Patriarchal logic includes the symbols and the images that we use to communicate and to understand ourselves and our place within the social order. I am especially indebted to the manner in which Klein has exposed some of the gaps and inconsistencies in Freud's theory and the way she has reformulated many of his concepts, including his theorizing of the relation between melancholy (or depression) and gender identity.

Kleinian psychoanalysis (the British School) takes as its primary focus the manner in which psychical processes mediate the relationship between the self and the external world. This particular iteration of psychoanalysis also explores how these psychical processes shape the form and content of art and how it is experienced. Building on Klein's initial insights, subsequent theorists in the British School have concentrated on aesthetic experience; they have specified the role of unconscious processes in the creation of art as well as in its appreciation. For my analysis of Cobain's creative output, Kleinian psychoanalytic aesthetics are germane precisely because they do not resort to an artist's biography in order to explain her or his works. Rather, Kleinians consider all art to result from a process, one that can be reconstructed (Glover, 24). In the forthcoming chapters, I retrace the process by which Cobain produces enigmatic lyrics and fills his journals with disaffecting images and disquieting narratives, all of which readers can indeed understand independently of his life story.

As Kent Brintnall explains, however, one does not have to buy completely into the empirical claims within Freudian or Kleinian theories in order to recognize how "culturally pervasive and persuasive [their theories are]; they provide fruitful points of access into the symbolic logic of patriarchy and its mechanisms of masculine domination" ("Masochism, Masculinity, and the Crucifixion," 18). In addition, psychoanalysis not only convincingly explains how our particular social order works, the theory operates also in part to create this very order. For Cobain's writings, psychoanalytic theory provides insights into how heterosexuality, as represented in his texts, constitutes a discourse and an institution that inaugurate and police a system of power and coercion. As a result, these insights provide a key to understanding how Cobain's writings constitute not only a reaction and a resistance to conventions of gender and sexuality, but also how his texts, simultaneously, reproduce and abet gender hierarchies and compulsory heterosexuality.

In using the theories as well as the clinical observations of analysts and theorists, I appropriate some of their conclusions and, especially, some of their models in order to understand both the structuring and the content of Cobain's writings. Therefore, in adapting a psychoanalytic lexicon, I am, above all else, appropriating and redeploying metaphors. I do not reify psychoanalytic precepts or suggest that these models of psychic life are ahistorical and universal. Thus, I follow in the tradition of Lewis Aron, who undertakes a trenchant critique and revision of traditional psychoanalytic concepts (198).

Just as I do not psychoanalyze Kurt Cobain, I do not use psychoanalytic aesthetics in order to induct his lyrics and journal writings into the canon of "great literature." I do suggest, however, how his creative writings might both fit into, and go against the grain of, the traditions of postmodern American literature. At the same time, my close readings, specifically of Cobain's lyrics, reveal the extent to which these compositions, as an ensemble, are uneven and flawed. In a similar manner, my examination of his journal entries confirms the assessment made by some of Cobain's harshest critics that these entries frequently devolve into the "gibberish" of a madman. At their very best, critics complain, Cobain's journals expose the mundane, adolescent musings of the kind that readers might encounter in the writings of a typical white American teenage boy.

Therefore, I do not intend to contribute to the process through which Cobain has been mythologized as a Romantic, artistic genius who tragically takes his own life at a young age. Rather, I deploy a critical vocabulary and logic that have been informed by psychoanalysis in order to understand how Cobain's creative writings function as aesthetic objects and, therefore, *how* they make sense (or create nonsense), even more so than *what* his lyrics and journal entries *mean*. In the process of conceiving and writing this study, however, I have discovered that certain psychoanalytic concepts, masochism and melancholy in particular, and the specific persona and certain narrative episodes that appear within Cobain's creative writings are mutually explicative.

As I reveal in parts II and III of this study, while psychoanalytic accounts of the construction and experience of gender help readers to understand the structure and content of Cobain lyrics and journals, the ensemble of his creative texts, in turn, helps scholars to understand some of the enigmas and contradictions within psychoanalytic theory itself. These theoretical conundrums include, for example, the complex interrelations that exist between masochistic, melancholic, and narcissistic identifications and comportments. In addition, an analysis of Cobain's lyrical and narrative texts confirms that masculinity, music performance, masochism, and melancholy are irreversibly interconnected; they "lean on" each other, in the psychoanalytic meaning of the expression. Therefore, these four terms can be used to illuminate each other. Although in examining Cobain's writings, one could analyze representations of music (as social critique and as performance) and representations of a specific white masculine identity as distinct literary productions, these representations intersect in complex and unpredictable ways.

In the literary analysis contained in the next two chapters, I first examine Cobain as a lyricist before turning my focus to his journal writing, while paying some attention also to the visual art contained in his handwritten notebooks.

Although my study of Cobain examines discrete texts and, therein, has a narrow focus, I mitigate some of the methodological challenges found in other studies that also examine individual artists by presenting close readings of specific texts. These studies frequently do not give adequate attention to, or they ignore altogether, how individual artists and specific texts are embedded within a broader historical and cultural context. To begin with, I do explore how Cobain's writings have emerged within a broader historical context. This context includes writers of the 1950s Beat generation as well as American film and fiction from the 1990s to the end of the twentieth century. This historical context explains, in part, why Cobain's creative writings enter into an intimate dialogue with European Romantic traditions.[1]

I begin with aesthetics. Therefore, it is by examining the lexical, grammatical, and syntactical features of Cobain's lyrics and journal entries that I reveal how these texts function to produce meaning and to tell us something significant about certain experiences of heterosexual masculinity. This initial examination leads me to consider the creation of images and narratives in Cobain's writings, though I do not assume that the meaning encoded in his texts is simple or self-evident. For any particular Cobain lyric or journal fragment, the answer to the questions "what is this text saying?" and "what and how does this image mean?" can lead to multiple, nuanced answers. That his writings and some of his images speak to me—in this specific time and place, more than a quarter of a century after his death—suggests that the meaning and the "pleasure in these texts," to appropriate another of Roland Barthes's expressions, cannot be taken to be static or universal.[2]

Further, one can conclude from the way Cobain's words, sounds, and images currently circulate on social media that his creative works continue to convey new meanings to new audiences in many parts of the world. Members of several Facebook groups, some of which have thousands of active adherents, routinely post excerpts from Cobain's lyrics in particular. Members then comment on and vigorously debate the meaning of his words.[3] All of Cobain's texts operate, then, in the precise manner that representation works in general, and his creative writings produce meaning in the same way meaning is produced in any act of reading and interpreting texts. As Stuart Hall writes about the nature of cultural representations and signifying practices in general, engaging with Cobain's creative writing confirms that

Meaning is not straightforward or transparent, and does not survive intact the passage through representation. It is a slippery customer, changing and shifting with context, usage and historical circumstances. It is therefore never finally fixed. . . . It is always being negotiated and inflected to resonate with new situations. It is often contested, and sometimes bitterly fought over. There are always different circuits of meaning circulating in any culture at the same time, overlapping discursive formations, from which we draw to create meaning or to express what we think. (9–10)

I do not, however, concentrate on the public consumption of Cobain's works. I put into parentheses, for example, the way the meanings within his lyrics have circulated among listeners and fans. Other scholars, in particular Catherine Strong and Jennifer Otter Bickerdike, have written persuasively on how audiences have received and interacted with Cobain's music and the various uses to which they have put his images as well as his music. Neither Strong nor Bickerdike, however, undertakes a close reading of Cobain's written texts. Nor do they explore how his writings might fit into the tradition of the cultural productions by certain white American men throughout the twentieth century, which constitutes one of the objectives of my analysis.

Bickerdike's *Fandom, Image and Authenticity: Joy Devotion and the Second Lives of Kurt Cobain and Ian Curtis* examines the parallels between the lives and the legacies of these two musicians. By using the familiar trope of authenticity as an aesthetic and political discourse within popular culture subgroups, she explores how Curtis's and Cobain's fans experience and respond in similar ways to the two men and their music. Bickerdike's analysis is thorough and persuasive, even though she seems more personally invested in Curtis, the man and his music, than in Cobain. In addition, given the nature of the study she undertakes, she does not attempt to examine Cobain's lyrical, narrative, or visual works of art. Moreover, even when she writes about Cobain, her principal target is not the historical, real Kurt Cobain. Nor is her main target the persona that Cobain cultivates in his media performances or that is embedded in his written texts. Rather, her primary objective is to examine the "hyperreal" Kurt Cobain, that is, the persona that has emerged via diverse traditional and social media in the wake of the performer's death.

In *Grunge: Music and Memory,* Strong sets out to fill a gap in academic studies of grunge by exploring grunge fandom and, therein, by including what she designates as "the voice of fans" in her analysis. Therefore, one aspect of her study is empirical. She uses interviews with Australians who were fans of grunge (at the time of its mainstream success) in order to explore how memory of the genre has evolved over the decades. She explores "the effects of grunge as a large-scale cultural phenomenon" (7) filtered through mass media. Strong concludes that grunge imparts a sense of connection among listeners and empowers fans. These fans, in turn, amplify the genre's cultural effects. In a chapter on Cobain ("The Memory of Kurt Cobain"), Strong concludes that Nirvana's music and images have been fashioned by the music industry and appropriated by others in specific ways for specific purposes. While acknowledging the value of analyses of music as text, Strong does not discuss Cobain's lyrics in detail or the content and structure of his journals at all.

Although I begin my exploration of Cobain's creative output with an examination of his aesthetic ideals and practice, aesthetics, of course, cannot be neatly separated from politics. A reading of his texts necessarily entails interrogating dynamics of power and pleasure and issues of self and other, identity and alterity. It is in this sense that his writings emerge from and engage with a particular social order that can be characterized as a racialized patriarchy. It is also in this sense that his texts critique and, at the same time, help to construct a particular cultural identity that is white, masculine, and heterosexual. Whether or not Cobain sets out deliberately in every single instance to communicate this specific identity is not a topic I dwell on. There are certainly particular lyrics and journal fragments for which the reader can clearly locate authorial intent, and this intent does help to shape how a text operates to produce meaning.

Just as I give some attention in the first part of this study to Cobain the performer, his audience, and his relation to the music industry, I also devote some attention to the influence of historical processes and geographical location. This kind of analysis, however, does not constitute my primary focus. On this topic, too, other writers have undertaken some significant studies. For example, in *White Boys, White Noise: Masculinities and 1980s Indie Guitar Rock*, Matthew Bannister explains how, historically and culturally, young white men from the 1970s to the 1990s produced independent rock predominantly for other young white men. He explores the relationship between gender and popular music during this specific era. In his account of alternative rock, Bannister examines a variety of bands and individual musicians to support his thesis concerning the performance of masculinity in American youth subcultures.

White Boys, however, includes only a very brief assessment of Cobain's influences and his specific contributions to alternative guitar rock. More significantly, like some other scholars who take on the same topic as he does, Bannister begins with the premise that the music of the period, as Frith and McRobbie suggest ("Rock and Sexuality"), does indeed simply reflect the masculinity of the musicians and their audiences. Finally, just like Strong and Bickerdike, he does not analyze Cobain's creative writings or attempt to understand his creativity within the broader context of American cultural productions of the twentieth century, the novels, poetry, and films, for example, that also engage with or that set out to represent white masculinities.

As is clear from my remarks in chapter 1, Ryan Moore's *Sells Like Teen Spirit* makes a significant contribution to popular music studies by attempting, in a more explicit manner than Bannister, to historicize the development of rock music and of popular culture more generally. In his materialist account, as I point out, Moore examines the role of social class and economics in the development of youth subcultures. Moore, unlike Bannister, does not see music production and consumption as mirrors that serve to reflect the gender and racial identities of musicians and audiences in alternative rock. But he does not sufficiently call into question the ways in which the masculinity in question intersects with a particular hegemony underpinned by sexist, heterosexist, and racist dynamics. Further, in spite of the implication of Moore's title, which is a riff on Nirvana's most popular song ("Smells Like Teen Spirit"), he does not examine Cobain's lyrical or journal writings.

My own readings of Cobain's written oeuvre has also been informed by older publications like Roger Beebe's *Rock Over the Edge,* studies that take an even wider angle than either Bannister or Moore in providing a history and a critique of the development of popular music culture. These studies typically examine multiple forms of popular music that, in addition to white-male-dominated rock, include black, country, and folk texts and performances. Although one essay in *Rock Over the Edge* undertakes a comparative study of Cobain and Tupac Shakur, Cobain's creative works, as opposed to his biography, remain but a mere footnote in this essay and in the collection as a whole. In this regard, this collection of insightful essays is representative of studies that generally dismiss grunge as another form of commercialized rock and that reduce Cobain to some of the discrete events in his life story. These studies, when they do include a discussion of grunge, such as Rupa Huq's *Beyond Subculture,* also generally fail to examine thoroughly the role of the male body and experiences of masculinity in the genre's production and appeal.

THE WHITE MALE BODY AS SYMBOL AND SYMPTOM IN COBAIN'S CREATIVE WRITINGS

My body is damaged from music in two ways. I have a red irritation in my stomach. It's psychosomatic, caused by all the anger and the screaming. I have scoliosis, where the curvature of [my] spine is bent, and the weight of my guitar has made it worse. I'm always in pain, and that adds to the anger in our music.

—KURT COBAIN (cited in Jessica Wood, "Pained Expression," 342)

It is because evocations of a rock musician's body suffuse Cobain's lyrics and journal entries that the concept of a gendered and racialized body constitutes one of the pillars upon which I construct my thesis. Given the parallels that exist between the ideals of grunge and the values and traditions of Romanticism, it should not be surprising that Cobain's writings spotlight the status and function of the body. As a renunciation of the pre-eminence that the Enlightenment had bestowed on progress, science, and rationality, the early Romantics prioritized not only nature and art but also individuality and emotionality in such a way that the body itself served as a means of expression and resistance. As Bickerdike explains, "Death, then, becomes part of this palette for expressing authenticity as the act of dying, especially the taking of one's own life, is the ultimate culmination for illustrating the connection between nature, physicality, and emotions" (44).

Some of Cobain's biographers, as well as other writers, have also recognized that the body features prominently as a theme in his lyrical and journal writings. They base their conclusions on Cobain's own pronouncements concerning the physical condition of his body and its relation to his music production, as articulated in the epigraph above, for instance. In *Heavier Than Heaven,* to cite one well-known example, biographer Charles Cross confirms that Cobain was "obsessed with the human body, bodily functions: Birth, urination, defecation, and sexuality" (90–91). Cross estimates that 90 percent of the themes that one encounters in Cobain's lyrics have to do with the condition and experiences of the human body.

In a similar manner, and based on a comparable reading of Cobain's interviews and written texts, scholar Jessica Wood asserts that Cobain's body ailments "shaped his life and his subjectivity" (332). She uses excerpts principally from Cobain's journals, in addition to the conclusions of biographers, to validate her thesis that the musician's experience of his overall physical health played a major role in his aesthetic ideals and his creative output. Further, as Nick Soulsby has unwittingly revealed in the foreword to *Dark Slivers,* an early sign of the nature and the all importance of the body, at least for Cobain's lyrical production, can be found in the manner in which he revised Shocking Blue's "Love Buzz," a song that Nirvana covered on their first album. Soulsby is correct in suggesting that it is easy to understand why the music of the original would appeal to the members of Nirvana and to other musicians with proto-grunge sensibilities. It is the lyrical changes that Cobain made, however, that explain why this song appealed especially to his imagination in a specific way. These changes are predictive of his future lyrical and journal writings.

First, the mere fact that a female character narrates the original song would have been particularly alluring for the persona the young songwriter was cultivating. And although he changed, as one might expect, the original second line from "You are the *king* of my *dreams*" to "You are the *queen* of my *heart,*" Cobain's lyrics still retain the feminine perspective of the Shocking Blue version. That is, his adapted lyrics retain what I postulate in the coming chapters as "the feminine cultural and social position" of the original song. This gendered position points to a persona, a narrative identity, that will prove to constitute the default perspective within Cobain's lyrics overall. Second, by transforming "dreams" to "heart," Nirvana's "Love Buzz" now suggests, as other songs written by Cobain will reconfirm, that love is made apparent by its bodily manifestation. As a result, love ceases to be simply a psychical and emotional phenomenon to become corporeal, inscribed indelibly in or on a body part.

When compared to his lyrical legacy, however, it is the way Cobain modifies the chorus of the song that will reverberate in his journal entries. This reverberation appears also in some of the illustrations that punctuate this text. As Soulsby begins to explain, the original chorus, "Can you hear my love buzz?" is, arguably, more logical than Cobain's modification, "Can you feel my love buzz?" for two principal reasons. To begin with, the word "buzz" indicates that love is indeed something to be "heard" primarily. The onomatopoeia also signals that the reception of the narrator's emotion (by the object of her affection) constitutes the song's focus. By changing "hear" to "feel," Cobain shifts this focus ever so slightly to make the song about the narrator's own perception and bodily experience of his love.

Next, the question posed in the original song, "Can you hear my love buzz?," anticipates an affirmative response, just as Cobain's modification does. But unlike the original, in which the singer and her lover remain separate beings, Cobain's adaptation suggests that the lover and the object of this love share the same body, or at least that there exists between them a flesh-to-flesh connection that cannot be sundered. Consequently, as Soulsby also suggests, his "buzz" is *felt* by her. As I explore further in part II of this study, the transformation is consistent with what readers encounter elsewhere in Cobain's original writings. In addition to love, other emotional and psychical states, like fear, anxiety, sadness, and guilt, are often represented as *physical* manifestations that are shared between two bodies that are inextricably bonded, for better or worse.

In their observations and analyses, most critics, and specifically both Cross and Wood in addition to Soulsby, often write as though the body that they take as the object of contemplation and representation in Cobain's texts is unmarked and, therefore, universal. Wood does contend that "Cobain's understanding of the *sick* body came from his life experiences as a thin male with chronic stomach problems, scoliosis, a heroin addiction, and a performance routine that featured regular stage diving, equipment smashing, and prolonged screaming" (332, emphasis added). She concludes that the sick body functions as a metaphor for Cobain's status as outsider, his antiestablishment cultural politics, and for the authenticity of his music. That is, although Wood does indicate, somewhat parenthetically, that the body evoked in Cobain's texts is gender-specific, neither she, Cross, nor other commentators have paid sufficient attention to the ostensible race and the sexuality in addition to the gender of this represented body. As a result, they have tended to overlook the way whiteness, masculinity, and heterosexuality are represented as coextensive in Cobain's written texts.

Therefore, what I am calling the Cobainian "creative project"—the ensemble of Cobain's creative output, visual as well as written—is constructed around representations, not only of a mode of masculinity presumed to be heterosexual, but also around representations of a specific male body that is evoked as intrinsically and irreducibly white. It is for these reasons that this specific mode of masculinity and this specific male body constitute the target of my analysis. It is, precisely, by focusing on the cultural identity associated with this body that I reveal how Cobain represents this identity as constructing and, simultaneously, as being constructed by a racialized, patriarchal order.

This focus in part distinguishes my study from previous ones. I maintain that when Cobain evokes "his" body in diverse writings and drawings—whether this body is real or phantasized—he is necessarily evoking a *specific* corporeal surface rather than an unmarked or universal body. But even when the human body as a general concept becomes a discursive object—that is, a theme and a subject of philosophical reflection—in Cobain's writings and visual art, he imagines a white body. In addition, his reflection on and representation of the male body challenge what Josep Armengol has identified in his history of the male body as "the traditional dichotomy established in visual culture between masculinity / activity / looking, on the one hand, and femininity / passivity / to be looked-at-ness, on the other" (3).[4]

The body that emerges within Cobain's writings might seem at times to correspond to his actual body at a specific moment in his life. At other times, the body he represents is clearly a phantasized corporeality, a surreal or cartoonlike image as seen also in some of his drawings. In either case, the body evoked verbally or represented visually, whether realistic or distorted, is specific. It can still be identified, as I suggest, as the product of a precise historical moment and a particular cultural practice. Therefore, implicit in my analysis of the status and function of the body within Cobain's creative productions is the acknowledgment that there is no essential or "natural" male body. On the contrary, all bodies are already always shaped and given meaning culturally and historically. In other words, as Cobain's lyrics, journals, and illustrations make evident, the body has always been and "remains the most visibly gendered [and racialized] social and cultural construction" that exists (Armengol, 1). In addition, when Cobain writes specifically of his corporeal surface and thus of his whiteness and maleness, he is also evoking necessarily a particular *psychical* experience. As I indicate in discussing Nirvana's cover of "Love Buzz," the corporeal and the psychical are represented as irreversibly intertwined in the texts that he writes. They form a composite in an interesting manner that ricochets throughout all of his written texts.[5]

My focus on the conception and on various representations of the male body in Cobain's creative writings leads me to postulate a complementary relationship, rather than an oppositional one, between the *phallic* and the nonphallic, or *testerical,* psychical makeup and comportment of the persona Cobain creates. In his texts, phallic masculinity presents itself as an aggressive, destructive, and sterile interaction with the world. Testerical masculinity, by contrast, emerges as a passive, protective, and productive engagement with others and with the self. I come eventually to employ "testerical" as an umbrella term to designate all those actions and psychical traits of the Cobain persona that are represented as "feminine" or nonmasculine, as defined culturally.

I first put forth the rationale for designating a certain mode of masculinity as testerical some years ago in an essay titled "The Male Body and Literary Metaphors for Masculinity." Then in a second essay, "Testeria: The Dis-ease of Black Men in White Supremacist, Patriarchal Culture," I elaborate more fully how what I theorize as "testeria" constitutes an analogue of hysteria, as understood within psychoanalytic theory. Both hysteria and testeria manifest a relationship to the body and both indicate that there is, necessarily, a relation between the unconscious and the body. Testeria, like hysteria, indicates that a subject is conflicted and identifies as male and female.[6] I also suggest in the second essay why testeria can be theorized as operating to challenge the very division of gender into a masculine articulation and a feminine one, as binary categories. As I shall establish in my reading of Cobain, a principal theme within his texts also functions, both implicitly and explicitly, to call into question the logic of conventional gender categories.

In addition, the theorizing of testeria serves to further elucidate, but also to render more perplexing, the manner in which heterosexuality, masculinity, and whiteness are represented as concomitant in Cobain's texts and within the culture at large. The very notion of testeria, therefore, underscores the way hegemonic culture operates to correlate femininity with the body, queerness, and blackness, while masculinity is aligned with the mind, heterosexuality, and whiteness. As will become clear in my analysis of Cobain's creative writings, I insist on designating as "testerical" the so-called feminine posturing of the persona Cobain assumes in order to retain, metaphorically, its connection to male corporeality. In Cobain's writings, what narrators in his lyrics and journal entries represent as a feminine or feminized self cannot be separated from the experiences of a body that is depicted as composed of decidedly *male* parts (penis, testicles, prostate [rectum]).

Throughout both my literary analysis and my cultural commentary, therefore, my focus remains on Cobain's discursive and representational praxis, that is, how he reflects on masculinity and the male body and how he uses language and images to communicate specific ideas. Yet I do not propose a historicist consideration of the body in general, an examination that would draw necessarily from the works of theorists like Michel Foucault and Susan Bordo, among others. Nevertheless, Cobain's writings, although creative and fictive, can be read into the history of the male body that scholars (such as Josep Armengol and Esther Zaplana) have been writing, especially in the past four decades. By focusing on the economic and cultural transformations that characterize American society from the 1920s up to the twenty-first century, these studies constitute a history of American culture that examines the male body as an erotic object and the precise manner in which it functions, both symbolically *and* as a real instrument of individual and institutional power.

Finally, it is through a reading of Cobain's journal entries that I uncover how and why "writing itself, as Calvin Thomas reminds us, is a 'bodily function' which has the potential to 'alienate, to abject, to feminize'—even to 'queer'" (Armengol, 5) hegemonic men. Certain men who self-identify as heterosexual, as Thomas suggests and as Cobain's journals confirm, necessarily reveal a different aspect of their identity when they write about themselves. And it is also through a reading of specific Cobain lyrics that it becomes clear that just as he sings, Cobain writes with his body. He composes in such a manner that the representation of his real or phantasized body skews and poses a challenge to the hegemony of heterosexual masculinity. He crafts both his lyrics and his journals in a way that calls into question the presumed naturalness and superiority of heterosexuality.

I designate the dominant mode of masculinity that Cobain's writings challenge as "heteromasculinity" and the "heteromasculine." It is in contesting conventional notions of masculinity, for example, that the ensemble of his texts countermands the patriarchal imperative that divorces masculinity from embodiment. Therein, his creative writings reveal an alignment with a certain feminist strategy. In the coming chapters, I expose precisely how and why Cobain's themes and his literary techniques—which, along with his visual art, make up his overall discursive practice—engage with different modes of masculinity, both hegemonic as well as nonhegemonic and queer.

THE COBAIN PERSONA AND THE WRITING OF FICTION
AS AUTOBIOGRAPHY

> A guard roughly pulls Cobain back, then smashes him in the head and knocks him down. As Cobain pulls his arms and legs into his chest, the guard stomps him. This wasn't staged, it was real—and yet there is a way in which this event was staged, because it was always present in the music. The glimpse you are given of the man inside the publicity, a defenseless loser named Kurt Cobain, inside a star who merely happens to have the same name—something the thug in the guard has suddenly glimpsed, and just as suddenly acted upon— is shocking.
>
> —GREIL MARCUS, "Artist of the Year: Kurt Cobain" (47)

Marcus is describing a scene from the 1994 documentary "Live! Tonight! Sold Out!!" in which Cobain performs on stage with shorter red hair and wearing no outer garments except what appears to be a black slip. His interaction with the guard encapsulates the essence of the slippage between person and persona to which I draw attention in my reading of Cobain's creative writings. It is this very distinction that I maintain throughout the following chapters between Cobain the person and the narrative perspective (or subject-position) in his lyrics and journals. In this respect also, I take a different strategy from previous writers who have commented on Cobain's writings only to the extent that these texts describe or seem to explain the events and circumstances of his real life. Thus, I follow José Muños's strategy as he reads the lyrics and analyzes the stage performance of the tragically doomed punk icon Darby Crash. Muños makes a critical distinction between the "figure" of Darby Crash and the "actual historical" Darby Crash, the closeted-gay lead singer of the Germs who committed suicide in 1980 from a heroin overdose (99). At the same time, Muños realizes, as I have discovered in distinguishing the Cobain persona from the historical Kurt Cobain, that what Muños calls the "figure" and the "historical person" can bleed into one another. The distinction cannot always be discerned or maintained.

In my readings of Cobain's lyrics and journal, I consider each of these texts, separately and collectively, to constitute a performance. As I have already indicated, these texts do not mirror or explain an identity, rather they perform one. A performance, in the narrow sense, designates a presentation of events during which the presenter is bodily present before an equally and bodily present audience. I am, of course, using "performance" in a broader sense, one that considers written narratives as performative.[7] Specifically in contrast to the way scholars within performance studies employ the terms "performance" (an embodied presentation) and "performativity" (evoking or mimicking a performance), when I write of the performance of gender, sexuality, or race in conjunction with Cobain's writings, I am referring to the images and messages his texts produce for the reader/viewer. I am also describing the physical sensations and the emotions his texts elicit. In focusing on the narrative strategies and lyrical flourishes within Cobain's writings, I use "performance" in the same way as Leerom Medovoi does in his study of "rock as a masculinist *performance* of generational rebellion" (156). I am also using "performance," then, as does Cortney Alexander in her "feminist analysis of Kurt Cobain's gender *performance*" (1).

I differ, however, from Alexander and other scholars who examine Cobain because I establish that it is a phantasized male body, one that is penetrated and thus feminized, that anchors the performance in certain lyrics that I identify as signature songs within Cobain's lyrical works. This testerical body is put on stage also in a number of signature journal entries, ones that constitute variations on a single theme. All these entries persist in exposing the burden and the abomination that is male flesh. Further, representations of this testerical body, I argue, suggest a specific kind of masculine identification and the adoption of a specific persona.

In each of the signature texts that Cobain produces, when he writes in the first person, the "I" of the text could potentially signal three referents. First, Cobain could be referring to himself, a real person born on February 20, 1967, in Aberdeen, Washington. Second, he could be playing a role and presenting a persona, specifically a producer and consumer of music and a reluctant rock star. And, third, the "I" of the text could represent the voice of a fictional character whose existence is limited to a specific song or journal entry. This character may or may not be an analogue of the real person or of the persona.[8] What each of these performative instances shares in common is the complex intertwining of the autobiographical and the fictional. The real person, the persona, and the character, as Cobain performs them in any particular text, are most frequently neither wholly real nor, in some respects, strictly fictional.

Of the three instances of "I," the real person is the most furtive and appears the most stealthily, if indeed at all, in any particular text. On the other hand, the persona-character, as he emerges within lyrics and journal entries, is the most consistently observable and assessable. Thus the persona-character constitutes the principal object of my analysis as I examine the social identity of the Cobain persona when he appears as narrators and characters in specific lyrics and journal fragments. The persona-character, which I shorthand simply as "persona," also appears invariably during Cobain's stage performances as well as in formal interviews, neither of which can be taken unproblematically as giving access to the real person. Further, as Philip Auslander writes about entertainers in general and glam rockers specifically, even off stage and during casual public appearances, it is the Cobain persona rather than the real person that is more readily accessible (6). Like many other music artists, such as David Bowie, for example, but to a much lesser extent and also in a more unselfconscious manner, Kurt Cobain continued to play a role when offstage and out of the range of the camera.

My own analysis of Cobain's writings suggests that the persona itself becomes so entangled with the person that the latter, in a sense, ceases to exist in these texts in any unadulterated manner. In other words, the persona functions to inflect the person and to determine, to a significant degree, how the real Kurt Cobain represents himself in pubic and how he speaks and behaves. Although all his biographers document the musician's propensity to effortlessly reinvent and thus fictionalize himself and the circumstances and events of his life, it is not always apparent, as I read Cobain's interviews, if he himself is always fully aware of when he is "reporting" and when he is "inventing" or embellishing.

This distinction, however, is not a subject I take on. This topic constitutes yet another one that commentators of Cobain's lyrics, such as Soulsby, invariably address. In my analysis, what I am calling "persona" in Cobain's interviews and public appearances corresponds to what David Graver in "The Actor's Body" labels "personage," because it is not "a foundational reality but simply another way of representing oneself" within a particular ideological discussion and cultural context (164). In Cobain's specific case, American popular culture and, specifically, alternative, white-male-dominated rock music makes up this discussion and context.

Although the real person and the persona cannot always be clearly distinguished from each other in Cobain's writings, the notion of the persona as a construct still holds significant interpretive value. The ensemble of Cobain's texts provides a propitious opportunity to examine the coming into being and the performance of a specific kind of masculine subject for three reasons. First, the historical moment during which Cobain writes (post–civil rights, feminist, and gay movements); second, the geographical location (predominantly white youth subcultures of the Pacific Northwest); and, third, the personal and interpersonal circumstances under which he was writing (chemical addiction, membership in an all-male band). It is also for reasons of history and geography that his lyrics and journals represent this subject in a manner that exposes the structure and the internal logic—including the contradictions—of whiteness, masculinity, and heterosexuality as normative positions within American culture.

In the typical Cobain text, one might say that it is because memory, phantasy, and the fictional elaboration of real events and circumstances are so intermeshed that disentangling them becomes impossible. Not only is it frequently impossible, in the reading of any single text or any combination of texts, to clearly demarcate person and persona, it is also heuristically unproductive to do so when attempting to understand the aesthetics and cultural politics represented in Cobain's lyrics and journals. I shall return to this point below. In this sense, my reading of his creative writings can be opposed to a traditional reading of his biography, or a reading of some of his texts that journalists and critics have presumed to be autobiographical. In the writing and reading of biography and autobiography, there would be historical value in attempting to distinguish between the real person and the persona.

Yet Cobain's texts do not have to present the "truth" about the events and circumstances in his life; they produce, nevertheless, meaning about his life, and about life in general, by the very fact that they speak to aspects of a real existence. The content of Cobain's texts requires readers to pose the exact question that preoccupies his fans, biographers, and many music journalists concerning the relationship between fact and fiction in his lyrics in particular. This question is, of course, one that many literary critics and historians of literature have invariably posed over the centuries about many other writers. It is the same question that Freud, too, broaches in a 1907 essay titled "Creative Writers and Day-Dreaming." In this essay, Freud proposes that phantasy plays a more determinant role than memory (of real events in a subject's life) when it comes to daydreaming and creative productions like literature and art. Cobain's writings also suggest that psychic reality overrules external reality when it comes to representing aspects of one's own existence.[9]

Further, as my analysis of Cobain's lyrics and journals will confirm, C. Fred Alford's account of the relationship between autobiography and fiction accurately describes the reparative and compensatory function of Cobain's creative texts:

> The artistic representation acknowledges the external world, even as it goes on to create another one. In creating another world of perfect wholeness and reconciliation, art calls attention to the contrast between this perfect world and its damaged, fragmented, empirical counterpart. It is in this contrast between phantasy and reality that the emancipatory power of art resides. (116; also cited by Sánchez-Pardo)

Because of the way Cobain's songs and journals compulsively conflate reality and fiction by confounding real and imagined experiences, some of his most poignant texts are infused with a rich and subtle emotional and psychical discernment. In this respect, in my analysis of his writings, I am inspired by Susan Suleiman's reading of a short story by twentieth-century French writer Louis Aragon titled "Le mentir-vrai" ("Truthfully Lying").

Suleiman's examination of the way Aragon frequently comments on the relationship between truth and the act of writing has informed especially my reading of Cobain's journals. Like the Aragon text that Suleiman analyzes, the fragments in Cobain's journals also call into question the necessarily problematic border that putatively separates autobiography and fiction. But whether reading Cobain's journals *or* his lyrics, attempting to distinguish verifiable, historical fact from demonstrably fictional invention does not get readers very far in their effort to understand how gender, sexuality, and race appear conceptually and rhetorically within his writings. What Cobain writes in a song like "Smells Like Teen Spirit" does not transcribe events or simply represent a masculine subject. Rather, the text *creates* these events and this subject.

Therefore, attempting to align a specific narrative or lyrical detail found within a Cobain text with a detail from his biography does not facilitate an understanding of how and why his texts represent masochism and melancholy as constituent components of normative masculinity. To cite just one illustrative example: In one of the longest and most affecting entries in his journals, Cobain invents the story of a serial killer. The narrative includes a description of the criminal's childhood and the family dynamics between the son and his mother, father, and sister. This entry is examined in detail in chapter 4. But whether or not readers realize that the killer's name ("Chuck Taylor") corresponds to the brand of Converse sneakers that Cobain preferred in real life sheds no light on how this journal entry proceeds to tell us something significant about father-son relationships and about the abuse of masculine power. Further, Cobain employs specific literary techniques, including a narrative that shifts between the first and third persons, in a way that skillfully suggests already the parallels that exist between the narrator (the Cobain persona) and the character (the serial killer) in this episode. As a result, the origin of the killer's name becomes superfluous, if not completely immaterial, in how the story produces a specific and uncanny effect on readers.

If I were obliged to insert Cobain's creative writings into a specific genre, I would characterize the ensemble of his texts as a fictionalized autobiography, or "autofiction." In literary criticism, the term autofiction, in the broad sense, refers to any form of autobiographical writing that has been fictionalized to some extent. French novelist and critic Serge Doubrovsky coined the term in 1977 in order to describe his novel *Fils,* a title that can mean either "sons" or "threads," depending on whether or not the "s" is pronounced in French. Doubrovsky presents his novel as an amalgamation, the "threading together" of fiction and autobiography. He contends initially that autobiography is the reserve of important people; he indicates also that the autobiographer writes in a refined style.

By contrast, autofiction, the fictionalizing of events that are manifestly real, according to Doubrovsky, results when the language that describes an adventure becomes itself a specific kind of adventure, an adventure of language; that is, when the language with which a story is being told becomes the story. When reading Cobain's creative writings, and his journal entries in particular, I would paraphrase Doubrovsky by specifying that in Cobain's autobiographical fiction, writing about an event has itself been turned into an event. As I shall reveal, the recounting of ostensible episodes in the musician's life, like a particular Nirvana concert, constitutes an act for which the writing takes precedence. Writing becomes more important than what is being written about. In Cobain's texts, the act of narrating is liberated, in a sense, from the narrated events since the telling of any story becomes independent from the story being told. The narration, the telling, takes on its own strategies and objectives, all of which operate to represent masculinity as a troubling and troubled identity.

Further, autofiction, for Doubrovsky, appears outside of the logic, the linguistic codes, and formal strictures of all versions of the novel, a characterization that also applies to Cobain's efforts to relate the story of his inner, phantasy life. The French critic concludes his initial definition of the genre by analogizing it to music in a way that further implicates Cobain's creative writings. The genre consists, Doubrovsky writes, of "juxtapositions, the threading together of words, alliterations, assonances, dissonances, writing that must have existed before, and that will surely outlive, the very history of literature. Autofiction has a natural form. It is 'concrete,' just as we characterize a certain kind of music" (10). The next two chapters of this book explore in detail how Cobain's lyrics and journals do indeed resort to the juxtaposition of disparate ideas and images and to an inventive wordplay, techniques that exploit the sound as well as the meaning of words, often to discomfiting effects.

In the four decades since the publication of *Fils,* the distinction that Doubrovsky establishes between autofiction and autobiography has inspired a continuing polemic on the part of creative writers, journalists, critics, and theorists, with Philippe Lejeune's *The Autobiographical Pact* and Philippe Gasparini's *Autofiction* featuring among the most influential theoretical texts. There are websites and at least one English-language academic journal devoted to the interrelations between autobiography, autofiction, and fiction.[10] And Cobain's autobiographical fiction, clearly, must be distinguished not only from autobiography but also from pure fiction. Notwithstanding this ongoing, intense debate concerning generic borders, including more generalized discussions about how texts are written, read, and interpreted, "auto-fictional"—an adjective signifying the construction of the self through fiction—best characterizes Cobain's lyrical and journal writing overall. In composing these texts, he is "truthfully lying."

Given the manner in which autobiographical fiction and pure phantasy fuse together within Cobain's written texts, throughout my analysis I use the terms "subject-position," the "Cobainian subject," and the "Cobain persona" in distinct but overlapping ways that reflect this fusion. I use "subject-position" to refer to the overall, defining aesthetics and politics embedded in his written texts. I use "Cobainian subject" to refer to the specific narrators and characters that populate Cobain's imaginary universe. And, in the way I use "persona," the term refers to the musician's performance on stage and during interviews, in addition to the subject-position that he constructs in his creative writings.

As I suggest above, Cobain is not radically different from other entertainment personalities, be they Bob Dylan, Bruce Springsteen, or Darby Crash, who all have engaged in self-creation to varying degrees. One especially evocative sign that Cobain was engaging in an especially ingenious and revealing form of self-creation is the variant spelling of his name, "Kurdt Kobain," which he began to use early on in his career.[11] The alternate spelling of the family name seems obvious, one could surmise, in that it turns an alliteration (words commencing with "K" and "C") into an orthographic repetition (K/K) as well. But given, on the one hand, Cobain's affinity for the ethics and aesthetics of the independent record label K Records and, on the other, the attention he accords to the Ku Klux Klan (KKK) in his journal entries and illustrations, the double "K" has a certain ironic resonance. In addition, as I also reveal in the forthcoming chapters, a particular kind of repetition or "stuttering" characterizes some of Cobain's writings at every level: letters of the alphabet, words, sentences, paragraphs, and entire narrative episodes.

Still, it is the spelling of his first name, which he often wrote with a capital "D" ("KurDt"), that is especially revealing because it points to and further underscores a recurring theme within Cobain's writing, namely, that of a natural, infrangible bond—but an extremely fraught relationship—between a son and his father. It is in his journals that Cobain most frequently wrote his first name with a capital "D," thereby accentuating the importance of this inventive spelling in his imaginary world. Cobain's father is Donald Cobain; the musician's own given name is Kurt Donald Cobain, which might be written on official forms in the United States as "Kurt D. Cobain." So, as some fans online suggest, with the choice of "KurDt" as a forename, Cobain was not adjoining a "d" but rather displacing one that is already present in his official name, one that links him forever to his father. As I shall also explore, a desire, both implicit and explicit, to displace the father emerges as a defining theme within his writings. Cobain also returns obsessively to the notion of a son's fear that he is destined, or perhaps condemned, to take on the father's characteristics, to turn into the father. With this orthographic gesture, or spelling trick, then, the persona that Cobain compulsively assumes in his written texts is revealing and, simultaneously, concealing his paternity, at least for those readers clever enough to figure it out.

In addition, Soulsby writes in *Dark Slivers* that "KurDt" was most probably meant to be pronounced "Curd," in a way that would make his name rhyme with "turd." The notion is not far-fetched, given that Cobain skillfully draws a foul-smelling, fresh pile of turds for the cover of a recording of the songs performed by his pre-Nirvana group. He names this group Fecal Matter. The beige background of the cover contrasts with the dark-brown, shit color of the pile of turds itself. Cobain expertly captures the "freshness" of the pile by drawing three squiggly parallel lines to represent the steam produced because the feces are still at body temperature. Further, although the pile has been freshly excreted, it is swarmed already by *buzzing* blowflies. For the cover's final and somewhat disgusting touch, Cobain inscribes the name of his group in large letters at the top. It is obvious that the name is represented, appropriately, as if the letters have been finger painted using the pile of "fecal matter" captured on the cover itself. The cover also artfully foreshadows the lyrics to the album's premier song, "Buffy's Pregnant": "We [men] are all the same, just flies on turds."

Soulsby's speculation about how "KurDt" is to be pronounced has credibility also because of the way Cobain characterizes himself and his lyrics in certain journal entries as a "pile of shit." Further, his alter ego appears in one illustration in his journals as a bowel movement, quite literally as a piece of shit ("corn poop"), represented as both a process and a product (fig. 1). Finally, Cobain's lyrics and journal writings are replete with examples of first-person narrators and characters who are compulsively self-critical and self-deprecating; they present themselves in varying ways as "little shits." His writings also abound with various third-person male characters—typically represented as racists, misogynists, or violent abusers of women, children, and nonwhites—who are in effect even bigger "pieces of shit" because they wield more power and cause more seemingly irreparable physical and psychic damage to others.

In chapters 3 and 4, I examine in detail Cobain's creative process. In exploring the specific way his inventive texts operate to condemn and to resist the masculinist ideology of the alternative rock subculture, I demonstrate precisely how the persona he creates comes to espouse a testerical identity, revealed to be arrantly antimacho, profeminist, gay-affirmative, and, tacitly at least, anti-racist as well. Cobain's lyrics and journals succeed in censuring conventional masculinity by rendering gay-male identities visible and by valorizing queer possibilities. But his creative texts also operate to reclaim heterosexual masculinity itself as a possible site of resistance to conventional notions of gender and sexuality. At the same time, his lyrics function implicitly, while his journals operate explicitly, to put forth a specific kind of white straight man as antiracist.

TEXTS
LYRICS AND JOURNALS

3

COBAIN'S LYRICS
The Anxiety of Living as Male and Straight in a
Misogynist and Heterosexist Culture

Kevin Allman: Does it make you laugh when people take apart all your songs and
try to figure out what you're saying?
Kurt Cobain: Oh, yeah. At the time I was writing those songs [*Nevermind*], I really
didn't know what I was trying to say. There is no point to analyze or explain it.
That used to be the biggest subject in an interview: "What are your lyrics about?"
  —KEVIN ALLMAN, "The Dark Side of Nirvana's Kurt Cobain" (381)

Cobain was a master practitioner within a genre known for producing innocu-
ous, ambiguous, and, at times, unintelligible lyrics. He wrote songs that would
seem, then, to resist a classic literary analysis in part because of the challenge
of assigning a fixed, coherent, and comprehensive meaning to texts that often
turn out to be "a fragmentary and elusive set of lyrics that sometimes degenerate into nonsense" (Beebe, 318). Even within the genre, however, Cobain has
become a cliché in the sense that he is viewed by some listeners of independent
guitar rock as the performer par excellence whose vocalizing, imprecise diction, awkward phrasing, elision of words, and muddled pronunciation often
render his already difficult lyrics even more challenging to comprehend.

   As Nick Soulsby indicates, *Mad Magazine* once gently poked fun at Cobain's
singing by proclaiming that all singers should be taught to "mumble like Kurt
Cobain so there'll be fewer incomprehensible lyrics [for fans and cover bands]
to memorize" (*Dark Slivers*, chap. 8). In addition, in 1992 Weird Al Yankovic
exploited the fact that much of the buzz surrounding the commercial success
of *Nevermind* centered on listeners' inability to decipher what Cobain was

singing. In a song Yankovic titles "Smells Like Nirvana," he expertly mimics Cobain's singing. He begins the first verse of his version of Nirvana's most popular song by asking "What is this song all about / How do the words to it go?" He then pleads with listeners to provide him with his own words. Yankovic concludes the verse, ironically, with a crisp diction that contradicts the very singing technique that he is satirizing: "Now I'm mumblin' and I'm screamin' / And I don't know what I'm singin'." In Cobain's case, even when listeners succeed in deciphering his words, they typically deem his laconic lyrics to be especially cryptic, opaque, or nonsensical. And, as he himself writes in "On a Plain," in a self-contradictory manner and with a certain degree of elfishness, "It is now time to make it unclear / To write off lines that don't make sense."

Most observers, like Sub Pop's owner Jonathan Poneman and entertainment journalist Chuck Crisafulli, agree that Cobain's lyrics display "a bent toward meaningful meaningless" (Crisafulli, 18). Yet most observers also insist that Cobain's voice and his stage performance give sense to his nonsense and meaning to his meaninglessness, whether this unintelligibility is willful or inadvertent. In a similar manner, Cobain's onetime girlfriend Tobi Vail asserts that listeners of certain songs, such as "Drain You" and "I Hate Myself and Want to Die," often "respond to the emotional quality of [Cobain's] voice and the phrasing of his words rather than to the actual meaning of the songs (True, 228). And when assessing Cobain's songwriting, Soulsby characterizes his genius as resulting from the combination of three features: the singular way he adopts a narrative perspective in his lyrics; the way he delivers lines in his most affecting songs; and the way he succeeds in expressing a specific take on contemporary social and cultural issues (*Dark Slivers,* chap. 10).

Contrary to the kind of analysis of Cobain songs that Soulsby, Crisafulli, and others propose, I take the written word as the principal object of my analysis. I put delivery and music performance in parenthesis. There exist already detailed commentaries on Cobain's voice and style of singing. Nick Kent writes in *The Guardian,* for example, of the "full death-moan vocal effect of Cobain's voice. His larynx-shredding voice," Kent concludes, "is probably the key to his enduring appeal: It still delivers, [for instance], as he turns the word 'pain' into a multi-syllable crescendo screech on the otherwise forgettable . . . song 'You Know You're Right'" ("Isn't There Somebody?"). There are also excellent analyses of the evolution and the significance of Nirvana's guitar, bass, and drum sounds. Kent, Soulsby, and Crisafulli, among others, have provided comprehensive accounts and convincing analyses of all the music Nirvana has recorded. These studies include the specific sounds on each song and, quite often, a description of the relation between the music and lyrics as well as the musical connections between individual songs.[1]

Even though my introduction to most of the songs examined in this chapter has been by way of Cobain's recorded voice and Nirvana's music, I conclude that his written lyrics can and do stand alone as literary texts. Based on these written texts, I examine Cobain's overall aesthetic and discursive practices by exploring how he goes about composing songs and inscribing them with specific meanings. I analyze his lyrics in order to demonstrate the ways some of the stories Cobain relates and some of the images he creates in his songs succeed in sketching the profile of a particular kind of masculine subject, one who experiences an acute anxiety about living as male and straight in a misogynist and heterosexist culture.

I do not comment on every song that Cobain has written; I direct my attention to a select group of lyrics that defines his signature style and that exposes the themes that preoccupy him. In particular, I refer to, but do not comment in detail on, several songs that critics have already thoroughly examined, like "Polly," "Been a Son," or "Smells Like Teen Spirit." Similarly, I shall not be especially concerned with the order in which he wrote songs. The chronology of composition is another topic that other writers have thoroughly covered. Some commentators, including Clark Humphrey and Gillian Gaar, as well as most of Cobain's biographers, have documented the dates and circumstances of the writing and the recording of all the songs in Nirvana's catalogue.[2] Although I do not comment on the order in which Cobain composed his songs, chronology does tell us something significant about his lyrics because songs composed during the three distinct periods of his career display a similar structuring and content. One can distinguish between the songs written during the pre-Nirvana years (Fecal Matter), during the Sub Pop and early Nirvana period (pre-*Nevermind*), and the during the later Nirvana period (post-*Nevermind*).

In the pursuit of my ultimate objective in this chapter, it does prove at times to be daunting to attempt to ascribe a coherent meaning to any individual Cobain song. But in revealing the literary techniques that characterize Cobain's lyrical production and in exploring the subjects he writes about and the images he creates, I demonstrate the precise manner in which his lyrics make sense or create nonsense. Through this process, instead of focusing exclusively on the content and the meaning of any particular song in isolation, I also highlight the interrelation between the songs. I examine how they dialogue with each other, thereby revealing the overarching themes and recurrent images that appear throughout Cobain's lyrics as an ensemble. Beyond my immediate aim in this chapter, my ultimate objective remains to explore how Cobain's creative writings, his journals as well as his lyrics, function to create a specific persona that Cobain takes great pains to cultivate.

Since Cobain has provided the transcription for only a few of his songs, primarily in his journals, it has been left to others to transcribe recorded versions of his lyrics. Fortunately, hundreds of Nirvana fans have done a commendable job in transcribing and posting lyrics on several websites.[3] These fan-generated transcriptions have facilitated my work, but they do present a challenge. To begin with, Cobain is, as I suggest, notorious for mumbling as well as for his tendency to punctuate his singing with screams and other vocalizations. As a result, there can be a wide variation in what listeners hear on a recording. Frequently, listeners disagree on what constitute single words or phrases in many songs. Like most listeners, I find no song to be completely incomprehensible from first line to last. Some lyrics, however, like "In His Room" and "Endless, Nameless" are especially difficult to decipher.

In addition, the matter of exact wording is further complicated because there can be lyrical variation of a song depending on which recorded version one transcribes. Gaar reveals, for example, how different recordings of "All Apologies" sport different lyrics (14). "Very Ape" is another example of Cobain singing different versions of a song at various times, resulting in the online circulation of different transcriptions of this song. In this chapter, I take the studio-recorded versions of songs as they appear on *Bleach, Nevermind, Incesticide,* and *In Utero* to constitute the definitive versions of Cobain's lyrics. Even though Cobain revised and edited certain songs, I subscribe to Soulsby's conclusion that "once a song was brought to the studio, [Cobain] committed to that edition of the lyrics as the conclusive rendition" (*Dark Slivers,* chap. 10). For the songs on *Illiteracy Will Prevail,* which Cobain wrote prior to forming Nirvana, I use the demo recording posted on YouTube (https://www.youtube .com/watch?v=zTnPdp_Vt3Y).[4]

THE ORIGINS AND INSPIRATION FOR COBAIN'S LYRICS:
PHANTASY AND AUTOBIOGRAPHICAL FICTION

Even a cursory analysis of Cobain's music and lyrics reveals that other musicians of his generation and from preceding generations have influenced him. He himself has indicated a fondness for American and British popular music of the '60s and '70s and an affinity for new wave, metal, hardcore, and alternative musicians of the '80s and early '90s. In fact, his songs reveal musical and lyrical influences from John Lennon and Paul McCartney (The Beatles); from Iggy Pop (The Stooges); from Eugene Kelly (The Vaselines); from Kathleen Hanna (Bikini Kill); and from Buzz Osborne (Melvins), among others. In particular, Cobain's songwriting and singing share features in common with the lyrics and stage presence of two of his contemporaries, Michael Stipe (R.E.M.) and Morrissey (The Smiths). Stipe and Morrissey are two of the performers that Cobain cites in his journals as paradigmatic of a certain kind of songwriter he prefers:

> It seems like there are only two options for [songwriters'] personalities. Either they're *sad, tragic* visionaries like Morrissey or Michael Stipe . . . or they're the goofy, nutty *white boy,* hey let's party and forget everything, people like Van Halen or all that other heavy metal crap. (*Journals,* 44, emphasis added)

In addition, the lyrics and performance style of these two artists, like Cobain's, also engage with the interrelations between music performance, masculinity, masochism, and melancholy.[5]

I do not, however, enter into the full details of these comparisons. This topic is yet another one for which biographers, as well as other scholars and music commentators, have already provided convincing accounts. These studies contextualize Cobain's music and lyrical production within the overall history and evolution of twentieth-century American guitar-rock in general, and grunge specifically.[6] Beyond Cobain's place in the history of popular music songwriting, I am more interested in how his creative writings, overall, fit into the broader tradition of autobiographical and fictional writings that engage with notions of masculinity, masochism, and melancholy.

Although in this chapter I drill down into the content of Cobain's lyrics in order to ascertain the nature and scope of the images and the subjects of his compositions, I do not set out, as indicated in the introduction, to uncover some previously undisclosed truth about Kurt Cobain the historical person. This chapter examines the structuring and the internal logic of his *imaginary world,* that is, the persona, characters, and narratives he invents. Therefore, I focus on how songwriting provides a way for Cobain to recreate himself by creating a persona. It is for this reason that I consider not only his lyrics but also his journals to constitute a fictionalized autobiography. His lyrics end up creating an imaginary subject that is neither real nor altogether made up. Instead, his songs present a phantasmatic version of Cobain's *subjective* truth. As a result, they provide access to an emotional and psychical reality. In a 1991 interview, Cobain explains how at an early age he used writing "to escape from what . . . [he] had been surrounded by [and] to vent" his frustrations (Spiccia, 210). He has also spoken of his sense of isolation that writing partially succeeded in mitigating (Mullins and Mullins, 120).[7]

There is quite clearly a relationship between Cobain's lyrics and his visual art. He recognizes and comments on this relationship on several occasions. Both forms of expression constitute a kind of collage, a juxtaposition of disparate words, images, or ideas. In the end, both modes of expression are nonlinear undertakings that possess a dream-like quality:

> **Phil Sutcliffe:** A lot of time with your lyrics . . . it seems you use images within . . . one song which are very different [from one another]. Not obviously connected.
>
> **Kurt Cobain:** Right.
>
> **PS:** I wondered if that had anything to do with your painting and sculpting approach to things at all?
>
> **KC:** Yeah, it does. I've always painted abstracts. I've always thought abstract. I love dreams that don't make sense. I'd much rather watch a film that doesn't have a plot. For me, the reason why most of my lyrics don't connect is that they're all pieces of my poetry. I've used lines from all these different poems—and in the first place none of the poems are about anything. They're not thematic, and then I take lines out of each of them, put them together—and I make up a theme to the lyric well after the fact. (Sutcliffe, 425)

After the release of *Nevermind,* when disclaiming any specific meaning for the songs on that album, Cobain contends that for all the songs he has ever written he has followed his usual practice of using ideas that came into his head and that he had written willy-nilly in his notebooks. With this method, Cobain affirms, it is impossible that even his most famous song could have a particular meaning. Though in these interviews he is speaking about *Nevermind* specifically, Cobain uses this same logic to deny that his lyrics in general have a direct connection to the people and events in his life: "When I say 'I,' I don't mean me. I am not autobiographical. My lyrics are often just bits of sentences put together without any particular meaning" (Pécker, 300). Cobain makes the same assertion in his journals: "When I say 'I' in a song, that doesn't necessarily mean that the person is me and it doesn't mean I'm just a storyteller; it means whoever or whatever you want" (120).

Although he may have genuinely believed these assertions as he was uttering or writing them, Cobain does seem aware, at least on a superficial level, of the relationship between his real life and his creative productions, the persona he takes on. Like many other artists, he is aware that he is creating an imaginary world as a way to escape from, and, I would add, as a way to understand his real world, one that he experiences at times as unrelentingly disconsolate. He later acknowledges in a 1992 interview that there is a certain autobiographical aspect to some of his lyrics: "My songs have always been frustrating themes, relationships that I've had. And now that I'm in love, I expect it to be really happy, or at least there won't be half as much anger as there was. . . . I don't know how my music's going to change. But I'm looking forward to it" (Kelly, cited by Pécker, 301).

But Cobain need not have corrected or amended his earlier statements. Even the casual Nirvana fan, while listening to *In Utero*, for example, can readily identify some of the personal references in these songs. In fact, in numerous subsequent interviews, if Cobain does not admit outright to personal references in his songs, he ceases at least to disclaim these references when journalists bring them up. Based on an exhaustive reading of some of Cobain's lyrics, however, Soulsby concludes that his "songs did not become [progressively] more autobiographical, they always were. What . . . [changed] was how explicit [his songs] were about the subjects and objects of his writing" ("Analysing Nirvana's Songs"). I contend, by contrast, that in the interval between *Bleach* and *In Utero*, Cobain simply becomes less cryptic and mysterious in certain songs that have particular significance for the *persona* he is creating and projecting.

THE SEARCH FOR MEANING IN MEANINGLESSNESS:
UNDERSTANDING THE INDIVIDUAL SONG

In his blog "Analysing Nirvana's Songs" and in his book *Dark Slivers: Searching for Nirvana in the Shards of Incesticide,* Soulsby provides some of the most trenchant interpretations of Cobain's lyrics that have been published in English to date. He writes explicitly as a Nirvana fan for other fans, those whom he assumes to be equally touched by Cobain's "genius." He specifies that the primary objective of everything he writes is to "enhance the listening experience" of fans (*Dark Slivers,* foreword). Although Soulsby occasionally conflates lyrics and music in his attempt to identify the inspiration behind Cobain's songwriting, he does succeed in suggesting why many of Cobain's songs—though uniquely flawed—are nonetheless complex and enigmatic sources of pleasure. He also succeeds in suggesting why, when performed, Cobain's lyrics are especially seductive to so many listeners.[8]

As other commentators have observed, Cobain wrote, generally speaking, three kinds of songs, though I would characterize these three genres somewhat differently than most observers. Of the scores of original songs that Cobain wrote, only a few, such as "Floyd the Barber" and "Sliver," can be characterized as "narrative" in that they relate, in a more or less chronological order, an event or episode. By comparison, a larger number of his original songs, such as "Scentless Apprentice" and "Even in His Youth" constitute "profiles" in the sense that they describe, to varying degrees, specific traits attributed to identifiable characters. But the vast majority of Cobain's songs must be described as "lyrical." The songs in this genre neither narrate an event nor do they profile a character; rather, they consist frequently of the interweaving of disjointed images or vague ruminations on a number of specific topics. The lyrical genre seems to be Cobain's default mode of writing, especially during the later years of his career. In this genre he is prolific and he excels in creating insightful, affecting lyrics. In reality, however, many of Cobain's songs consist of a combination of the three genres. A narrative song can be composed as the profile of a character, as in "Laminated Effect," or the profile of a character can be accomplished through a lyrical elaboration of specific character traits, as in "Heart Shaped Box."

Cobain evolved as a songwriter. During the early part of his career, his lyrics are often simplistic and repetitive. The repetition in these songs serves more of a sonic or locutionary function than a narrative, profile, or lyrical purpose.

Just as Tobi Vail asserts, the sound of the words and the way Cobain enunciates them, more so than what the words signify, take precedence. During the later part of his career, his lyrics typically are more verbose, if not more complex. In these later songs, repetition, in addition to its sonic and locutionary function, often serve to evoke a specific emotion or to reinforce an image or an idea presented in a song.

Notwithstanding the different writing styles that Cobain adopts during the three phases of his career, a common writing technique stamps all the songs he composes in a way that makes them identifiable as Cobain compositions. All of his songs do indeed resort, to varying degrees, to techniques of juxtaposition. The subtle humor that runs through Cobain's lyrics is often a result of the unusual conjoining of words, such as the fusion and confusion of incest with insecticide ("Incesticide") or anorexic with exorcist ("anorexorcist"). Cobain juxtaposes not only single words; he also conjoins ideas and images in a canny and entertaining manner.[9]

"On a Plain," for example, contains the amusing phrase "blackmailed by black sheep." Other examples of humor can be found in otherwise serious or even seemingly high-minded lyrics like "Radio Friendly Unit Shifter," in which one reads the following lines: "Second-rate, third-degree burns" / "Afterbirth of a nation" / "Bipolar opposites attract." Thus it is in the juxtaposing of ideas that Cobain often creates enigmatic images. In "Scoff," for example, one encounters contrasting imperatives: "*Heal* a million, *kill* a million." Or in "Blew," one confronts an arresting, antithetical request on the part of the narrator in the song: "If you wouldn't mind, I would like *to bleed*" / If you wouldn't mind, I would like *to breathe*." In this specific instance, the juxtaposition produces the charged conflation of images of life (breathe) and imminent death (bleed), an image that circulates in Cobain's journals as well.

It is, however, the juxtaposition of different narrative perspectives that accounts for *the* defining stylistic feature of Cobain's lyrics. I explore this feature by providing a close reading of several songs I identify as signature Cobain songs because of how they are structured, the mode in which they are written, and because of the themes they obsessively take on. When Duane Fish writes of "the sensory images of confusion" (89) that are created through Cobain's use of language, I contend that a perplexed and perplexing use of narrative perspective is principally responsible for this effect. A creative use of narrative perspective also accounts for how the reader/listener is constrained to experience the palpable angst that underscores many of Cobain's songs. He manipulates narrative perspective in a manner that confuses and disorients. In a typical narrative song, for example, the perspective of a first-person narrator abruptly and inexplicably shifts to, or is conflated with, a third-person perspective. The reverse is also frequently the case, wherein a "story" that begins in the third person shifts to the first person. Sometimes the slippage in perspective occurs within the same stanza or within a single line, as in "Frances Farmer Will Have Her Revenge on Seattle" and in "Beeswax," respectively.

In addition to the merging of first- and third-person points of view, a second-person perspective often complicates even further the point of view in a Cobain song. As a result, the entirety of the song's images becomes blurred and the song's ostensible message is corrupted. That is, many songs, whether in the narrative, profile, or lyrical mode, are addressed to a "you" whose perspective or whose actual voice can be heard in the text. Frequently, the perspective of a first-person narrator also fuses with, and cannot always be readily differentiated from, this second-person perspective. As a result, in songs like "Milk It" and "Drain You"—analyzed below—the reader is left rudderless, often ill-equipped to navigate the waves of meaning within the story being told. Even the attentive reader is unable to discern whose perspective is being presented or who is telling the story in question. Unable to identify completely or consistently with the narrator, addressee, or the characters, the reader of songs like "Beeswax" and "Spank Thru"—which I also examine—struggles mightily to make sense of it all. Frequently, as Cobain asserts, the song could mean "whatever you want."

Shifts in Narrative Perspectives as Symptomatic of a Divided Identity

A particularly arresting example of the juxtaposing and shifting of narrative perspectives occurs in "Mr. Moustache," a song in which there is an explicit conjoining of narrator ("I") and interlocutor ("you"). In most songs, the convergence of "I" and "you" is usually merely suggested, left open to interpretation. In "Mr. Moustache," by comparison, the instability and the shifting nature of the narrator's identity constitute the most salient feature of the song. In the postchorus, the narrator poses and then answers his own question as to his identity: "I'm who? / I'm you."

In other songs, like "Lounge Act," not only is the first-person narrator conflated with the person he is addressing ("I can't let you smother me"); he is, at the same time, fused with other characters in the song ("he"/"she"). In the chorus to "Lounge Act," the reader confronts four ostensibly distinct characters: "you," "her," "a friend," and "they." All these characters are interchangeable and they intersect with the "I" of the narrator. For example, the narrator describes a "friend" with whom he is bonded ("made a pact"). He alludes to an unspecified, absent woman ("her") whose odor lingers on the person the narrator is addressing. By the concluding lines of the song, a mysterious "they" appear in the guise of several, unspecified characters who take the place of the narrating "I" in the story. As a result, what is rendered in the initial chorus as "*I* still smell her on you" modulates into "*They* still smell her on you" in the final chorus. The shift functions precisely to jumble narrator, interlocutor, and characters in complex and confounding ways.

Though "Lounge Act" may represent a paramount example of this literary feature, the multiple shifts in narrative perspective that occur in this song constitute, as I suggest, a common Cobain technique. It turns out to be the default position in many of his lyrics. The technique functions, in the end, to render the song's message ambiguous. It blurs the distinction between self and other, me and you. In this sense, the narrator macho jerk in "Mr. Moustache" or in "Very Ape," just like both members of the couple in "Swap Meet" and just like the authoritarian character in "Big Cheese," all have filiations with the dominant narrative perspective in these songs. In this sense also, the narrator in these songs is "complicit" with all the subject-positions and points of view put on stage. Cobain is deftly playing all of the parts in the phantasy universe he constructs.

When one considers all of Cobain's songs in which there is a perplexing narrative perspective, "Frances Farmer Will Have Her Revenge on Seattle" represents the most inscrutable example of a text where the fusing of "I," "you," "she," and "they" operates to create an irremediably disjointed text with a maddeningly ambiguous, malleable message. Verse 1 begins in the first person singular with a female-identified narrator expressing three specific sentiments: "It's so relieving . . . to know that you're leaving"; "it's so relaxing to hear you asking"; and "It's so soothing to know that you'll sue me." Further, the initial chorus confirms that the voice heard in the first verse is that of Frances herself: "I miss the comfort of being sad."

Verse 2, by contrast, shifts from the first-person singular to the first-person plural ("we"). The second verse also introduces the second-person addressee ("In a false witness, we hope *you*'re still with us"), indicating that Frances is also the person being spoken to and, in addition, that the narrator is part of the group of people holding her captive. This perspective is confirmed in verse 2 with the reintroduction of Frances, this time in the role of a third-person character ("Our favorite patient. . . . *She*'ll come back as fire"). In addition, the second verse indicates that Frances herself is part of a larger group of misunderstood, persecuted women (witches): "We hope you're still with us" / "To see if they float or drown."[10]

The end result is a confused and confusing narrative perspective. The reader does indeed find it challenging to keep track of the following: Who is speaking? Who is being spoken to? Who is being spoken about? The ambiguity results in a recognizable persona, a poetic voice that is fragmented, unstable, and constantly shifting. Even in this song, however, the psychical and emotional state the song evokes, melancholy, is clear and consistent. As in other lyrics, though the story being related seems surreal, sense-destroying, and impenetrable, the song succeeds nonetheless in conveying an engaging, melancholic experience. In spite of its noise and clutter, the song clearly communicates an experience of persecution, desolation, and impending death.

When analyzing certain songs, both Soulsby and Crisafulli insist on making a distinction between the narrator in a first-person lyric and the historical Kurt Cobain, just as Cobain himself suggests. At the same time, the two commentators insist on differentiating between Cobain's first-person narrators and his third-person narrators. They also acknowledge that such distinctions are not always self-evident. For the difference specifically between songs written in the first person and those written in the third, I argue that it proves also to be heuristically unproductive to distinguish between them, if one's ultimate objective is to analyze representations of masculine subjectivity and agency within Cobain's lyrics.

Crisafulli observes, for example, that the writer (the historical Kurt Cobain) and the character (the macho jerk) in "Very Ape" are clearly distinct. Even though Crisafulli does not seem to recognize that both writer and character must also be distinguished from the narrator in the song (the Cobain persona, the poetic voice), he does make a significant observation. He indicates that "throughout 'Very Ape'—especially when the singer takes pride in being 'the king of illiterature'—it's not entirely clear where *Kurt* leaves off and where the 'Very Ape' character begins" (182, emphasis added). I would modify Crisafulli's conclusion by parenthesizing the historical Kurt Cobain altogether and by designating both the narrator *and* the character in "Very Ape" as versions of the persona that Cobain is trying on.

For his part, Soulsby, while advocating against an autobiographical reading of some of Cobain's lyrics, concedes, after some equivocation, that songs like "Dumb," "Very Ape," and "Pennyroyal Tea" all constitute "screens" for different aspects of Cobain himself (*Dark Slivers,* chap. 10). Once again, I argue that it would be more accurate to state that these songs constitute representations of the Cobain *persona* rather than the historical person per se. Superposing the content of any song with Kurt Cobain's historical reality risks distorting the song's cannily crafted, internal logic. It forces the song to conform to Cobain's authentically felt emotions and his sincerely held beliefs, both of which may be, ultimately, unknowable.

Narrative Dissonance/Thematic Harmony

Because Cobain resorts to juxtaposition as a literary technique, in a song like "In Bloom" the chorus is not necessarily tied thematically to the verses. The verses in this song relate to the title because they concern nature and reproduction ("Spring is here again" / "Reproductive glands"). The chorus, by contrast, takes up a seemingly different subject. This part of the song criticizes a certain kind of male consumer of Nirvana's alternative music ("He's the one who likes the pretty songs" / . . . "But he don't know what it means"). Soulsby considers the obvious disjunction between the verses and chorus in "In Bloom" to be typical of the tracks on *Nevermind.* He characterizes the album as one "where numerous songs have almost no connection between verses and chorus" (*Dark Slivers,* chap. 11). When examining the song's grammatical and syntactical structure, however, "In Bloom" is atypical of Cobain's overall lyrical work in that this song is written in cogent phrases and complete sentences.

Although Cobain rarely writes in clauses (subject + verb) or complete sentences—excluding one-word or two-word imperatives—all of his songs tend to contain a prominent idea. If this idea is not precisely central, in the sense that the song is structured around it and all the images are connected to it, then the idea constitutes at least a kind of portmanteau. The idea stands out because the concept is especially evocative when it comes to notions of a problematic identity and the understanding of one's place in the world. In each song, Cobain layers or complements the central idea with a seeming elaboration and with seemingly related images.

Many of these complementing ideas and images, however, do indeed have only a tangential or tenuous connection with the central notion itself, while others are completely disconnected from it. For this reason, it can be challenging to ascribe one particular meaning to an individual song. Like the particular literary technique in Cobain's journals that mimics the effects of intoxication and addiction, his songs, too, often seem incomplete, as if they were structured around a number of missing ellipses. Further, the imperative mode or the interrogative mode frequently dominates Cobain's lyrics. On the one hand, a narrator is making a demand as in "Smells Like Teen Spirit" ("Entertain us") and "Mr. Moustache" ("Lead the way to my temptations"). On the other, he is either interrogating himself or posing questions to an interlocutor, as in "All Apologies" ("What else should I be?") and "Radio Friendly Unit Shifter" ("What is wrong with me?"). In each case, the lyrics communicate a certain resignation and passivity on the part of the narrating voice. As a result, often the dominant voice in a song is that of a man acknowledging his shortcomings and expressing contrition.

Given Cobain's consistent use of juxtaposition, as evident in his recourse to wordplay and especially to shifting narrative perspective, there is a structural unity to his songs. But it is the thematic unity within his lyrics that constitutes a compelling feature of his songwriting. Whether writing in the narrative, the profile, or the lyrical mode, all of Cobain's songs return obsessively to the same cluster of themes. After confirming which themes dominate in his lyrics, I show that even though individual songs may be confounding and challenging to understand, Cobain's lyrical works, taken as a whole, possess a definite consistency and an overarching logic because of their thematic unity. This harmony of themes does not preclude his lyrics from being structurally flawed or built on faulty logic, in addition to containing many contradictions, malapropisms, and frustratingly inscrutable lines.

In the next section of this chapter, I begin to explore Cobain's themes by examining the representation of masculinity and masculinist culture as contaminated and diseased and in need of purification. I reveal how Cobain's lyrics create a specific persona, a young man who focuses on the debility of male corporeality and the lapses in the moral makeup of men. As a result, these songs put forth an unrelenting critique of a specific mode of masculine comportment. Then in the following section of the chapter, I pay special attention to how songs from Cobain's pre-Nirvana days and his Nirvana compositions reinforce and complement each other in specific ways. Thus I confirm the consistency and the overarching logic of his lyrical production. In the final section of this chapter, I examine the theme of death and dying in Cobain's lyrics. This section confirms why all of Cobain's songs, in various ways and to varying degrees, represent heterosexual masculinity (in a culture that marginalizes women and delegitimizes homosexuality) as a masochistic and melancholic identity.

For the moment, by "masochistic" I mean simply that male narrators are represented as divided, conflicted subjects. They derive solace or some degree of pleasure, either implicit or explicit, in being imprisoned or threatened with imprisonment and in being debased and hurt, or threatened to be debased and hurt.[11] And by "melancholic," I do not mean solely a profound sense of sadness. But, for the moment, I do mean simply that the narrator in a song is, once again, represented as experiencing a conflicted identity. Further, he experiences an acute sense of inadequacy and unworthiness and a desire, either implicit or explicit, for self-destruction.

MASCULINITY AND MASCULINIST CULTURE AS DISEASED: "I FEEL STUPID AND CONTAGIOUS" / SO MILK ME, DRAIN ME

Since representations of masculinity and experiences of male corporeality shore up all of Cobain's signature lyrics to some extent, one can group all the recurrent, besetting themes within his songs into four broad, interconnected categories. All these categories begin with and return to the male body: disease, violence, reproduction, and death. In the first instance, disease is conceived of as a kind of violence. It is revealed to be a symptom on or in the body that is responsible for its deterioration. The overall theme of violence itself emerges, on the one hand, as violence perpetrated on the bodies and psyches of others. In this instance, violence is manifest in themes of captivity, torture, rape, spousal and child neglect or abuse, and authority in general. On the other hand, violence is represented in Cobain's lyrics as injury inflicted upon the self, both physically and psychically. In this second instance, violence to the self is apparent in themes of anxiety, guilt, shame, self-criticism, self-debasement, and fantasies of emasculation, castration, and death. All these themes exhibit a masochistic component because all these actions constitute sources of pleasure. There is, of course, a nexus between violence and death (of the self and of others) in Cobain's songs.

The four broad thematic categories that recur throughout Cobain's lyrics all have a common element. These themes, no matter how they are initially posited and developed textually, do indeed return to one overarching motif: Conventional masculinity is unremittingly troubled and troubling. These themes posit traditional masculinity as an intractable problem. Cobain's songs, however, do not necessarily follow through with or develop this theme in a logical manner. His lyrics are more likely to expose this theme in a circular, iterative manner. Therefore, particular songs prove to be more lyrical and impressionistic than narrative or properly discursive.

In exhibiting a self-evident fascination with disease, infection, and the body's degeneration, Cobain lyrics at times incite readers' disgust. As the following excerpts illustrate, "Mexican Seafood" provides the most detailed example of an infected, degenerating male body. The song begins with a long, rhyming list of repulsive afflictions and conditions that includes "fungus mold cured by injection" and "yeast infection." In the second verse, the song shifts from the third to the first person: "Now I vomit cum and diarrhea," but the list continues to include "cloudy puss" and "chowder rust." The final verse concludes with a description of the narrator's repugnant bed invaded by insects and other vermin ("lice," "bugs," "fleas," "worms"). His bed is also saturated with foul body fluids and secretions ("toe jam," "booger," "stomach acid," "sugared sludge").

The theme of an unclean or unhealthy body is one to which Cobain is consistently attracted. He develops the theme in curious ways to the extent that filth, disease, and corporeal degeneration constitute also a source of delectation, a palpable pleasure. The oft-cited line from "Heart Shaped Box" has come to encapsulate this feature of Cobain's lyrics: "I wish I could eat your cancer when you turn black." Because of the conflation of self and other through a blurring of narrator and interlocutor, the male body in Cobain's lyrics is typically represented as being composed of male and female features. In addition, from the notion of hegemonic masculinity as iniquitous, Cobain's lyrics proceed to evoke many aspects of the very culture itself, dominated as it is by men, as equally contaminated and contaminating, as suggested in the following phrase from "Frances Farmer": "Disease-covered Puget Sound." Within the context of the song's overriding theme, this city could be designated "Putrid" Sound in the sense that the location is foul, characterized by the threat of violence (to women in general and to one specific woman in particular), and by ethical depravity.

Fans readily recognize the sentence that serves as my subtitle above, "I feel stupid and contagious," as a line from "Teen Spirit." As it appears in the song, the line might not seem immediately comprehensible within the context of the lines that directly precede and follow it. Ever since the song's release, listeners often cite this line as a curious and memorable lyric, but they do not generally accord it any special interpretation. Yet when considered within the context of Cobain's complete lyrical work, this line, just like the phrase "Diseased-covered Puget Sound" from "Frances Farmer," has a distinctive *resonance,* in the original meaning of this noun and its derivation from the verb "resound." The line constitutes a clear echo, a strong reverberation, of a masochistic and melancholic phantasy that appears to give structure to and to provide the content of Cobain's most affecting songs. Within this phantasy, the dominant mode of masculinity is experienced as an incurable affliction. Further, any nonconforming man and any resisting masculine mode necessarily reveal nonhegemonic or counterhegemonic men to be deeply disconsolate (melancholic) and inexorably self-punishing (masochistic).

There are lines in other songs that function in the same manner as the above lines from "Frances Farmer" and "Teen Spirit." These lines also either do not necessarily make sense, or they are not especially evocative, within the song as an individual text. In a pre-Nirvana song like "Blather's Log," for example, one reads these lines: "Your body burns in me" / It's really like a disease." Within the context of the song, the narrator has been confronted by bullies. Yet this line, too, as it appears in this individual song, is ambiguous at best, even though, like the corresponding lines from "Teen Spirit" and "Frances Farmer," it presents a provocative image of male corporeality and, by extension, of patriarchal culture.

Or, to cite another example but from the Nirvana canon, the following line in "Stay Away" (aka "Pay to Play") functions in a similar manner: "Have to have poison skin." When examined as a phrase in this individual song, this second-verse line is amusing, but it does not appear particularly to make sense, given the content of the preceding first verse and chorus. Again, like its counterparts in the three songs cited above, this line could easily be perceived as a throwaway, another instance of the songwriter just willy-nilly adding an idea, albeit an intriguing one, to a composition. But it is by reinserting these four songs within the entirety of Cobain's lyrical works that the reader realizes the significance of images evoking masculine defilement and self-defilement embedded in these specific lines.

Cobain's lyrics are indeed replete with references to bodily injuries such as sores, cancer, viruses, infections, and medical procedures. Soulsby has produced a convenient chart listing all references to "medicine, disease, and injury" that he has found in twenty-eight different songs (*Dark Slivers*, chap. 12). Within the entirety of Cobain's lyrical writings, however, there are two songs in particular, "Milk It" (*In Utero*) and "Drain You" (*Nevermind*), that posit more comprehensively this notion of masculinity as diseased and that provide more sustained, disaffecting images of this theme. These two songs are also remarkable in that they underscore another notion as well, one that has escaped the attention of other commentators. In addition to the phantasy that the more fully realized body is both masculine and feminine, it is in these two songs that we see the most compelling affirmation that disease and debility, for the male subject, are to be experienced as sources of delight for a particular reason. These songs represent male corporeal and psychical distemper as a necessary, delectable intoxication because disease and debility can and should bring on the destruction of a pernicious mode of masculinity and, again, one is to infer, the upending of the masculinist culture to which it gives rise.

"Milk It"

"Milk It" constitutes a prime example of a signature Cobain song. It combines the three genres of his songwriting: narrative, profile, and lyrical. The lyrics expose a narrator who revels in his own inherent parasitic and infected nature ("I am my own parasite / I don't need a host to live"). In the recorded version of the song, Cobain screams the words "shit," "viruses," and "parasites" with discernible relish and as "terms of endearment" (Crisafulli, 164). The song commences as a profile in the first-person singular; it does not appear to be addressed to a specific interlocutor. The shift to the first-person plural ("we") in the second couplet of the first verse suggests, however, that the narrator is addressing himself. He is speaking to his "own parasite." The organism is represented as part and parcel of the narrator's physical and psychical self.

The shift to "we" in the first verse also establishes that the narrator and his parasite are not only lovers, as some commentators have suggested, but that they are also a parent and gestating child. The appearance of the biological terms "ecto-plasma, ecto-skeletal" (read: "ectoplasm" and "exoskeletal") in the song's outro confirms its context of organic and human development. But since "exoskeletal" describes certain insects such as grasshoppers and cockroaches (as well as crustaceans), this song also reflects Cobain's captivation by the idea of humans and insects interbreeding, as can be seen in the cover art he produced for different singles and albums like "Lithium" and *Incesticide*.

The cover of *Incesticide* is especially striking in the way it displays a curious connection to "Milk It." The drawing depicts the skeletal head and shoulders of an adult with an insect-like trunk and limbs. This humanoid-insect is cradling in its right arm what could be Cobain's version of the pennyroyal plant, the allegedly miscarriage-inducing flower. The cover also depicts a near-monstrous, yet strangely familiar-looking infant. It possesses a partially bashed-in skull, giving it the appearance of possessing devil horns. At the same time, the infant possesses the innocent-looking face of one of the baby dolls that Cobain collected.[12] The doll's face is attached to a puppet-like body sporting limbs that can be disarticulated. In a gesture of apparent protest, the child is tugging at the missing breast of its presumptive, undemonstrative parent, as if the offspring were pleading for some nonexistent "milk." This parent-child couple, as we shall see, resembles several others that readers encounter in Cobain's creative writings. One version of this breast-less, milk-less parent reappears several times in Cobain's journals as a young man desiring and sometimes even phantasizing the possession of breasts: "Let me grow some breasts" (224), he wails on one occasion. On another, he proclaims in all sincerity to be "a male, age 23 and lactating" (138).

In addition to the ambiguity in the relationship between the couple depicted in "Milk It," the song utilizes a technique that Cobain returns to not only in his lyrics but also in his journals: He "feminizes" either the body or the psyche of a male character. In this particular song, a presumptively male narrator envisions himself inhabiting a female body and possessing feminine characteristics. The narrator conflates his body with that of a defenseless "angel" with a "broken wing." And angels within Cobain's writings and drawings are exclusively feminine. In other songs, most notably in "Been A Son" and "Oh The Guilt" as well as in "Milk It," Cobain creates a male narrator or character who either simply identifies with or outright adopts a feminine perspective.[13] In other instances, Cobain constructs a song in such a way that the reader is constrained to identity with the position of the victimized, whether this victimization is at the hands of an individual man (as in "Polly") or the result of a sexist and misogynist culture more generally (as in "Frances Farmer").

"Milk It" showcases injury to and deficiencies within the body in a way that suggests that no healing, repair, or recovery exists. In addition to the song's diagnosis of visible injury to the body's exterior ("broken wing"; "lost eyesight"), it also catalogues, in the chorus, the body's interior and its invisible damage and deficiencies ("Lack of iron and sleeping"). What begins in the first verse as the evocation of a pregnant narrator evolves, in the second verse, into him having given birth ("I own my own pet virus / I get to pet and name her"). No longer are the narrator and his offspring in a relationship of "parasite" and "host"; they are now parent and child, master and pet, possessor and possessed.

The second couplet of the second verse confirms the remerging and the ultimate indistinguishability between the narrator and his virus/parasite because, at this juncture in the song, it is the virus/parasite that nourishes the narrator/host. This second couplet also confirms the complete erasure of any border between masculine and feminine ("Her milk is my shit / My shit is her milk"), such that this song could just as well have been titled "Milk *Me*" rather than "Milk It." In this sense, the song has parallels with the imperative to "Dive in me" that constitutes the repeated refrain in "Dive" (*Incesticide*).

"Milk It," as the song concludes, makes another ingenious use of juxtaposition as a literary technique in a specific way: The song fuses life and death. This conflation is signaled in this text by the confounding use of "obituary" as an adjective to describe "birthday," a juxtaposition that constitutes the two-word, penultimate line of the song. The line is, by and large, inexplicable within the context of the song itself. But as is often the case, it takes on a distinct meaning when read concurrently with other lyrics (or journal entries) that also present life and death as convergent.

"Drain You"

The closest lyrical analogue to "Milk It" is "Drain You." This *Nevermind* song contains the same overarching theme and the same defining images as "Milk It." It includes a comparable blurring of a relationship between two lovers and a concomitant relationship between parent and fetus. The parent-fetus dynamic is signaled in "Drain You" in two lines that suggest the presence of amniotic fluid: "The water is so yellow . . . / Vacuum out the liquids."[14] The parent-child relationship in this song, however, elides into an in-utero-like communication between twin infants who, like the parent and unborn child couple, constitute a dyad that cannot be easily decoupled. They represent the conjoining of two bodies that are mutually dependent; and, in essential ways, the two bodies are indistinguishable the one from the other. "To drain" and "to milk" are, therefore, synonymous in Cobain's universe. Milking can sustain one life while sapping another.

"Drain You" begins as a third-person narrative, but unlike in "Milk It," there is no ambiguity as to the person being addressed. It is clear that one member of the dyad is addressing the other, as evident in the first line: "One baby to another says / I'm lucky to have met you." The "I" of the text constitutes the voice of one of the characters. Therefore, except for the first two lines, the entire song should be presented in quotation marks. The narrator intends to completely "drain" his interlocutor and, at the same time, to enter into a symbiotic relationship and dissolve his essence into hers ("Chew your meat for you, pass it back and forth in a passionate kiss"). In addition, in its second verse, "Drain You" contains another canny example of Cobain's skill at wordplay: "With eyes so dilated / I've become your pupil." The second verse cleverly goes on to shift the meaning of "pupil" (as body part) into its meaning as "apprentice," when the narrator asserts that he has learned a lot from this unusually intimate relationship. "I'm a healthy *student*," he declares.

As in "Milk It," "Drain You" also presents the notion of disease and corporeal contamination as a desired, felicitous condition because it confirms that the couple is indissolubly conjoined: "A travel through a tube / And end up in your infection." This notion is also expressed in "I Hate Myself and Want To Die" in the following lines: "Even if you have a cold still" / "You can cough on me again." These songs indicate that several Nirvana albums include songs in which the notion of infection and cross-contamination signifies a passionate bonding of two aspects of a single subject. This dual identity is represented as a more complete subjectivity because it is, at one and the same time, lover and loved one, parent and child, masculine and feminine.

Purifying Masculinity and Masculinist Culture

Because masculinity, like patriarchal culture as a whole, is represented as diseased and as a condition in need of purification, it is not surprising to find in Cobain's lyrics references to cleansing, hygiene, and health. As Soulsby has also remarked, these references appear in numerous songs. "Punk Rocker" provides a challenging example. The chorus to the song blends the perspective of a first-person narrator with the second-person addressee, whom the narrator quotes in the first person. The story is further complicated by the presence of a third-person character ("best friend"): "And you and my best friend, you came over to me" / "And you said, 'Hey, jerk' / 'I've got this good thing going here.'" Therefore, it is not clear if it is the narrator/addressee or his friend who utters the subsequent lines: "My mind must be" / "Washed with bleach." And even though references to cleansing, hygiene, and health do not always refer specifically or unequivocally to the male body or to masculinity, they do invariably suggest either an unsanitary environment or a pathogenic person that a narrator or character has to endure.

In the first verse of "Paper Cuts," for example, a narrator finds himself confined animal-like in a room lined with newspaper that has been put down in order to absorb the human waste. But this method of disposal does not suffice: "Newspapers spread around" / "Soaking all that they can" / "A cleansing is due again" / "A good hosing down."[15] The lines project an image of a person imprisoned in his own waste and in need of deliverance from his unhygienic confinement. In other songs, the reference to cleansing appears in one line or in a couplet that does not seem connected to the remainder of the verse. "Mr. Moustache," for example, finds a narrator in the position of many of the narrators in Cobain's lyrics in that he is making a request of an unspecified interlocutor: "Take my hand and give it cleaning." This specific request, however, does not explain, follow up, or contradict the two preceding requests in the strophe, and it has only an ambiguous connection with the line that follows it: "Yes, I eat cow, I'm not proud."

A similarly beseeching narrator appears in "Come As You Are," one who requests that an unspecified addressee "Come doused in mud, soaked in bleach." Here, as in other songs, the image is vivid, but the expression "soaked in bleach" seems to function merely to contrast with the preceding phrase "Doused in mud." The line is, therefore, ambiguous, open to interpretation. As we see with baffling images and inexplicable ideas in other songs, references to cleansing and hygiene in both "Come As You Are" and "Mr. Moustache," as individual songs, may not seem particularly noteworthy. But the recurrence of these images and ideas throughout Cobain's writings functions to retrofit them with a potent, singular significance. As I shall demonstrate, this theme takes on its full significance when we read Cobain's lyrics alongside his journals.

The notion that masculinity and masculinist culture are diseased and contaminated lead not only to references to cleansing, hygiene, and health as specific types of actions; the notion leads also to implicit and explicit references in Cobain's lyrics to products or agents used to cleanse, cure, and purify. These agents include bleach, isopropyl alcohol, insecticide, and the pennyroyal plant. *Bleach*, of course, is the title of an album, and two Cobain songs are titled "Gallons of Rubbing Alcohol Flow Through the Strip" and "Pennyroyal Tea." The pennyroyal plant is alleged to have cleansing and curative effects as well as the potential to induce miscarriages. This same pennyroyal plant, according to Soulsby, "can also be used as a bug repellent" (*Dark Slivers*, chap. 3). The notion of an insect repellent would constitute an especially evocative notion for a specific kind of creative artist, one for whom a dominant theme in some of his visual art consists of discomforting images of insectoid-humanoids. These creatures, as seen on the *Incesticide* cover, invite viewers' fascination but also their ill-ease, if not their repulsion.

In some of Cobain's songs, allusions to the themes of cleansing, hygiene, and health appear to be especially fortuitous and parenthetical. For example, in "Laminated Effect" (*Illiteracy Will Prevail*), what initially appears as an offhand reference to the male body and hygiene ("[He] Kept his body clean") takes on a special resonance in Cobain's lyrics. The line is echoed and amplified elsewhere. It constitutes the only line in all of Cobain's songs that he repeats verbatim in another song, "Even in His Youth" ("Teen Spirit" B-side). And, as suggested below, the line takes on the same "queer," metaphoric value in the two songs. As such, this line operates, ultimately, to call into question the logic of the hetero/homo distinction. I explore this topic in the next chapter of this book because Cobain's journals also establish a relationship between a clean body and male sexuality.

REACHING NIRVANA VIA A RETURN TO COBAIN'S FECAL MATTER: EVEN IN HIS YOUTH, HE WAS LAMINATED

Critics consider Fecal Matter Cobain's first serious effort to form and record with a band.[16] Before the group's compilation demo *Illiteracy Will Prevail* was made public in 2005–2006, there had been much speculation about the lyrical content and the musical quality of these tracks and their relationship to the songs penned for Nirvana. Two of the songs, "Downer" and "Spank Thru," would survive to become ones that Nirvana recorded and performed live. I explore two songs from Cobain's Fecal Matter period because of the way they are predictive of his Nirvana compositions. Comparing the songs penned for the two groups allows for a deeper understanding of Cobain's overall aesthetic and cultural practice. Reading these songs in tandem reveals how the ensemble of his lyrical production constitutes discrete literary texts and, at the same time, these discrete texts operate as parts of an eclectic, indissoluble whole.

If the differences between the songs composed for Fecal Matter and those composed for Nirvana provide an accurate reflection of the evolution of, but also the consistency in, Cobain's songwriting, one concludes that as he becomes more experienced in composing lyrics, his writing becomes more concise and focused. His songwriting also tends to be less frequently tied to concrete referents or characterized by a specificity of narrative details. Although his writing becomes more pared down and more concise thematically, however, it continues to exhibit a structural complexity that makes his later lyrics just as circumspect and conceptual in nature. I examine "Laminated Effect" and "Spank Thru" in order to demonstrate how they dialogue with two Nirvana songs, "Even in His Youth" and "Beeswax," respectively. This dialogue demonstrates most clearly the consistency in the content and the structuring of Cobain's lyrics. The two Fecal Matter songs contain arresting lyrics; they merit special attention because of the specific manner in which they forecast the thematic obsessions and the recurrent images that characterize not only Cobain's overall lyrical production but his journal writing as well.

"Even in His Youth" was first recorded in 1989 for the "Blew" EP before Nirvana rerecorded it in 1991 as the B-side for "Smells Like Teen Spirit." It is both a narrative and a profile song. The episode related can be succinctly summarized in a couple of sentences because, in the style of other songs composed during the early Nirvana years, "Even in His Youth" is narrowly focused. The song recounts the story of a young man and his father. There are no secondary characters or events; the narrative lends itself to a summary account:

A young man is a source of disgrace and shame for his father because the son shares the father's prominent last name ("He was something"). But the son, no longer a youth ("Who was nothing"), is still worthless in his father's eyes, just as he was defective and a disappointment "even in his youth." Presently, as a young man, he has no future ("going nowhere").

As in other narrative songs, this one begins as a third-person narration with two characters. The lyrics dramatize an irresoluble conflict between a young man and his "daddy," both of whom are introduced in the opening chorus. The conflict between father and son is reinforced by the repeated juxtaposing and rhyming of "nothing" and "something": "He [son] was nothing" / "He [father] was something." But, already within the opening lines, the song suggests a possible slippage between the behavior and sentiments of the father and those of the son. This possibility is borne out in the subsequent verses when the song resorts to the juxtaposition of different narrative perspectives.

"Even in His Youth" begins with the chorus. And although it begins in the third person, the first line of the first verse brings about a change in perspective. The seemingly omniscient third-person narrator (who is not a character in the story) shifts abruptly into the limited perspective of a first-person narrator ("I've got nothing to lose"). By contrast, this narrator is a character in the story being told. But it is unclear to whom the narrator is speaking ("Read this form before *you*'re through"). The collating of two different narrative perspectives and the introduction of an ostensible interlocutor who is listening to the narrator's story succeed, as in other songs, in disorienting the reader. In addition, the first verse is ambiguous since it can also be read as the voice of the son, rather than the voice of the father: "I've got nothing left to prove." In fact, the childlike cadence of the next line ("If I die before I wake") argues for this reading.

In this sense, "Even in His Youth" takes up and expands on other defining themes and images that recur in Cobain's work. This song spotlights the following: The male body ("He kept his body clean"); experiences of guilt, shame, and immorality ("Daddy was ashamed / Disgraced the family name"); themes of captivity and powerlessness ("come back as a slave"); and, finally, an allusion to death and dying ("If I die before I wake"). By its conclusion, the song has indeed succeeded in conflating son and father. As I explore in the next chapter, Cobain's journals consist of several entries that also present a scenario wherein a son who fears turning into his father, inheriting his sins, so to speak, is conflated with this very parent.

Although the initial reference to the male body is cryptic in the chorus ("Kept his body clean"), the fact that this reference occurs in the third line of the song suggests the importance of corporeality, even though the song does not offer a sustained reflection on the body proper. As the line appears in the song, its meaning is baffling. The words are enigmatic, however, only if the reader is not already familiar with the Fecal Matter song that predates it and that constitutes its correlative. "Even in His Youth" has connections to and converses with "Laminated Effect" in such a manner that the very meaning of the expression "clean body" is made unmistakably clear only if one reads the two songs in tandem.

"Laminated Effect"

"Laminated Effect" constitutes one of the earliest versions of what I label a signature Cobain song because of the themes it explores and the images that the lyrics create. Written and recorded in 1985–86, it is both a narrative and a profile song. Compared to "Even in His Youth," however, the narrative in this earlier song is more challenging to summarize succinctly because the episode related is not as clearly focused on the central character and his father. "Laminated Effect" stands apart from other songs in Cobain's repertoire, and from "Even in His Youth" specifically, in that it introduces a named female character in the second verse.[17] The song introduces this character in a manner that complicates the implicit message about masculinity and sexuality that the text communicates. Here is a précis of the story that the song relates:

Johnny, a young gay man, was raped by his father; he contracted AIDS as a result. He was an unhappy son made to feel guilty and ashamed by his father. Meanwhile, Lucy, a young lesbian, moves to Mexico. Disdainful of relating to men, she, nevertheless, meets, dates, and sleeps with Johnny. Both appear to have found new lives away from parental and religious authority.

"Laminated Effect," like "Even in His Youth," also begins as a third-person narration about a father and son. Unlike other songs that profile identifiable characters—in which the characters remain unnamed—Cobain gives a name to the central character in these lyrics. In addition, compared to other songs, he specifies the character's sexual orientation ("Johnny was a homo"). The attentive reader who is familiar with Cobain's entire lyrical output recognizes that the character is an analogue and a precursor of the nameless protagonist in "Even in His Youth." The third line of the Nirvana song does repeat the second line of "Laminated Effect": "Kept his body clean."

The meaning of this line, however, is not cryptic here as it is in "Even in His Youth." On the contrary, the precise meaning of the adjective "clean" when used to characterize the male body is unequivocal: The adjective signifies "virginal," "innocent," "disease-free." This particular meaning of "clean," as I suggest, also surfaces in Cobain's notebooks. In one of the more sexually graphic entries found in Cobain's journals (examined in detail in the next chapter), Cobain presents a jumble of different narrative fragments describing various American male musicians, actors, and television characters engaging in intercourse. This third-person journal entry shifts to the first person when the narrator poses a question to himself: "Why am I so sexually conscious? Why can I not be *clean?* Have I read too many porns?" (*Journals,* 78, emphasis added).

In "Laminated Effect," after having rhymed "homo" and "San Francisco" in lines 1 and 3 of the song, Cobain creates an approximate rhyme, or pararhyme, by opposing "clean" and "disease" in lines 2 and 4, suggesting indeed how "clean" should ultimately be understood. Since the disease in question is AIDS ("a big disease" that originated "in San Francisco"), and since it is presented in the song as a sexually transmitted disease, its obverse, the reader can surmise, is sexual self-denial and, specifically, abstinence from gay sex. It is in this sense, therefore, that the meaning of "kept his body clean" in the song written for Nirvana makes sense when read concurrently with the Fecal Matter song. "Laminated Effect" predicts and, proactively, solves the enigma presented in the later-composed "Even in His Youth."

At the same time, the Nirvana song represents a simplification, a paring down of the narrative details in the Fecal Matter composition. For example, what will be depicted in "Even in His Youth" simply as an unspecified conflict between father and son, is expressed explicitly in "Laminated Effect" as a sexual assault committed by the father. In addition, whereas the dismal future of the son in "Even in His Youth" is left vague, Johnny's fate is explicit: He is condemned to a future of suffering and premature death because of the incurable disease with which his father has infected him. In spite of these differences, the essential message and the overall literary effect of the two songs coincide. First, the father-son relationship is oppositional and perverted by its very nature. Just like the unnamed character in the Nirvana song, Johnny, too, is shamed and lives a miserable life because of his father ("Told he was at fault / Living life unhappy"). Second, through the juxtaposing of narrative perspectives, the two songs succeed in blurring the distinction between son and father. Once again, a son is poised to "inherit" the disease of his father. In addition to re-emerging within Cobain's journals, this theme also reappears, as revealed in chapter 6, in his suicide letter.

In spite of the similarity in the young male characters depicted in the two songs, and notwithstanding an engagement with the same themes of shame, guilt, and reprehensible fathers, the two songs are structurally quite different.

Although "Laminated Effect" presents a more expansive narrative with concrete details, it exhibits, nevertheless, a simpler structuring in that it remains a third-person narrative throughout. Yet the song still presents a complicated narrative perspective. It introduces an interlocutor in the chorus, an addition that causes the meaning of the entire chorus to be ambiguous: "You're living in a time of change" / "Too many things to feel afraid" / "To think against the will of God." At the same time, the presence of a third-person plural "they" in the chorus further complicates the matter of determining from whose perspective the story is being told: "Maybe someday soon *they*'ll realize they're wrong." If one reads the song line-by-line, the "they" of the chorus, grammatically, would designate Johnny and his father, since these two characters are, so far, the only ones presented. The chorus is equally ambiguous for another reason. In addition to the jarring juxtaposition of "you" and "they," the character Johnny himself appears to be the "you" being addressed by the unidentified narrator.

Nevertheless, upon further analysis, it becomes clear that the "you" in the text could also be the father. That is, the father could be the one who "feels afraid / To think against the will of God." In this way, the Fecal Matter song employs a favorite Cobain technique, one that confounds the narrative perspective within a text. The inclusion in particular of an interlocutor in the chorus functions to intertwine even further the perspective and the experiences of the father and those of the son.

As with many of Cobain's songs, his fans, biographers, and some scholars attempt to read "Laminated Effect" as a *roman à clef,* as providing insights into Cobain's external life. Efforts to align details from "Laminated Effect" with Cobain's biography in order to determine the possible historical referents for the characters and the scenario represented in the song are entertaining. But, as with other songs, such efforts do not enhance the reader's understanding of how the song works to provide a commentary on paternal authority or sexual conventions. On the contrary, as soon as commentators identify the historical Kurt Cobain as the song's narrator, they have already positioned themselves to misread or overread the work.[18]

Besides not illuminating the song's themes or its take on cultural and social issues, these efforts do not illuminate the song's aesthetics, such as the use of rhyme, alliteration, and assonance and the clever juxtaposition of disjointed images and concepts. For example, Cobain juxtaposes and rhymes a slang word for female genitalia ("her hole") with the male's moral and emotional nature ("his soul") in a way that produces an indescribable effect on the reader. This aesthetic maneuver creates mystery and confusion; it renders the song obtuse. Further, the juxtaposition functions manifestly to posit the kernel of another notion, one that is more fully developed in Cobain's later lyrical and journal writings. This notion can be summarized in the following manner: In the universe that Cobain imagines, men are cursed with an unseemly, abject body. The superior, if not ideal, male subject, by contrast, possesses female body parts and functions. Such a subject is both masculine and feminine, *body* and *soul*.

Further, it would be a mistake to assume that the narrator's voice in "Laminated Effect"—or in any other song—corresponds to the voice of the historical Kurt Cobain. Therefore one cannot assume that the sentiments expressed in the lyrics echo the musician's genuinely held social and cultural beliefs. The narrator in this song, just like "Daddy," "Johnny," and "Lucy," is merely another character that Cobain creates. Does the narrator speak for Cobain the writer? Within the context of the kind of analysis that I am undertaking, it is impossible and pointless to attempt to respond comprehensively to this question. For example, there is no record of Kurt Cobain, the publicly gay-affirming musician, ever using the word "homo" as an invective. This observation does not mean, of course, that he never did so. It simply does not matter for determining how this particular song works as a literary composition, that is, *how* it makes sense and produces a particular effect on the reader. One has only to specify that in this song the term is meant as an insult when voiced by the narrator. But for the songwriter (Cobain)—as opposed to the narrator/character in the song—"homo" simply provides a convenient, amusing, and sophomoric rhyme for "San Francisco."

Understandably, readers pose questions about the relationship between the narrator in this song and Cobain. The narrator may not be pantomiming Kurt Cobain. Yet a relationship does exist between the two as producer and product, as dreamer and his dreamed-up character or persona. As specified in chapter 2, there exists throughout Cobain's creative works a correlation between person and persona. But posing the question as to how the two might converge in this specific instance, as in other texts, does not get readers very far in an attempt to comprehend how the song produces meaning about gender and sexuality and how it evokes emotions on the part of the reader. Nevertheless, just as in a dream the dreamers disperse their psychical reality throughout all the characters that populate their sleeping vision, the persona that Cobain creates in

"Laminated Effect" and "Even in His Youth" is a composite of all the characters and events that he has conjured up. To paraphrase lines from "Lithium," he has found his friends and his enemies, and they are all in his head. They are all him.

Given the nature of the study of gender that I am advancing, it is inconsequential whether or not the characters in "Laminated Effect" are based on real people and events in Cobain's outer world. What is important, on the contrary, is how the characters in his *inner,* imaginary world interact with each other: For example, what are the dynamics of power within this scenario involving a gay son and his disapproving father? How does the song suggest a relationship between power, on the one hand, and gender identity, on the other? Further, how does the text suggest a relationship between cultural power, sexual practice, and an individual's pleasure? In order to assess the content and structure of this song, one must consider how the various ideas and images exposed in the lyrics are connected (or left disjointed) and developed (or abandoned) as the song progresses. This song, as a literary text, has its own truth and coherence that do not depend on the presumed relationship between these phantasy characters and any actual person or event in the writer's life. Therefore, my reading of "Laminated Effect" necessarily neither confirms nor confutes Cobain's real attitudes about gender or his actual experience of paternal authority, the two principal themes the song broaches.

FROM MASTURBATION TO CASTRATION
"Spank Thru"

"Spank Thru" epitomizes the way castration and emasculation constitute themes that are rehearsed in Cobain's creative writings. Even though there is a focus on the male body and bodily processes, functions, and fluids in Cobain's written works as a whole, there is a conspicuous absence of references to the penis itself as an emblem of power, pleasure, and authority.[19] In addition, as I indicate, Cobain's lyrics, in terms of representations of masculinity, can be characterized more accurately as testerical: antimacho and antiphallic.

Similar to all the other images and themes that predominate across the entirety of Cobain's creative writings, the near absence or the abjection of the penis first emerges in his pre-Nirvana lyrics. In this particular instance, the subject is put center stage in "Spank Thru." This song constitutes one of only two exceptions within Cobain's lyrics in that the penis appears to be the main "character" in the text.[20] Yet the organ remains unnamed, designated simply by the pronoun "it." "Spank Thru" proves to be ingeniously composed because of the way an ostensible paean to male masturbation ends up, on the contrary, demystifying and devaluating the penis, if not actually advocating and staging its destruction altogether.

Several versions of "Spank Thru" have been recorded, including a home demo that dates from 1985.[21] Although Nirvana would record a live performance of the song at the 1992 Reading Festival, the lyrics began as a pre-Nirvana text. The mythology regarding the origin of Nirvana as a group revolves around an earlier home recording of "Spank Thru." In order to introduce Krist Novoselic to his musical tastes and talents, Cobain included the song on a tape he passed on to his friend. In *Rolling Stone,* Daniel Epstein relates the now familiar story about the role of the song in the very genesis of Nirvana and the group's eventual mass appeal:

A good argument can be made for "Spank Thru" as *the song that started it all.* Dating back to his 1985 Fecal Matter demo, it was the first Cobain-penned song that got Krist Novoselic's attention, thus kick-starting the formation of Nirvana. "One of the songs on [the tape] was 'Spank Thru,'" Novoselic recalled in a 1992 interview. . . . [Kurt] turned me on to it, and I really liked it, it kind of got me excited. So I go, 'Hey man, let's start a band.'" . . . Once the band had mobilized, it became the third Nirvana song to find official release . . . and [it] has continued to make appearances on most of their official live albums. ("All 102 Nirvana Songs Ranked")

It is perhaps not fortuitous that the song that is reputed to have ignited the whole Nirvana phenomenon is one that demystifies and problematizes the male sexual organ and function.

The first verse of "Spank Thru" begins ostensibly as a love song with a spoken preamble: "This is for the lovers out there." With tongue decidedly in cheek, the narrator evokes a romantic scene comprising blissful birds soaring above a landscape of flowers singing "in D minor." The first-person narrator addresses his message to a female lover he has lost: "I need you back, oh baby, baby / I can't explain just why we lost *it* from the start." The antecedent for the pronoun "it" in this line is not included in the text, but the reader might surmise the antecedent to be "our love." A grammatical ambiguity ensues immediately, however, since all the other "its" subsequent to the one in this line refer to the narrator's penis, and the pronoun is repeated some forty-odd times.

Clued in by the title of the song, the reader might also have expected the solitary sex act, the spanking, to serve as a mere replacement for the narrator's erotic interaction with the lost lover. But the act appears to be conflated rather with love itself. Thus masturbation does not replace the absent lover (a person) or the act of making love (a practice), it replaces the lost love, a sentiment. In this sense, "Spank Thru" displays a technique that Cobain uses frequently in his lyrical writing and in his journals as well, wherein as I have indicated, an emotion like love becomes inscribed in or on the male body. Soulsby also writes about Cobain's "tendency to equate love and biology" (*Dark Slivers*), an equation whereby an emotional/psychical experience becomes inseparable from the flesh.

Even more so than its association with the verb "to masturbate," "to spank" means to punish and, specifically, to punish a disobedient or misbehaving child. Thus, the verb signifies, simultaneously, a relation of parent to child and a relation of a male subject to his own body and, typically, to the organ that establishes his maleness and presumptive potency. This dual meaning and ambiguity are captured in the chorus of the song in which evocations of pleasure ("I can feel it, I can hold it") are juxtaposed with suggestions of punishment and pain ("I can cut it / . . . I can beat it"), the very definition of masochism. "To spank," of course, does take on a precise meaning in certain sexual practices between consenting partners.

The most jarring juxtaposition of pleasure with punishment and pain occurs in the third line of the chorus: "I can cut it, I can taste it." At the same time, the actions of the narrator in "Spank Thru" echo those of other dysfunctional fathers in Cobain's lyrics, as found in "Even in His Youth" and "Laminated Effect." In "Spank Thru," the narrator entertains a relationship of parent to his child-penis. He mimics the attitudes and actions of other fathers who endeavor to shape, indoctrinate, and control their sons. Finally, at the very end of the initial 1985 recording of the song, the equivocation that the verb "to spank" sets in motion is reinforced rather than resolved. The meaning of the title continues to toggle between the two possibilities: the disciplining of a misbehaving child and an act of autoerotic pleasuring. As the recorded song concludes, the quacking of a duck interrupts the singer who, continuing to play the role of narrator-father, reprimands the bird by shushing it to keep quiet and to behave.

Although "Spank Thru" constitutes a seeming celebration of the penis and masturbation, the ultimate image of the organ, as evoked in the final repeated line of the song, is not an image of active power, domination, or triumph. On the contrary, this line represents passivity, submission, and defeat: "I can make it do things you wouldn't think it ever could." The image, however, corresponds precisely to the image of masculinity that predominates throughout Cobain's lyrics. In many of his songs, a specific kind of pleasure is derived from a self-willed victimization, passivity, or submission. In his writings in general, but especially in his journals, there is an explicit desire and a need to be "spanked," to inhabit the physical, emotional, and psychical space of the subordinate person in a power relation. In other words, masochism constitutes the very essence of the masculine persona that Cobain cultivates. It is in part because of this feature that the male body is often represented in his writings as vulnerable, testerical. As indicated, this masculine mode is consistently presented as non-macho, lacking "balls," castrated.

Minding and Mining His "Beeswax "

"Beeswax" is the second song in Cobain's repertoire in which the penis makes an inauspicious appearance, this time in the thrice-repeated line of the choruses: "I got my diddly spayed." Whereas "Spank Thru," written for Fecal Matter, was first released in 1988, "Beeswax" was first released in 1991 on a compilation album (*Kill Rock Stars*). It reappeared in 1992 as a track on *Incesticide*. If the organ is punished and beaten into submission in the Fecal Matter song, in "Beeswax" it is completely destroyed. It is deprived of all potency and precluded from providing a potential source of pleasure. Whereas the penis remains unnamed in "Spank Thru," it is designated by three different terms in these lyrics.

The principal noun to designate the organ, "diddly"—a term repeated twenty times—confirms the organ's nature and status. The most common meaning of "diddly," according to the *OED,* is "a thing with little or no value." The noun also means an object that either malfunctions or does not function at all. Further, the *OED* specifies that "diddly" is a shortened form of "diddly-shit" and "diddly-squat," meaning zero, absolutely nothing. This definition, consequently, raises the question as to why the penis is being removed ("spayed") if it is, for the narrator, always already nothing, a nonfunctioning, impotent organ. As might be expected, then, "Beeswax," unlike "Spank Thru," is not about masturbation, although the act is briefly and cryptically alluded to in the second verse: "Jacking themselves off polyester."

It is, of course, female animals that are spayed to prevent them from reproducing. By citing this operation to designate the excision of male genitalia, Cobain accomplishes what I refer to as a "discursive maneuver" (as opposed to an aesthetic one). He will repeat the maneuver in various forms and to various degrees in other lyrics, as he does in "Milk It." The maneuver consists in feminizing the body (and/or psyche) of a male narrator. In this song, not only does the narrator voluntarily submit to a female operation, he is, or desires to be, the receptive partner in intercourse with another man, as indicated in the fourth verse: "Bill, just fuck me, take me anal." This discursive maneuver, in whatever form it reappears in Cobain's writings, ultimately functions to define a phantasied male body as possessing a "feminine," receptive function.

The maneuver also functions to posit a self-correcting masculine activity as nonphallic and nonpenetrative. In this specific instance, as in other Cobain texts that represent a desire for self-emasculation, the narrator distinguishes himself from other men who would be horrified by his voluntary castration ("Goring my manhood turns a man off") and by his welcoming penetration. For the narrator, by contrast, the very experience of dispossession and pain brings about an unmistakable sense of self-satisfaction.

In addition to "diddly," the narrator employs "penis" once and "dick" twice to designate the offending organ. In the first instance, there is no semantic or symbolic difference between "penis" and "diddly" when the narrator exclaims in the penultimate chorus, "I got my *penis* spayed." He specifies that the penis remains flaccid ("Nothing hard") and undesired. The song's employment of "dick," although complicating the meaning of the lyrics, functions to reconfirm the narrator's compulsive desire to rid himself of the organ that he abhors: "I've gotta dick, dick / Hear my fuckin' hate." The desire and the need to be castrated can be read as ironic in this specific instance since castration, properly speaking, does not mean the excision of the penis but rather the removal or neutralizing of the testicles. But just as in "Spank Thru," in "Beeswax," too, castration is put forth as a corrective and compensating procedure, a form of punishment but also as a specific kind of pleasure. This song proves to be yet another text, like many of the entries in Cobain's journals, that exposes the seemingly peculiar behavior of what turns out to be a masochistic subject who seeks delight in his own chastisement and affliction.

Given its overall structure, "Beeswax," again like "Spank Thru," constitutes another signature song. The very title is enigmatic. It does not appear to have a direct connection to the content of the lyrics, but the song does point to Cobain's tendency to resort to juxtaposition and wordplay. The word "beeswax" is both a noun and a verb. In addition to its literal meaning (a wax made by bees and used to make certain products like candles), as a noun "beeswax" is used metaphorically to mean "business." As such, it is most often used in colloquial American English in the expression "Mind your own beeswax," that is, "stay out of my business." As a verb, "beeswax" means "to rub or treat with beeswax." It also means simply "to clean" or "to polish," as in to beeswax one's car (*OED*), thus thoroughly embedding the song within one of Cobain's overarching themes.

"Beeswax" is also a signature Cobain song because of its structure. Each verse consists of the juxtaposition of dissimilar and unconnected ideas and images, and the narrative perspective shifts between and within the verses. The third verse represents an extreme example of this structuring in the way Cobain juxtaposes ideas and images. The first two lines are surreal, impressionistic. They introduce the character to whom the narrator is speaking: "If *you're* wondering, it's gaining monthly" / "Fiber glass insulated, the sky is cotton candy." The third verse also contains the following three features: Allusions to fish reproduction and ovulation ("Spanning downstream, el rancho ovulate"); the narrator's invitation, already mentioned, to be penetrated by another character's penis; and references to American pop music ("Toni Tennille") and prime-time television ("The Love Boat").

The collage of ideas and images presented in the third verse functions to alienate and disorient; the images and ideas are opaque, making additional, veiled references to a penetrated male body.[22] The collage itself, however, is difficult to break down. The verse thus operates to alienate and disorient a specific kind of reader, the one "who likes all our pretty songs … but he don't know what it means" ("In Bloom"). This particular kind of heterosexual and presumptively homophobic male reader appears to be the implicit target of "Beeswax," just as he is the mark in "In Bloom." At the same time that this collation of images and ideas remains confounding and seemingly impenetrable, though, it is also familiar and comforting precisely because these images and ideas refer to pop music and familiar television shows. The Captain and Tennille were a successful husband-and-wife recording duo who had their own television variety show in the 1970s. The couple in real life and their television personas, like "The Love Boat," a popular show from the late '70s, all romanticized and naturalized conventional masculinity and heterosexual relations. What type of images could be more effective in reassuring an unsettled listener/reader?

The first verse and chorus present the dominant image and announce the central idea of the song. The lyrics operate to profile a narrator who envisions inhabiting a body that is male and female, and he, like the narrator in "Spank Thru," fancies castration as punishment and as pleasure. This narrator also rejects traditional phallic masculinity, as emblematized by Pepe Le Pew: "Like Pepe Le Pew would say" / "Hey, hey, hey and we clash."

Pepe Le Pew, created by animator Chuck Jones (1912–2002), is a Warner Brothers' Looney Tunes, "French" character best known for his offensive, skunk odor. He is also infamous because of his equally offensive and aggressive romantic pursuit of a frightened, put-upon, uninterested "pussy" (a black cat named Penelope Pussycat), who rejects his advances. In earlier versions of the cartoon, Pepe (aka "Stinky") pursues, unwittingly, a *male* cat who is merely masquerading as a female skunk in order to evade his human hunters. In this respect, the character suggests the kind of sexual fluidity and gender plasticity that Cobain's journals in particular posit as desirable for a nonconforming masculine subject.[23] Finally, the name Pepe, when sung, easily elides into "pee pee," a child's word for penis, an organ usually considered immature and nonthreatening.

"Beeswax" employs the frequently used Cobain technique of conflating and confounding narrative perspectives. The first line of the first verse is indecipherable. The "she" in the text remains unspecified, although the character reappears in the second verse as an observer who mocks the narrator's impotence ("She laughs at it"). This female character, however, merges with another character, the one to whom the narrator is recounting his experiences: "If *you're* wondering its gaining monthly." And, as in many other Cobain songs, the perspective of the narrator and those of the other characters ("you"/ "she") cannot be easily distinguished, if at all. Pepe Le Pew is an apt example of the technique. He appears in the first verse, then disappears, and finally reappears at the conclusion of the song. It is his voice that is heard in the outro: "Nothing hard" / "I gotta be around pussy" / "I gotta hey hey" / . . . "*We* got my diddly spayed" (repeated six times).

Since the narrative perspective throughout "Beeswax" is ambiguous, it is initially unclear whose perspective is being presented at the conclusion of the song. The second line of the outro does suggest that it is Pepe speaking because the line summarizes his obsessive actions vis-à-vis the object of his desire: "I [just] gotta be around pussy," he insists. The fourth line also indicates that we are hearing the voice of Pepe since it contains an utterance that the narrator presents as Pepe's signature expression ("Hey, hey"), initially heard in the first verse.

I have italicized "we" in the above excerpt, however, because it is the introduction of the first-person plural pronoun in the final chorus that creates an even greater degree of ambiguity. I read the plural pronoun as designating the narrator and the "she/you" of the text. The narrator and his female addressee together, in other words, have gotten him "fixed." On the other hand, this single use (in the entire song) of the pronoun "we" can also signal the complicitous relationship that exists between the narrator and the offensive Pepe, since the narrator is ventriloquizing him at this very moment. In this instance, the reader understands that Pepe and the narrator, together, have divested the narrator of his penis: "*We* got my diddly spayed." Whichever interpretation the reader settles on, the ultimate message that the song communicates—regarding the male sex organ and traditional masculine behavior—remains unchanged.

LYRICAL CONCLUSIONS: FROM SELF-CRITICISM TO SELF-MURDER AND PHANTASIES OF DEATH AND DYING

Although Cobain employs both first-person and third-person narrators in his songs, he seems to prefer the former. After examining his signature songs, though, I conclude that these two modes of narration are indistinguishable. As literary techniques, they produce the same effect. In any particular song, the perspective of a Cobain narrator merges with that of other characters presented in the lyrics, often to the point, as demonstrated, that it becomes difficult to disengage narrator and characters. Further, it becomes heuristically counterproductive to attempt to untangle the different narrative perspectives present in any text if one's objective is to account for how gender and sexuality appear conceptually and rhetorically in Cobain's lyrics. As I have specified, it is as though narrators in Cobain's songs are dreamers who distribute different aspects of their psychical makeup among several characters.

If a certain mode of masculine behavior and psychology is represented consistently in Cobain's lyrics as reprehensible and in need of reprobation and/or total eradication, it would stand to reason that narrators would be presented primarily in two ways. On the one hand, first-person narrators paint their own portrait from a position of power. In this instance, no explicit, authorial voice comments on or condemns the narrator's attitudes and actions. Yet the profile is so unequivocal that the reader is horrified and is constrained to hold the narrator in contempt, or at least up to ridicule. One of the most dispiriting examples of this type of narrator comes to life in the pre-Nirvana composition "Control." The song's narrator represents the ultimate incarnation of the damnable man who emerges within Cobain's lyrics. He reveals himself to be a domestic abuser: "Kicking out your eye-sock" / "Then I dislocate your shoulder." He is also a misogynist, a hypocrite, and an overall moral reprobate who is incapable of changing his abusive behavior:

[Chorus]
All the blood has dried before you're forced to misconstrue
And I tell her I'm sorry and I'll make it up to you
. . .
Then I turn around and do it all again

On the other hand, there are first-person narrators in Cobain's lyrics who are represented as self-aware and who therefore recognize their incipient or their fully developed monstrosity. These narrators attempt, in various ways, to express their guilt and shame. Like the first kind of first-person narrator, this kind of narrator, too, speaks from a position of power, but he also identifies with the nonmasculine or nondominant position presented in the song. It is because these narrators explicitly cross-identify with a powerless position that they are represented typically as filled with anxiety, guilt, or shame. They are the ones who present themselves as diseased physically or as deficient mentally and morally. In precisely these instances, narrators are prone to self-criticism and even a masochistic self-hatred. Frequently, these narrators are also confronting, at the same time and in various ways, experiences of loss; therefore, they are also melancholic.

Experiences of loss that engender self-criticism, self-punishment, and possibly self-destruction emerge in a song like "Lithium." In asserting that he has *found* his "friends" and his "god," the narrator is unwittingly acknowledging his loss, which in addition to his friends and his god also includes his hair and physical appearance. The recovery of his losses is only imaginary: "I'm happy 'cause today I've found my friends, *they're in my head*." Since his recovered friends exist only in his imaginary world, the narrator has failed to adequately recover them. His physical world, in other words, remains unchanged. Thus, he expresses ambivalent, contradictory feelings. He continues to be melancholic, in spite of his laconic denial: "I'm so lonely and / That's ok, I shaved my head / And I'm not sad."

In the second verse and in the chorus of "Lithium," the narrator's melancholy and loss are expressed more explicitly. For example, he continues to be lonely and sex-starved, but now he is also paralyzed by guilt ("I'm so lonely . . . I'm to blame . . . I'm so horny"), even though he attempts, once again, to mask his disconsolation. The chorus introduces the second-person pronoun and the character to whom the narrator is addressing his plaints. As in other songs, the identity of the interlocutor remains ambiguous. Familiarity with Cobain's literary techniques suggests that the narrator and interlocutor represent two aspects of the same subject. In "Lithium," the narrator reveals the relationship between the two aspects of this divided identity by repeating, seemingly ad infinitum, that he loves, misses, and has killed his partner. He has in fact killed himself, an aspect of himself:

I miss you

. . .

I love you

. . .

I killed you
I'm not gonna crack

In addition to "Lithium," "Negative Creep" and "All Apologies" may constitute more fully developed examples of self-criticizing narrators who are both masochistic and melancholic. This internal self-censure can be seen in the defining lines from these two songs, respectively: "I'm a negative creep and I'm stoned"; "Everything is my fault, I will take all the blame." Soulsby has produced another chart (*Dark Slivers*, chap. 10) summarizing this time the characteristics and the actions of this kind of self-blaming, self-chastising, masochistic, and melancholic narrator as found in other lyrics. In many of these songs, the narrator's actions and attitudes are represented as mere kernels of a theme in lyrics that do not then go on to develop the topic. In this way, a single line or fragment of a line functions in a manner similar to the isolated lines I have highlighted from "Frances Farmer," "Teen Spirit," and "Blather's Log." The verse appears as another one-off line, but it takes on its full impact when collated with similar lines from other songs.

Here is a partial list of the songs containing the more evocative of these seemingly one-off lines. I cite them because they will facilitate my reading of two songs—"Mrs. Butterworth" and "In His Room"—that constitute poignant examples of lyrics in which a narrator's self-criticism and self-hatred morph into phantasies of death and dying. It is in these two songs that readers confront narrators that are the most clearly represented as irretrievably both masochistic and melancholic.

SONG	LINES(S)
"Downer"	"I've had a lobotomy"
"Radio Friendly Unit Shifter"	"I hate you for what I am not" / "What is wrong with me"
"Negative Creep"	"I'm a negative creep"
"Scoff"	"I'm not worth it"
"Dive"	"I'm real good at hating"
"Stain"	"I'm a stain"
"Big Long Now"	"Shameful as it seems"
"Teen Spirit":	"I feel stupid and contagious"
	. . .
	"I'm best at what I do worst"
"Dumb"	"I think I'm dumb"
"Pennyroyal Tea"	"I'm a liar and a thief"
"Lithium"	"I'm to blame for all I've heard"
"Lounge Act"	"I'll arrest myself"
"All Apologies"	"What else should I be, all apologies"
	. . .
	"Everything is my fault" / "I'll take all the blame"

SONG	LINES(S)
"Insurance"	"Thank you for the shame"
"Accusations"	"All my lawyers say that I should plead totally guilty"
"Floyd the Barber"	"I was shamed"

Indeed, a logical extension of representations of a self-blaming and self-loathing narrator, as evident in the above lines, would be allusions to and images of death and suicide. This shift is manifest even in a song as exasperatingly incoherent as "Endless, Nameless." This beguilingly plaintive song contains the following succession of disjointed lines: "Here I am . . . I have died. . . . Death with violence, Excitement. . . . Death is what I am. . . . Here I am, Take a chance. Dead."

Since Cobain's death, it has been routine for fans, biographers, and commentators to underscore references to guns, death, and suicide in his lyrics. For example, writers invariably speculate on the significance of the first line in "Teen Spirit": "Load up on guns, bring all your friends." Likewise, many fans have debated the significance of the chorus in "Come As You Are: "And I swear I don't have a gun" / "No, I don't have a gun." But in addition to the lines from the sixteen songs cited above that point to self-blaming and self-loathing narrators, I draw attention to other lyrics in which readers confront explicit references to death and dying on the part of plaintive narrators:

SONG	LINES(S)
"Pennyroyal Tea"	"Give me a Leonard Cohen afterworld" / "So I can sigh eternally"
"Stay Away"	"I'd rather be dead than cool"
"Been a Son"	"She should have died when she was born"
"On a Plain"	"My mother died every night"
"Milk It"	"Look on the bright side is suicide"
"Token Eastern Song"	"Suicide is something mean"[24]

Not only do "Mrs. Butterworth" and "In His Room" offer lyrics in which it becomes difficult to differentiate self-criticism from phantasies of death, these two songs also put forth lyrics in which masculinity is represented explicitly as a masochistic subjectivity that *modulates* into melancholy. Although the two songs are not especially popular even among Nirvana fans, they constitute seminal texts to the extent that they underscore the role of death and dying in Cobain's lyrics. The two songs also predict how these themes operate in Cobain's journals and in his suicide letter.

"In His Room" in particular constitutes the most explicitly delineated example of this defining role. If one were to judge by the title of a song alone, though, then the role of death and dying would seem to be presented more unequivocally in another song, "I Hate Myself and Want to Die." In actuality, the lyrics to "I Hate Myself" only fleetingly and parenthetically hint at the notion of disempowerment and a desire for one's own demise that characterize the suffering, masochistic, and melancholic persona that is represented in Cobain's lyrics and especially in certain journal entries. Its suggestive title notwithstanding, the actual lyrics to the song, as opposed to its music, do not succeed in exposing the depth of the narrator's melancholy—and the joy he finds in dying—as found elsewhere in Cobain's writings.[25]

Therefore, I put "I Hate Myself" aside, though I do draw on the implication of its infamous title in order to examine "Mrs. Butterworth" and "In His Room." These two manifestly inscrutable songs evoke disempowerment and death in ways merely hinted at in "I Hate Myself." These songs represent the divestment of power and the narrator's pending death as both an aggravation of, and a cure for, the contagion and iniquity that is his very existence. Further, I reinterpret references to death and suicide in a way that departs from previous analyses of this theme in Cobain's songs. I examine these references as literary productions; I read them as *phantasies* expressed in poetic form.

Thus, I explore references to self-murder in Cobain's lyrics in particular as examples of a "discursive suicide," that is, as a literary strategy. I examine the songs as fiction and not as a sign or a confession, whether conscious or unconscious, on the part of the historical Kurt Cobain that he is contemplating taking his own life. Discursive suicide indicates simply that Cobain's writings represent masculinity as an unstable and untenable subjectivity. His lyrics represent masculinity as a gender identity that is, as I continue to emphasize, both troubled and troubling in specific ways and for specific reasons, including—but not limited to—the challenges of navigating a sexist and heterosexist culture as a straight man.

Mrs. Butterworth and Death in a Jar / Dying in His Room and on the Cross

"Mrs. Butterworth" provides yet another example of a Cobain text in which the narrator's point of view merges with that of the character he is addressing. In this particular instance, the merging is revealed in the chorus. This section of the song is characterized by a subtle shift from previous descriptions of *"your"* life to evocations of *"my"* death. As in "Drain You," the narrator is in fact addressing himself. He is assessing his own dismal life and then proposing a solution to his discomfiture. The first verse begins with the narrator proclaiming that "your life" is "shit," "bogus," a "crime," and "hell." Although he is ostensibly addressing another person, the chorus confirms that he is fact describing the iniquity of his own existence. The chorus proceeds, *in the first person,* to specify how the narrator will rectify his miserable existence: "I'm gonna die, start a new union" / I'm gonna die, with my libido."

"Mrs. Butterworth" also follows the typical pattern in a signature Cobain song in the way the verses seem to entertain, at best, a tenuous relation to the chorus. In this case, the first four lines of the chorus merely repeat, in four different ways, the bleakness and comfortlessness of the narrator's existence. In the subsequent four lines, the narrator simply reiterates the irreversible solution that he has found to his wretchedness: A union with death. The subsequent verses, however, contradict the solution proposed in the chorus. In order to relieve his distress, the narrator lays out an elaborate plan to continue living. He will "open up a flea market" that will include the selling of his empty "Mrs. Butterworth jars."

In spite of the manner in which "Mrs. Butterworth" makes sense within the context of Cobain's overall lyrical production as an example of a narrator who is masochistic and melancholic, it is "In His Room" that most clearly and succinctly suggests how phantasies of death and dying function in Cobain's creative writings. The first two verses of this song constitute a soliloquy. The narrator does not appear to be addressing anyone in particular, though he seems aware that he is not alone, and that someone is listening to his anguished refrain, as the lines cited from the first and second verses suggest. Since I find the recorded versions of the song especially difficult to understand, I provide possible alternate versions of these lines.

The first verse, for example, includes the following two lines: "Wouldn't want to fake it, and I'm tired of this dream" and "Driven conversations, he died in June." Alternate versions of these lines could very well be *"He's going to chase*

you in and out of a dream" and "*If they don't show affection, he'll die in June.*"
The second verse contains two lines that are equally difficult to decipher: "Giving conversations to a friend of mine" and "Giving medications, in a lighted room," lines that might indeed be the following instead: "*He's not gonna catch you in a lighted room*" and "*He's going to chase you in and out of a dream.*"

Whatever the specific details, the two verses make several observations concerning the nonspecific, oneiric predicament in which the narrator finds himself: "I'm tired of this dream." While shifting from the first to the third person, the chorus proceeds to describe the main character "dying in his room." The third verse, by contrast, is written in the first person plural ("*We*'re not gonna make it, well I don't mind"), rendering the lyrics elliptic in two ways. First, the first-person plural pronoun here, as in other songs, complicates the narrative perspective: It is unclear if two or three characters are present in this scene. Nor does the relation between the narrator and the characters remain consistent. Second, the introduction of the first-person plural pronoun complicates the nature of the episode that is being related: It is unclear what kind of death story is being told, who is telling it, or who is listening to this narration. As opposed to the first two verses, the third suggests that the narrator is addressing the friend, the dead person. As in other lyrics, the choruses turn out to provide one key to understanding the overall structuring of the song and its central idea.

Given Cobain's aesthetic inclinations, it is to be expected that in "In His Room," the "I," "he," and "you" of this song all fuse together. This particular phantasy of death, dying, killing, and self-killing broadcasts the significance of discursive suicide within Cobain's creative works overall. I cite the two choruses because, unlike the verses, they point more directly to the reasons why the phantasy of dying constitutes such a poignant and potent feature within the complex, disorienting universe that Cobain assiduously creates: "See the stab wounds in his hands" / "See him dying in his room" / "Heading for me, heading this way" / ... "*He* is coming, *I* don't care."

In the first chorus, the merging of "I" and "he" establishes, in one more example within Cobain's lyrics, that the narrator experiences a divided identity and he is, therefore, witnessing himself in the process of dying. In "Mrs. Butterworth," the narrator's pleasure in recounting (witnessing) his own death scene is merely implied. In "In His Room," by contrast, the narrator's experience of the comfort and relief that result from a reunion with death is explicit: The character is described in the process of dying; further, death is coming for the narrator who welcomes it. Through death, in other words, the narrator, a divided subject, is reintegrated.

In the second version of the chorus, the introduction of the second-person pronoun establishes that the narrator reverts again to a bifurcated identity. In this instance, however, it is no longer an "I/he" divide, the one that makes possible the narrator's observation of his own dying. This second chorus establishes a mirror identity between the "I" and the "*you*" of the text. As a result of the merging of the first and second persons, in addition to beholding his own expiration, the narrator also fulfills at this moment the role of executioner: "You killed him, I don't care." In fact, these lines mean "You killed *me*, I don't care."

However, since the "I" of the text cannot be distinguished from the "you," the lines operate to confirm the notion that death occurs at the subject's own hands: "*I* killed me, I don't care." Further, death takes place in the fulfillment of a covenant. Within this phantasy, the subject's death is not only an imperative, an obligation to be met, it constitutes also a sacrifice, in the manner of Christ's death on the Cross: "See the stab wounds in his hands" / "You killed him, I don't care" / "Keep a promise, you would too" (repeated twice). From start to finish, the song continues to mimic a dream sequence in the way that the narrator plays all three parts in this scenario: He is the one being killed, he does the killing, and he witnesses the scene. As I shall explore in the next chapter, this very same dynamic repeats itself in a curious manner in Cobain's journal writings and in at least one illustration.

It is the first line in the two choruses—the only line that is identical in the different versions—that authorizes reading this phantasy within the context of the death of Christ: "See the stab wounds in his hands." As I shall also explore further when examining Cobain's published journals, there are allusions to Christ in his notebooks that recall the structure and the content of "In His Room." For example, there is a reference to a "Scarecrow Jesus" in one journal entry (243) and an actual sketch in another entry of this figure being crucified (127). The sketch constitutes one of the images in his notebooks that Cobain presents as a self-portrait. It depicts an emaciated, Cobainesque male figure in the process of dying.

In addition, a version of Scarecrow Jesus appears in the "Heart Shaped Box" video in which the character wears a Santa hat instead of a jack-o'-lantern on his head. Outside of his journals, other images—allegedly produced by Cobain and posted on line after his death ("Guide to Kurt Cobain's Art")—include Christ-like figures, one of which depicts another familiar-looking, Cobainesque figure. A different image depicts a male figure with bleeding hands.[26]

It may initially appear surprising that Cobain's lyrics, like his journals, would reveal a certain affinity with Christ, given the way the persona Cobain cultivates appears to dismiss certain tenets of Christianity. Christ is also the subject of two of Cobain's favorite cover songs: "They Hung Him on a Cross" and "Jesus Doesn't Want Me for a Sunbeam." Christ, or more specifically the crucifixion of Christ, epitomizes a mode of masculinity that can also best be characterized as masochistic and melancholic. On the one hand, Christ embodies a masculinity that is self-sacrificing and that masochistically takes on all the pain of the world; and on the other, he incarnates a divided subjectivity (human/divine), one characterized also by a profound sense of melancholy, loss, and abandonment: "My God, my God, why hast thou forsaken me?" (Mark 15:34 and Matthew 27:46).[27]

"Mrs. Butterworth" and "In His Room" do indeed, just like "Spank Thru" and "Beeswax" in their own inimitable way, exemplify the principal aesthetics and the underlying philosophy espoused by the persona that Cobain unfailingly creates. This aesthetics and this philosophy reverberate throughout the majority of his lyrics. Further, the representation of death and dying in "Mrs. Butterworth" and in "In His Room" finds echoes, as I suggest, in certain passages in Cobain's journals, a text in which these themes are expressed even more explicitly and dishearteningly. It is in his fragmented, handwritten, and illustrated notebooks that readers encounter vexing representations of melancholy as a phantasy of self-murder. As Cobain suggests already in these two remarkable songs, his journals will confirm that three characters, a specific trinity, are essential for this phantasy to function and to produce the desired result: There must be a killer, a person killed, and a witness to the execution. Each of these roles, as it turns out, must all be performed by the same male subject.

4 THE PAGES OF COBAIN'S JOURNALS "SMELL LIKE SEMEN"
Writing (with) the Male Body

Cobain wrote the line "Electrolytes smell like semen" in "Scentless Apprentice," a song on *In Utero* that continues the obsession with male corporeality—including the effects of its ostensible "odors"—that characterize his lyrical production. Since his lyrics and his journals exist in a symbiotic relationship, they are mutually explicative. Metaphorically, seminal fluid conjugates these two related but quite distinct creative writings; thematically, representations of experiences of the male body and an irremediable anxiety about one's value and place in the world link them inextricably. Cobain's handwritten and illustrated notebooks provide a rehearsal space where the lyricist launches and edits many of the songs he later records. I shall return to the details of this function of Cobain's journals in the second half of this chapter.

The two sections that make up this chapter correspond to the two principal methods I use to read the fragments that make up Cobain's notebooks. Selections from his personal writings were initially published in 2002 as *Journals*. In the first section, I examine the text as it was augmented, annotated, and republished in the 2003 paperback edition. I read it as an independent text with its own thesis and internal logic. In this instance, I read *Journals* as an imaginary universe, a phantasy. As such, the text does not reproduce an external reality, but it does, like Cobain's lyrics, capture an emotional and psychical truth.[1] It is in the second section of this chapter that I read *Journals* as a phantasy text that dialogues with and complements Cobain's lyrics. In this second instance, I read the text as an inadvertently racialized space, one that seems gaslighted by a seductive but illusory blackness. This black presence appears in the guise of a revealing yet problematic homage to an African American songwriter, musician, and performer.

Written between the late 1980s and the early 1990s, *Journals* constitutes a collation of mostly undated and sundry texts. In addition to song lyrics, the text includes proposals for video versions of songs, letters to friends, letters to the editor of national magazines, open letters, lists of favorite songs and musicians, several biographies of Nirvana, two recipes, and hundreds of drawings, sketches, and illustrations. According to the publisher, *Journals* is a compilation of materials "from 23 of Cobain's personal notebooks (some 800 pages)" (Wood, 332).

As an ensemble of recursive and fragmented texts, the writing in these notebooks seems symptomatic of the much-heralded crisis of straight white masculinity that some scholars have identified as characteristic of the late twentieth and early twenty-first centuries in North America. Fred Pfeil attempts to identify the causes of this crisis in *White Guys: Studies in Postmodern Domination and Difference*. "The contemporary crisis of straight white masculinity," he writes, "is precisely a function of the degree to which those men incarnating it have been forced to see it for what it is: A subjectivity that is organized within structures of control and authority" (xi).

If Pfiel is correct, then *Journals* appears to constitute a prognostic; it seems to put forth a solution to the crisis. Cobain's text functions, implicitly, as an impassioned plea to men to reflect on the meaning and the consequences of conventional masculine behavior. Like some political treaties written by twentieth-century, progressive white men, Cobain's illustrated notebooks furtively but passionately solicit straight white men to consider a different gender mode. *Journals* encourages these men to construct a "new" masculinity with three distinct features. It proposes a gender identity "whose desire is no longer dependent on oppression"; [one that is] no longer policed by homophobia; and [one that] no longer resorts to violence, [racism], and misogyny to maintain its sense of coherence" (Chapman and Rutherford, 11).[2]

The 1990s saw the emergence of a particular iteration of the crisis of white masculinity, what Kyle Kusz refers to as the "youthification of the white male as victim trope" (390). This trope, already prevalent for decades in American literature and popular culture, becomes, in the final decades of the twentieth century, evident in alternative music as *young* white men present and represent themselves as neglected, disadvantaged, or in some way oppressed. Later on, this particular version of the crisis is especially evident, as indicated in chapter 2, in emo chat rooms, lyrics, and stage performances.

But when *Journals* is read as a self-contained, self-referential, autonomous text, rather than reflecting simply a specific historical moment of crisis, or even the dire straits of a specific person or persona, the text offers an auspicious example of how creative works in general can vividly illustrate the dynamics of unconscious phantasy and the complexities of subjectivity. As indicated in the introduction, I use the "ph" spelling of phantasy to underscore what the concept of "unconscious phantasy" means within Melanie Klein's theory. For analysts and scholars who subscribe to Klein's original idea, unconscious phantasy determines both the structure and the content of psychical life. Cobain's journal writings and illustrations, even more so than his lyrics, bear out Klein's insight that there is an interrelation between our unconscious phantasy life—and in particular how we experience and resolve anxiety—and our corporeality, how we come to know and experience our bodies.

The separate fragments that constitute *Journals* allow readers to follow the psychical and emotional development of a subject attempting to come to terms with a profound and irresolvable inner conflict. The persona that emerges within this text, as within Cobain's lyrics, cannot be identified in any direct and unproblematic way with the historical person, the writer of the text. In fact, the cogency of the representation of the persona Cobain creates would be compromised if the tenets, characters, and episodes in *Journals* were to be "reality tested" against the events and people in Cobain's external life. Such a compromise occurs whether one considers Cobain's life as his biographers have chronicled it, or as Cobain himself reveals aspects of his life in interviews.

Therefore, reading *Journals* primarily in order to understand the historical Kurt Cobain—the son, brother, boyfriend, husband, father, and bandmate—leads invariably to a disappointing reading. In particular, some critics in the popular media, some historians of popular music, and at least one prominent rock musician have all dismissed this text as unworthy of serious attention. They conclude that *Journals* is incoherent, practically illiterate, pitiable, and merely symptomatic of a run-of-the-mill addiction. They suggest further that this addiction is itself likely camouflaging an impenetrable pathology:

The abuse heaped on Cobain's *Journals* by the mainstream media is at once staggering and unsurprising. In a brief, dismissive piece in the *New York Times,*

King Kaufman tosses aside [the text] as nothing more than "the musings of anyone in his 20s: letters to friends, naïve whining about politics, lists of favorite records [. . .], equivocating about the severity of his drug problem, even the occasional recipe." Pete Townshend, writing in the *Observer,* calls [*Journals*] "the scribblings of some once beautiful, muddled, angry, petulant, spoiled, drug-addled middle-class white boy from a divorced family"; they're not even real journals for Townshend, they're "so-called." The disparaging terms reviewers use—"semi-coherent," "puerile," "obviously sick," "mentally deranged," "ridiculous," "pathetic," "torturous"—issue from the sober light of day, where no sense can be made of nocturnal fascinations. They "provide no insight," Kaufman harrumphs. "I picked up this book searching for connections," moans Townshend [. . .] who uses *Journals* as evidence that Cobain must have plagiarized in his recorded output: based on these "infantile scribbling," he sniffs, "Cobain had a lot of help for [the writing of] his albums." (Sirc, 19)

The critical reception of *Journals* parallels in some ways the 1994 reception of Elizabeth Wurtzel's memoir *Prozac Nation* (Marlan). In addition to Wurtzel's comments on Cobain and her initial intent to title her memoir *I Hate Myself and Want to Die,* the two texts coincidentally reveal the same truth. Both books confirm that certain psychical and emotional experiences are unrepresentable, even though Cobain, unlike Wurtzel, does not set out to write a conventional memoir.[3]

In addition to journalists from the national press, insightful commentators on Cobain's life and music, such as Nick Soulsby, and even some die-hard Nirvana fans have also dismissed *Journals* as an irrelevant text. Judging from blogs and online posts, in spite of an overall positive reception, many fans are disappointed with these published notebooks. Some who idolize Cobain, for example, are still seeking to reconcile, if not to distinguish, the performer/persona and the real person. They seem to sense, or perhaps to hope, that what might have been censored from these journal entries must be more probative.[4]

Other readers with an interest in the history of popular music conclude that *Journals* is not especially informative if one is seeking to write the history of Nirvana and grunge. They are correct. When read in tandem with the biographies of Cobain and with accounts of grunge that have appeared since his death, his published notebooks offer no additional insights into the creation of Nirvana; nor do they illuminate Cobain's artistic and personal relationship with the other members of the group. Neither is the text immediately revelatory for anyone seeking to appreciate the degree to which Cobain both influenced and was himself influenced by the aesthetics and politics of his generation.

Finally, most of Cobain's biographers suggest that many fragments in *Journals* should be read as pure fiction. Nevertheless, they cite these notebooks to substantiate many of the details in the biographies they compose. As a result, these writers unwittingly confirm that the border separating biography and autobiography from fiction is indeed porous. Jesse Kavadlo, in his analysis of the theme of self-destruction in literature, argues that there is a continuum between contemporary American fiction (the rock-and-roll novel specifically) and Cobain's biography. As I also argue, many of Cobain's journal entries constitute a particular kind of autobiographical fiction.

Rather than reading *Journals* exclusively as source material to write Cobain's life story, one can successfully read the text outside of the gravitational pull of his biography. In particular, one can understand the text outside of the mythology that Cobain himself consciously constructed about his life in general and about his politics, his sexuality, and his music specifically. The content of *Journals* does not convincingly substantiate, nor does the text successfully belie, certain claims that Cobain repeats publicly. He insists, for example, that he espouses a feminist and antiracist political ideology; that he identifies with certain aspects of African American culture; that he is bisexual and gay "in spirit"; and that, in spite of the mass appeal of his later recordings, his music remains authentically punk. In fact, on these specific topics, *Journals* may appear on the surface to be evidentiary, but the text frequently complicates, if it does not outright contradict, these very claims.

Although I contend that *Journals* may not necessarily serve up the kind of biographical details that some fans and scholars seek, I do realize that the text has a history. Cobain wrote these entries within a specific social and cultural context. Therefore, the text does speak to certain sociological phenomena and historical processes having to do with making and listening to rock music. Even as I read Cobain's personal writings as distinct from his biography, I am not impervious, to paraphrase Nicky Glover writing in a different context, to the more challenging question as to why *Journals* is so "precious" and speaks so intimately and powerfully to certain readers. This effect on readers has been so profound and pervasive that the notion of pursuing postgraduate Cobain Studies is not considered preposterous (Callies; Alexander).

When read as a text that is complete in and of itself, one that is propelled by an interstitial logic, the structure and content of *Journals* do give readers an unusual glimpse into the creative process. Further, the text confirms, as certain psychoanalysts theorize, that subjectivity is predicated necessarily on an experience of anxiety and on attempts to come to terms with it. Cobain's personal notebooks also validate the thesis that anxiety itself appears invariably as a bodily manifestation.

In my literary and cultural analyses of *Journals,* I am putting into parentheses the problematic questions surrounding the publication of the text, including whether or not the original notebooks were even intended to be made public. I am also setting aside the extent to which the notebooks may have been censored or edited prior to publication. As I suggest, Cobain's published journals, like his lyrics, do not provide readers with raw material. That is, these notebooks, necessarily, have been mediated by editors prior to publication. After publication, their reception has been further mediated by book reviews in traditional and social media. As the comments cited above by Townshend and others confirm, this mediation has affected how the text is currently read and interpreted.[5]

With *Journals,* readers have enough contiguous material from individual notebooks to allow us to conclude that the published text is representative of the ensemble. The nature and scope of this material authorize a specific kind of reading. Therefore, I do begin by reading these handwritten, illustrated journal entries as a dream space for Cobain to reflect on, prepare for, and understand aspects of his life. In the process, however, his real life is transformed because, in this text, emotional and psychical reality comes to supplant experiential reality in the overall story that Cobain is attempting to tell. In order to relate this story, he creates and then attempts to inhabit a specific persona. *Journals* epitomizes journal writing in the sense that French philosopher and literary theorist Maurice Blanchot defines the genre: Cobain's text is composed of self-reflective questions and snippets of writing. It constitutes a space of contemplation in which the writing subject creates, rehearses, and then recreates all the significant and insignificant details that might give structure and meaning to his fear and desire.

"A POOL OF RAZOR BLADES AND SPERM": A PHANTASY OF WHITE, HETEROSEXUAL MASCULINITY IN JOURNALS

I like to feel guilty for being a white, American male.

I like the comfort of knowing that women are superior.

I like the comfort of knowing that the Afro American invented Rock and Roll.

I like the comfort of knowing that women are the future of Rock and Roll.

I find a few things sacred such as the superiority of women and the Negro to art.

Uh, god is a woman and she's back in black.

God is gay and so am I.

I hate myself and want to die. (*Journals,* 109–230)

These discrete, sequential declarations punctuate at irregular intervals the nearly three hundred pages that make up the second edition of *Journals.* These seemingly simple assertions undergird the text and point to an acute anxiety about gender and racial identity that generates and modulates the writing. The very act of writing, in turn, further fuels the narrator's manifest anguish. One of the text's signal expressions, "a pool of razor blades and sperm," a phrase that appears twice in the text, emblematizes this inner conflict. The expression encapsulates a series of themes that revolve around questions of power, violence, pleasure, and creativity. In addition, iterations and variations of this unusual expression, and the themes it puts into play, are emblematic of the striking poetics of *Journals:* The text is fluid, redundant, and elliptical. Cobain constructs it often as a series of concentric circles. The expression "a pool of razor blades and sperm" also presents in miniature form the text's tentative, inchoate thesis concerning the relation between gender (masculinity), authority (power), violence (racism/sexism), and youth subcultures (resistance):

And hairy, sweaty, macho-sexist and racist Dickheads who will soon drown in *a pool of razor blades and sperm* from the uprising of your children, the armed and de-programmed crusade, littering the floors of Wall Street with revolutionary debris, assasinating [*sic*] both the lesser and greater of two evils [,] bringing an everlasting sterile and bacterial, herbacious [*sic*] corporate cleansing for our ancestors to gaze in wonderment and awe [emphasis added].

The representatives of the American Male RAPES [*sic*] in more ways than one. Posing as the enemy to infiltrate the mechanics of the empire and slowly start its rot from the inside [,] it's an inside job—it starts with the custodians and the cheerleaders, oh well, whatever, nevermind. (145)[6]

Thirty pages and some twenty-two entries later, a variation of the above passage—which contains fragments of a storyboard for a "Smells Like Teen Spirit" video—is embedded within an extended journal entry. This five-page entry constitutes one of the longest continuous fragments in the text (177–82). It constitutes what I identify as the central entry in *Journals*. The nature and scope of the themes within this entry function to italicize it in relationship to the remainder of the text. This long entry not only repeats elements from several other entries that appear before and after it, the central entry also self-consciously repeats itself. In effect, Cobain composes the central entry in the text in three "movements." Together these three movements replicate a particular song structure (chorus/verse/chorus) that appeals to him. Further, these very words, "chorus, verse, chorus," constitute a locution that appears repeatedly in *Journals* within varying contexts, some having nothing to do with music composition (99, 153, 154, 159, 164). The chorus-verse-chorus structure is one that applies equally to the composition of *Journals* in its entirety.

It is precisely because the central entry signally reproduces in miniature form the overall structure and content of Cobain's published notebooks as a whole that I cite below three passages from it. Composed ostensibly as a letter to his girlfriend Tobi Vail, this entry echoes, and adds details to, a discussion of gender and racial politics exposed in embryonic forms earlier in the text. Since snippets and variations of this discussion erupt throughout the pages of *Journals,* they give the text a particular cadence. Although these eruptions further fragment the text, which thereby appears even more disjointed and provisionally incoherent, they in fact lend the text a salient cogency and coherence.

The entry is positioned, appropriately, near the very center of the published text. It functions, however, as would a trailer if *Journals* were a feature film. The kernel theme the entry announces is replete with references to violence that include self-penetration, invasion, contamination, and self-destruction, all presented as a means to a masculine self-purification and salvation. Though his girlfriend is the letter's presumptive addressee, Cobain composes it as an open letter. He begins by explaining how sexism, homophobia, and racism are interconnected:

Hi,

Yeah, all isms feed off one other, but at the top of the food chain is still the white, corporate, macho, strong ox male. Not redeemable as far as I'm concerned [. . .] He's in charge. He decides. I still think that in order to expand on all other isms, sexism has to be blown wide open [. . .] The most effective tool is entertainment [. . .] Major labels, the evil corporate Oppressors (god, I need a new word!) the ones who are in Kahoots with the government [. . .] are finally allowing supposedly subversive, alternative thinking bands to have a loan of money to expose their crusade [. . .] because it looks to be a money-making comodity [*sic*], but we can use them. We can pose as the enemy to infiltrate the mechanics of the system to start its rot from the inside. (177)

Cobain then proceeds to explain precisely how young white men who are punk musicians can deploy their music to disrupt the system of male oppression. As if he were indeed composing a song, he further develops this atypically long entry by repeating its "chorus":

Sabotage the empire by pretending to play their game. Compromise just enough to call their bluff. *And the hairy, sweaty macho, sexist dickheads will soon drown in a pool of razor blades and semen.* Stemmed from the uprising of their children. The armed and deprogrammed crusade, littering the floors of Wall Street with revolutionary debris [. . .], [presenting an] everlasting, sterile and bacterial herbacious and botanical and corporate cleansing for our ancestors to gaze in wonderment and awe. AWE! geezus Christ. (repeat): Posing as the enemy to infiltrate the mechanics of the empire and slowly start its rot from the inside, it's an inside job. (179; emphasis added)

Finally, Cobain concludes this remarkable entry, which serves as both a love letter and a manifesto, with an imperative written in all capital letters: "HOMOPHOBE VACCECTOMY." In the development of a politics embedded within a manifestly punk aesthetics, however, the entry has parenthesized one of the defining features of the declared enemy: "the white, corporate, macho, strong ox male." His whiteness, though featured first in his profile, has completely disappeared at the entry's conclusion. In this same manner, as I shall reveal, whiteness becomes an unconscious identity feature of the persona Cobain takes on. Nevertheless, the central entry in *Journals* puts forth a solution to the seemingly intractable problem of homophobia and the rape of women, a solution that contains both an impossible, phantastical component and a practical, real-world one:

> It's like what Kathleen [Hanna] said about how in school there was this class that you went to and they were teaching the girls how to prepare themselves for rape and when you looked outside and saw the rapers [*sic*] outside playing football and you said they are the ones who should be in here being *taught not to rape!!* How true. Suck 'em in with quality entertainment and hit em with reality [...]
>
> I totally love you,
> Kurdt (182).

Throughout *Journals,* Cobain writes in the first person in a manner that creates a persona represented foremost as an artist, a performer. At critical moments in the text, the persona he cultivates is preoccupied with fame and with the relationship between fame, the right to privacy, self-definition, and self-determination. In addition, he is frequently preoccupied also with artistic authenticity and with his own legacy as a lyricist and musician. As a result, the narrator in *Journals* seems especially attuned to the rewards and challenges of membership in an all-male rock band. Unlike other performers to whom he refers, however, he evinces an awareness of the continuum that exists between the homosocial dynamics (male bonding) that undergird membership in a rock band and the erotic implications of these dynamics. Within a heterosexist culture, this continuum, as Eve Kosofsky Sedgwick and other scholars have explored it, invariably incites various expressions of homophobia.

It is with an irrepressible sense of despair that the narrator in this text also represents himself as male, the son of a white working-class family, and as an adolescent and young adult who rejects the politics of his parents' generation. He represents himself explicitly as above average in intelligence but as an underperforming high school student. Cobain creates the persona of a young man who is conflicted about his intellectual acuity, his socioeconomic status, and his relationship to black cultural production. Moreover, as his self-portrait emerges, the narrator in *Journals* seems hopelessly insecure about the color and the fortitude of his body. His insecurity modulates everything he does, including making music. He gives signs that he is suffering "from a profound identity crisis that result[s] from a combination of his fame, his heavy drug use, and his ... depression" (Mazullo, 738).

Above all else, *Journals* constitutes a narrative and lyrical attempt at self-reflection, an attempt that undermines, and may ultimately occlude, its own internal coherence. The writing reveals an inner vision, a process of self-examination but also of self-affirmation, as tentative and as full of contradictions as this process may appear. In other words, the text points to an inner scanning, even if this inventory is in part unconscious. It is in this sense that *Journals* constitutes a deft representation of an unconscious phantasy in the specific way that the term has come to be understood within Kleinian theory. The different entries Cobain composes do not necessarily set out deliberately to be introspective and self-revealing. Nevertheless, the text offers an apt example of the way journal writing can graphically illustrate how self-knowledge is achieved. Put quite simply, Cobain's writings mimic the complex mental processes wherein meaning is generated. We can read the contents of his notebooks as an attempt to arrest the unending fluctuations and the illogic of an unconscious phantasy. The text does so by attempting to superimpose a logical structure and the semblance of a permanent, external reality onto the ever-changing structure and content of a phantasy life.

To summarize Klein's theory, "phantasy" refers to an infant's state of mind early on during its development. Because the prelinguistic infant does not differentiate between what it imagines and what it experiences consciously and concretely, Klein theorizes that phantasies are unconscious. They are set in motion because of natural needs, drives, and instincts. Phantasies, however, are made up of both real and imaginary experiences. These experiences are "plastic" in that they are reshaped and redeployed as needs, drives, and instincts evolve. In addition, according to Klein, "unconscious phantasy does not refer only to the *content* of psychic experience; it also refers to the actual *mechanisms* ... that structure inner life" (Glover, 44). Klein does not limit her theory to children but rather considers unconscious phantasy to be implicated in the way all humans perceive, think, and create. Her description of how we become subjects can help explain how creative works in general come into being and, specifically, how the written fragments and illustrations in *Journals* bring to life "KurDt," the Cobain persona, as a particular kind of subject with a specific story to tell.

Klein specifies that phantasies emerge in symbolic form in child's play and that they emerge in dreams and neuroses. As she lays out her theory, it can facilitate an appreciation of how Cobain's "infantile scribbling," as critics describe Cobain's writings, tell us something significant about depression and how a subject comes to think of himself as male and as white. Klein specifies further that the infant comes to understand its external world, including its own body, through unconscious phantasies. And via mechanisms of externalization (projection) and internalization (introjection), the infant interacts with and relates to the external world. In other words, for Klein, phantasy is an inner experience that projects what is on the inside of the subject outward, onto the external world. At the same time, phantasy takes in what is on the outside of the subject, making what is external an intricate part of the self.

The written entries and illustrations in Cobain's notebooks operate according to these same dynamics. As the narrator of the text, KurDt begins the story he sets out to tell by projecting his internal reality—his insecurities and his anguish—onto the outside world, including onto his own body. He then internalizes aspects of the outside world, such as the music industry, into his phantasy life. And his inner life henceforth includes a phantasied version of his corporeality. The structure and content of *Journals* confirm, as Klein theorizes, that subjectivity is predicated not only on an experience of anxiety but also on the compulsion to restage this anxiety in an attempt to mitigate it.

In particular, an acute distress about the insufferably abject consequences of what it means to be a white, heteromasculine subject animates the writing in *Journals*. The text represents a young man who appears at moments paralyzed not only by depressive anxiety but also by paranoia. It is for this reason that psychoanalytic theory is probative for an understanding of Cobain's writings, in spite of the limitations of Freudian psychoanalysis in particular to explain how racial subjectivity comes about (Lane). Nevertheless, the theory offers one way to penetrate what appears to be the impenetrable clutter and static found in Cobain's notebooks.[7]

In the way *Journals* presents narrators and characters engaged in both deliberate and unwitting mental processes, the text might be said to combine daydreaming, or "fantasy" in the usual meaning of the word, and unconscious phantasy in the Kleinian sense. The persona Cobain creates, as he reveals himself in several journal entries, plays upon the dialectic between "fantasy" and "phantasy." For example, as a self-aware narrator, he writes a cogent letter to

Mark Lanegan, Screaming Trees' singer-songwriter, that includes specific, verifiable details about Nirvana's recording and touring activities. After the first four hundred words, though, the letter abruptly shifts its subject matter and point of view. It becomes an additional four-hundred-word, dreamlike meditation on the body-mind continuum by a narrator who is caught completely unawares, incognizant of who or where he is:

> Just before I fall asleep and when I'm really bored I . . . lay down and think
> for a while until I ~~subconsciously~~ fall into a ~~hypo~~ semi hypnotic state of sub-
> consciousness, some call it daydreaming, some call it just fucking spacing out.
> but I feel like I'm not here and it doesn't matter . . . some call it thinking but when
> I'm in this particular state of mind I forget to think. (21; first ellipsis in original)

JOURNALS, UNCONSCIOUS PHANTASY, AND CREATIVITY

If Klein's theories can help readers break through the opacity that characterizes the writing in *Journals,* the content and the structure of the text itself, in turn, have implications for psychoanalytic aesthetics and, in particular, for a deeper understanding of the intriguing parallel that exists between unconscious phantasy, depression, and creativity. I return to this topic in the concluding chapter of this book. In some of her most influential essays, Klein explores the relationship between unconscious phantasy, the nature of art and creativity, and, indirectly, the construction and experience of gender. The thrust of this work facilitates an understanding of the inventiveness of Cobain's journal writings and his uncanny representation of gender anxiety.[8]

Klein was initially concerned with visual art. She demonstrates how an infant's genetic tendency to succumb to an elaborate phantasy life is a prerequisite for ingenuity. Whereas for Freud unconscious phantasies are manifest primarily in dream life, Klein, as indicated above, theorizes that in addition to subtending all dreams, they "underlie both the form and content of [all] thinking, perception and creativity" (Glover, 47). In exposing the parallels that exist between the dynamics of a work of art and unconscious phantasy, Klein also establishes that we can understand both phantasies and works of art as closed systems with their own distinct logic. Both can make sense in and of themselves. They do not have to be interpreted according to the ways in which a particular phantasy or a specific work of art might communicate something about the subject's or the artist's external reality. It is the persuasiveness of

Klein's arguments that has inspired me to read Cobain's journal writings independently from the events in his brief life.

Through a creative use of language and images, Cobain's notebooks point to a fear and a desire that do not seem to make complete sense, as if they were just beyond the conscious apprehension of the writer of the text. As Ken Macrorie suggests about a particular kind of effective writing, the writing in *Journals*, just as one observes in Cobain's lyrics, is characterized in places by an ingenious play on words and by a skillful construction and subversion of metaphors (Schroeder and Boe). The writing is further characterized by vivid yet still elusive false starts and open-ended conclusions. The writing is frequently incoherent, just as Cobain's critics contend. Portions of the text are struck through or erased; some fragments are written between the lines and in the margins.

In addition, and most poignantly, the writing in Cobain's notebooks is often characterized by the disclosing of disquieting, intimate details that activate the emotional and psychical struggling of the persona that Cobain insists on taking in and projecting out. As a result, the story that *Journals* is struggling to tell, or at least the voice that strains to tell this story, lacks fluency. For example, in a rambling entry titled "Critic Goes God" in which Cobain's narrator attempts to articulate an aesthetic of contemporary popular music, he is reduced to stammering: "I'm crosslegged [*sic*], Rosary to ~~my right, Bible to my left~~ the left of me, Bible to the right, here I am stuck in the middle with you. Stuck in the middle with you. Who sang that song?" (86).

Besides the clutter and static resulting from portions of the text that are struck through, erased, or written between the lines and in the margins, the writing in *Journals* is also frequently distorted by spelling and grammatical errors and by syntactical infelicities. Faulty mechanics make Cobain's writing even more opaque and equivocal. Consequently, the structural noise in the text corrupts the overall message in *Journals* with a kind of cultural static and "white noise," as this term is used metaphorically. That is, as Bannister specifies when writing about other rock musicians of the 1980s, Cobain's journal writings, much like his lyrics, carves out a creative space where writing constitutes a pleasure, an end within itself, even though it does not always communicate a clear message.

In effect, Cobain's notebooks constitute a space, to use Bannister's words, that allows for "a free play of meaning," where writing seems "devoid of authorship." It is a space that is "quintessentially postmodern and fragmented" (158).

White noise suggests an indeterminacy in the writing; it suggests a disjuncture between the sender and the receiver of the message the writer is laboring to articulate. For example, it is evident in the letter that constitutes the central entry in *Journals* that the pleasure resides in the writing exclusively. This letter, like other missives to friends and strangers found in the text, is never destined to be read by its presumptive addressee. It constitutes the letter writer's revelations, ruminations, and confessions to himself. And, as demonstrated in the final chapter of this study, Cobain's suicide letter, though not included in his notebooks, is composed and functions in the same manner as the letters written in his notebooks. Together they constitute signposts on a tortuous journey to self-knowledge.

Since Cobain complements *Journals* with drawings and illustrations, the text is also visually provocative. It reveals Cobain to be a discerning and contemplative narrator at best, but one who is disconcerting and contemptuous of his reader at worst. Because the text is elaborately and skillfully illustrated and is often composed in a handwriting that is difficult to read, it constrains the reader to engage, ultimately, in a visual as well as a verbal decipherment, as evident in figure 1, for example. The illustrations and drawings, which include scripted comics, sometimes do complement the writing in the other entries, but at other times they deflect the writing. Images of the white male body in particular constitute evocative but vexing graphics. They suggest the way that visual creativity, according to Klein, can be a means of coping with depression ("Anxiety reflected in a work of art").

In *Journals,* however, the drawings of the male body do not manifest the restorative, reparative function that Klein theorizes. On the contrary, images of the male body underscore debility, disease, and disintegration. I draw attention to a few drawings from forty-nine pages that include hundreds of sketches, drawings, illustrations, and comics. I comment specifically but briefly on three drawings of the male body. I do so because these particular images make it easier to retrace, in a manner of speaking, the narrator's desire and his anxiety—concerning, in particular, masculinity and heterosexuality—in the specific way that his emotional and psychical states manifest themselves throughout the text. Two of these images, one depicting a hanged body and another that Cobain presents as a self-portrait, also forecast how, within *Journals* as a whole, fear and desire are projected upon a specific kind of male body.

As evident in the eight citations that make up the epigraph to this section, the persona Cobain is attempting to inhabit identifies both with and against women. He also identifies with and against men who are gay or black. He writes, "I like the comfort of knowing that the Afro American invented Rock and Roll. I like the comfort of knowing that women are the future of Rock and Roll. Uh, god is a woman and she's back in black. God is gay and so am I." Though Cobain composes his entries principally in the first person, he also writes some narrative and lyrical fragments in the third person. All together, these fragments introduce a cast of assorted characters. Many of the characters Cobain ventriloquizes are fictional, phantastical even, but some of the various actors who populate the pages of *Journals* are names that some readers recognize. In the central entry, for example, musicians and songwriters Robin Zander (Cheap Trick), Iggy Pop (Stooges), and Kathleen Hanna (Bikini Kill) appear. But all the characters in this text make up aspects of the persona Cobain takes on, as has been demonstrated concerning Cobain's lyrics. He invariably plays all the parts in the drama that he stages.

As the narrator's profile comes into focus in *Journals,* identifying as woman, gay, or black signals a refusal to identify as masculine and to be confined to a white male body and limited to heterosexual activity. But since masculinity, as Cobain represents it as a bodily experience, depends on and is modeled on whiteness—in the same way that some psychoanalysts contend that sexuality "leans on" gender (Freud, *Three Essays,* 182)—neither masculinity nor whiteness seems fully fleshed out, so to speak, in the text.[9] A defining question for me then becomes what values does Cobain ascribe to whiteness and to masculinity and how are these values made manifest in the specific persona that he assumes?

The Body in the Text: A Prescription for Self-Destruction / A Desire for Penetration

I was a rodent-like, underdeveloped, hyperactive spaz who could fit his entire torso in one leg of his bell-bottomed jeans. (115)

I am obsessed with the fact that I am skinny and stupid. (134)

I haven't masturbated in months because I've lost my imagination [...] I am seriously afraid to touch myself. (138)

My skin is goth rock pale. (141)

[White men] will be strung up by the balls with pages of the scum manifesto stapled to their bodies. (145)

I've kept and raised . . . my children . . . as if God had fucked me and planted
   these precious little eggs. (189)

Just as unconscious phantasy, for Klein, is rooted in bodily sensations and,
therefore, cannot be extricated from our corporeality, the declarations above,
and different iterations of them that appear throughout *Journals,* confirm that
the central, organizing phantasy in this text also has its genesis in the narrator's experience of his body. Further, the writings and illustrations in Cobain's
notebooks confirm Klein's contention that our sense of corporeality consists
of "the bodily processes out of which [identity/subjectivity] is formed" (Glover,
37). The narrator's corporeal capabilities and limitations appear left, right, and
center stage in the crises of identity that *Journals* enacts. Klein theorizes, more
specifically, that not only do phantasies evolve primarily from somatic origins,
but each bodily sensation, in turn, produces a mental experience. Once again,
specific fragments in Cobain's notebooks bear out this observation.

   Therefore, an assessment of the content and the structuring of *Journals*
and, in particular, insights into how the text represents experiences of white
masculinity, should track the evolving status of the male body as it is represented verbally and visually in the text. Such an assessment would specify the
body's presentation and its sensations and functions. Cobain's first-person
narrator experiences his body as the essence of his being because it mediates
his interactions with others and determines his relationship to authenticity
and creativity, a relationship that eludes him. He also *suffers* the actions of his
body as alien. The actions that our culture prescribes for his white male body
do not coincide with what the narrator feels and desires to be authentic and
subjectively real.

   The alienating experience of the male body that Cobain depicts is perhaps
more obsessively illustrated, properly speaking, in some of the drawings and
sketches in *Journals.* These visual depictions constitute a code meant to be
understood as the answers to two fundamental questions: Who am I? Who do I
desire to become? But the written entries, too, also revolve around bodily experiences that are estranging. One detailed entry, parts of which are strategically
crossed out, makes explicit the function of Cobain's written entries. This entry
constitutes another example of a fragment that "stutters." It begins as the description of an emergent "pedophile." After this false beginning, the entry then
begins anew and proceeds to present a surreal description of the body parts of

"an old man," including his "arm pits, ripe pink-prune skin . . . uncut, brittle, jaundiced fingernails [and] . . . smooth thighs" (124).

The entry continues, but it shifts to the first person. The shift in perspective occurs in a manner that confirms the inextricability of the corporeal and the psychical in *Journals* as a whole: "I only feel with grunts [,] screams [,] and tones and with hand gestures and my body. I'm deaf in spirit" (124). In a series of run-on sentences and muddled clauses that contain subjects without a predicate, this entry reinforces even further the image of the narrator's male body as alienating, dissected, and in disarray.

Nowhere is the status of the male body more graphically exposed than in a comic drawing titled "Crybaby Jenkins Fouls It Up Again" (100 [fig. 1]). The comic proves to be an analogue of the written entries in the text: Visually it stutters, and it is noisy and cluttered. The opening image foregrounds the male body as a smorgasbord of disconnected parts and fluids. The concluding image reveals that the body of Crybaby Jenkins has been "digested" to re-emerge as a pile of turd ("corn poop"). The dominant image in the upper panel is a drawing of the naked and partially transparent body of the protagonist: His genitals, liver, and brain cells are exposed. The action described in the illustration takes place at a "Benny Hannas" restaurant, where "dinner is cooked right at your table . . . special today: fry babys [*sic*] on toast with juice."

Consistent with the theme of the comic, the upper panel is saturated with filleted and seasoned body parts being prepared for consumption. These menu items include six arms (right and left) with hands attached; two hands without arms; teeth; four bodiless heads, one with its left eye penetrated by Crybaby's erect penis; one headless body displaying its back, buttocks, legs, and feet. The upper panel also includes intestines, livers, and innumerable sperm cells. The script accompanying the upper panel, written in the first person, appears to be the voice of the restaurant's chef, "Big Dump." The script could also mean that we are hearing the voice of Crybaby Jenkins, since he also ends up as feces, a big dump.[10]

It is the second panel that provides the plot of this comic. Except for a pair of lungs that function as "ash trays," the male body parts and fluids have all disappeared, the reader is left to assume, into the stomachs of Benny Hannas's patrons. The story is challenging to read in part because the compressed script is written partially in the spiraling form of an intestine, forcing the reader to

Fig. 1. "Crybaby Jenkins Fouls It up Again."

manipulate the page clockwise to follow the story line. The story concludes as a bowel movement accompanied by the phrase that provides the title for the illustration: "Crybaby Jenkins . . . fouls it up again." The verb "fouls" in this context has two meanings: The protagonist has failed at another task, and his very presence makes the world around him reek.

Mimicking the relationship between the verses and choruses in some of Cobain's lyrics, the coda to the comic appears to be a mere add-on that is not directly connected to the comic itself. As a result, this page from Cobain's notebooks presents yet another collage of ideas and images. The coda also constitutes the visual equivalent of stuttering. The word "Satan" is written in varying sized letters and with different spacing between the letters and between the words. The words themselves appear right side up, upside down, horizontally, vertically, and on a slant.

Consequently, like other written entries in the text, "Crybaby Jenkins Fouls It Up Again" is difficult to navigate and to decipher because it flirts, as a graphic as well as a narrative, ever so shrewdly with nonsense. Although the comic constitutes, in and of itself, a striking and befuddling visual pun, as an isolated illustration in *Journals* it does not appear especially incisive. But when reinserted within the text as a whole, this one-page comic reveals the degree to which white masculinity, represented unfailingly as "a pile of [smelly] shit," is posited in this text, as in Cobain's lyrics, as irreparably troubled and troubling. Everything I write, Cobain concludes at the end of another long, introspective entry, is "just a big pile of shit like me" (109).

More graphically than in the written entries, the evolving and at times devolving visual images of the male body throughout *Journals* suggests an irrepressible desire on the part of the persona that Cobain projects to "rewrite" his body, to disassemble it in order to reassemble and reinvest it with a different meaning and potential. As I suggest, it is as if the persona that Cobain inhabits senses that his body is not natural but rather has been, counter to his desire, culturally constituted. In addition to male bodies that are dissected, ill-defined, or incompletely formed, the narrator's anxiety is reinscribed in all the specific kinds of images that Cobain compulsively reproduces and that punctuate the pages of his notebooks. These obsessively reproduced images include drawings of guitars and seahorses. One of the dynamics within these reiterated images reproduces the white male body as an inherently abnegated object. In different illustrations, the white male body seems to toggle in a loop from (1) a young, blond, anorexic, male punk performer to (2) an executed, masked rapist disguised as football player-soldier-corporate executive to (3) a male body represented as female, that is, a seahorse giving birth.

I have already referenced this first image, one of Cobain's self-portrait that includes a likeness of his face and hair and a representation of his naked torso, depicted down to the navel, as frail and underdeveloped (214). The image also displays in the background lines from "Teen Spirit," lyrics that the subject appears to be screaming. The second image is disturbing. It depicts a male figure whose head and face are concealed under a football helmet (116). Dressed in a camouflage military uniform, the figure is sporting an assault rifle on his back and a hand grenade on his left side. Most significantly, however, it is impossible to determine if the man has been executed or, more likely since he retains his lethal weapons, if he has committed suicide. The third image in the toggle is actually a series of images drawn in different sizes and appearing at three places in the text (190, 272, 275). One drawing in this series constitutes a full-page image of a seahorse giving birth to eight offspring or sea foals. The following inscription appears handwritten in large black letters to the right of the image: "[T]he male Seahorse carries the children and gives them birth" (272). Throughout the text, it is clear that the narrator identifies with the seahorse. In one drawing, for example, the seahorse appears on a promotional Nirvana T-shirt instead of the group's lead singer (275).

Both the written entries and the illustrations in *Journals* capture the relationship between the narrator and his corporeality, and they suggest how he thinks *with* his body and not merely about it. Both suggest that he experiences his body as problematic. Throughout the text, he refuses to accept and, at moments, even to recognize his corporeal boundaries that prevent him from being black (that is, the forefather of rock and roll) and, most crucially, that prevent him from being a woman (that is, rock's progeny). As indicated in the discussion in chapter 3 of the connection between the song "Milk It" and the cover of *Incesticide,* a particular phantasy reoccurs throughout the pages of Cobain's journals. This wish fulfillment takes different forms, but it invariably points to KurDt's problematic relationship to his abject body: "I am male, age 23 & I am lactating" (138), he utters at an especially agonizing, introspective moment. That he employs the ampersand to connect the two clauses that make up this declaration, rather than the conjunction "but," indicates that he phantasizes lactation as a natural function of the body he imagines inhabiting.

As a result of the refusal to recognize or to accept his corporeality, the persona in which Cobain becomes progressively invested emerges as paranoid. In relation to his own body, he assumes an aggressive posture, represented in Cobain's notebooks, as in his lyrics, as an impulse toward self-destruction. In the central entry of the text, for example, this impulse begins with anorexia (he is dangerously thin) and concludes with bulimia (he vomits compulsively [181]). In between, the narrator experiences his body as irremediably languid and underdeveloped. He describes himself as "anemic" and deliberately "malnourished" (182).

Whereas the impulse toward self-annihilation is merely suggested in the central entry, it is articulated explicitly in others, as in a letter to the editor of a music magazine. In this letter Cobain, skillfully playing his role as self-effacing rock star, feels constrained to defend himself in face of an onslaught of negative press. Although he is writing ostensibly in order to counter his profile as captured in the national press, he ends up inadvertently reconfirming this very image. The image that he consistently provides of himself in several other entries in *Journals* corresponds in every detail to the press profile he is protesting in this letter:

I've heard so many insanely exhaggerated [*sic*] stories or reports from my friends and I've read so many pathetic second rate, Freudian evaluations from my childhood up until the present state of my personality and how I'm a notoriously fucked up heroine [*sic*] addict, alcoholic, self [-] destructive, yet overly sensitive, frail, fragile, soft[-]spoken, narcoleptic, *neurotic*, little piss ant who at any minute is going to O.D. Jump off a roof [,] wig out. Blow my head off or all 3 at once. (191)

I subtitle the above entry "Triple Suicide." Death as a trifecta constitutes a theme to which Cobain returns, as in the following entry: "If you want to know what the afterlife feels like," he writes, "then put on a parachute, go up in a plane, shoot a good amount of heroine into your veins and immediately follow that with a hit of nitrous oxide[,] then jump. Or set yourself on fire" (125). In fact, interspersed throughout *Journals,* there are nine explicit references to self-destruction and suicide (28, 29, 55, 88, 110, 125, 147, 191, 193), as well as scores of indirect and implicit references that are too numerous to cite.

One can characterize the experiences of the male body and the mode of masculinity that *Journals* represents as "male subjectivity at the margins." Kaja Silverman employs this expression to identify certain nonhegemonic masculine identifications and comportments. One could also characterize the corporeal experience that Cobain captures as "male hysteria," in the sense that Constance Penley and Sharon Willis define this erstwhile condition.[11] Penley and Willis's description of the relationship between masculinity and hysteria is also consistent with the way that Mark Micale, in his social history of male nervous illness, documents that hysteria can be, and has always been, mapped onto the male body. And as explored in the next chapter, the explicit masochism of the persona Cobain incubates can be read as a form of resistance to the constraints of conventional masculinity. Male masochism constitutes what Silverman characterizes as a "perverse" antiphallic strategy, one designed to resist, but that ends up reclaiming, a white, heteromasculine position of entitlement and power. In this sense, the masochistic alter ego with which Cobain is so enamored can be considered hysterical.

In addition, David Savran's description of the "masochistic male subject's conflation and then appropriation of femininity and blackness" (33) applies also to how the persona Cobain adopts identifies with women and with black male musicians. Like the masochistic male subject Savran exposes (in his study of the lives and creative works of twentieth-century white male writers and filmmakers), the masochistic persona Cobain embraces, in identifying with women and with black men, is also complicit in their marginalization and oppression. Before turning my attention to the way Cobain's alter ego appropriates blackness, I explore the conflicted nature of the identification with and appropriation of femininity that his journal entries put forth. This conflict is signaled already in the way male-on-male sex and the feminizing of the male body constitute intersecting themes in his notebooks.

The Penetrated Male Body

Cobain's notebooks present the white male body, both visually and verbally, in a manner that mirrors the inner conflict, the crisis of identity, that the narrator in *Journals* experiences. On the one hand, the male body is frequently phantasized as possessing female parts. As noted before, numerous expressions that appear repeatedly and in various forms throughout the text exemplify this phantasy: For example, the narrator pleads at a particularly stressful moment in his life, "Let me grow some breasts" (224). On the other hand, the male body is feminized in *Journals,* just as it is in "Beeswax," because it is represented as being penetrated by another man.

Cobain depicts penetration in two distinct ways. When it is a question of a well-known music or television celebrity, he represents penetration as pleasurable but atypical for these presumptively straight men. He presents these episodes as transgressive, exciting, and mysterious. Cobain also constructs these stories in order to amuse the reader: "TELLY SAVALAS greasing up his head and ramming it in and out! IN and out of another TV personalities [*sic*] ass. Who's [*sic*] ass? Who cares. either way it's a cheap way to get an immediate laugh" (78).

Overall, scenes describing the sexual activities of male celebrities are designed to disorient the reader. Cobain narrates them in the third person in a way that distances the reader from the action. But when accounts of penetration are narrated in the first person and it is a question of the persona Cobain is projecting, anal intercourse is still represented as transgressive, exciting, and mysterious. But Cobain represents these scenes as commonplace, normative. Penetration of the male body results in the reinvigoration of the narrator and the production of new life. The reader is constrained to identify with the narrator, to be drawn into the action.

Male penetration as comical, atypical, distancing, and disorienting is put forth, for example, in an entry titled "The Late 1980's." Under the guise of what Cobain characterizes as a "Punk-Rock collage," the episode emerges from and revolves around the image of Michael J. Fox, an iconic American television actor, and Bruce Springsteen, an equally iconic pop/rock American musician, penetrating each other (5). Later in *Journals,* another meticulously detailed entry features images of two couples (of familiar television characters and actors) engaging in mutual penetration. This second entry concludes with one of several graphic depictions of sex found in Cobain's notebooks.

To add to the tentative, mysterious nature of this particular entry, crucial fragments of the text are struck through: ~~"How about Goober and Gomer giving it to each other or Gary Coleman (Arnold on "Different Strokes") and Emanuel Lewis ("Webster") [,] reesus [sic] monkey love in the 69 tongue[-]butt position"~~ (78). The narrator seems tentative, perhaps unsettled himself by the scene he is evoking. Within this same entry, however, the first-person narrator phantasizes himself being penetrated, in this instance by the redundantly phallic actor Telly Savalas, in a matter-of-fact assertion that wavers between evoking the narrator's pleasure and his discomfort: "Telly's stubble scratched the inner walls of my colon" (78).[12]

Cobain represents penetration as normative, alluring, and a means to produce new life in several entries. One of the storyboards for the "Heart Shaped Box" video provides an evocative example of how the act gives the body a new, creative potential:

> William [Burroughs] and I are sitting across from one other . . . holding hands staring into each other's eyes. He gropes me from behind and falls dead on top of me. Medical footage of sperm flowing through penis. A ghost vapor comes out of his chest and groin area and enters my body. (256)

Several versions of this storyboard appear in Cobain notebooks. In this particular version, the new life that results from copulation ("a ghost vapor") comes in the form of Burroughs's literary creativity becoming implanted in the narrator. In other entries in the text as well, the narrator reveals his desire to absorb the essence of, to be impregnated by, other creative men.

A narrative snippet from the "Heart Shaped Box" storyboard reappears in another entry, one of the few in *Journals* that is typewritten, attesting perhaps to the importance that Cobain accords it. This provocative, confounding entry is also one of the few to which Cobain gives a title: "WOMBan DE-JA VOO-DOO BY: KurDt Kobain." Like many of Cobain's entries, this one consists of a collage of disparate images and storylines. The appearance of a Burroughs-like character ties the entry to the proposed "Heart Shaped Box" video: "An old man name Bob will travel miles to visit me. He will pull apart my pyles [sic] and stick it in. He will die just as he comes inside of me and all of his orgones and bad thoughts and desires for truth will soak into the walls of my intestines. I will be re-fueled" (196).

Although the narrator's anal penetration and subsequent impregnation are presented overall as desired, positive experiences because they reinvigorate the body and activate its potential to create, these acts are presented in one episode, nonetheless, as nonconsensual, torturous, and criminal. Cobain begins this revealing but disquieting entry by announcing an attempt to draw a distinction between an authentic "punk" musician and a fraudulent, "whiteboy, corporate rocker." The objective of the undated fragment, he writes, is to "decipher the difference between a sincere entertainer and an honest swindler"

(189). In defending authentic music, however, Cobain returns momentarily, and as if allured by some irresistible force, to the phantasy of an anorexic-bulimic male body with female parts as an ideal. Further, Cobain posits the notion of a superior, if not ideal, masculine subject as inescapably masochistic. In this instance, the feminized body is still capable of creating new life and authentic art, even though, or perhaps because, it is tortured and exploited:

> I've violently vomited to the point of my stomach literally turning itself inside out to show you the fine hair[-]like nerves I've kept and raised as my children, garnishing and maintaining each one as if God had fucked me and planted these precious little eggs. And I parade them around in peacock victory and maternal pride like a whore relieved from the duties of repeated rape and torture, promoted to a more dignified job of just plain old every day, good old, wholesome prostitution. My feathers are my pussy. (189)

All the excerpts cited above reveal the confused and problematic manner in which Cobain's notebooks construct the persona of a young man who identifies with and appropriates femininity. These fragments equate femininity with a masochistic desire, with pain, submission, and a need to be penetrated. I turn my attention now to the equally confounding and problematic way Cobain's journal fragments create the persona of a young male musician who identifies with and, to a degree, appropriates "blackness." Like femininity, a phantasized blackness constitutes an essential feature of the persona that so captivates Cobain in the writing of his notebooks.

JOURNALS AS A RACIALIZED, REHEARSAL SPACE FOR COBAIN'S LYRICS

In the previous section, I have been reading *Journals* primarily as a self-contained, self-referential, and autonomous text, one that allows readers to observe how a cleverly written and illustrated text takes on distinctive themes and assumes a particular literary structure. I now re-examine *Journals* as these written fragments and illustrations dialogue with specific Cobain songs. I explore how the text functions as a rehearsal space for his lyrics, a creative space in which racial difference has been reinscribed. Among the hundreds of entries in *Journals,* the reader encounters drafts of twenty-six different Cobain songs.[13] In addition, there are isolated words and phrases throughout the text that are not written as lyrics per se but that find their way, nonetheless, into particular songs as part of a line or as a title.

All of these isolated snippets and fragments stand out either because of the sound of the words, the wordplay, or because of their special significance within Cobain's overall thematic interests and obsessions. For example, "pennyroyal tea" first appears in *Journals* in an entry titled "Bitching About Prog-Rock" (73). This entry consists of a sentence salad that narrates a phantastical story involving numerous characters. This cast of diverse individuals appears to have no connection to each other except that they find themselves in the same unspecified physical space. As the noun "pennyroyal tea" occurs in this entry, then, it has no connection, seemingly, to the song that will come to bear that title. In a similar manner, the phrase "Oh, well, whatever, nevermind" appears several times in different entries in *Journals,* but not as a line in "Smells Like Teen Spirit," the song into which it will be inserted. And "nevermind," as a one-word imperative, will become the title of Nirvana's most commercially successful album.

In addition to the drafts and fragments of actual songs, Cobain's notebooks also connect to his lyrics in the way most of these entries, like his lyrics, are written in three modes: narrative, profile, and lyrical. In an unusually long entry mentioned in chapter 2, for example, Cobain invents a 1,600-word story about a serial killer, Chuck Taylor, who, the text specifies, has slaughtered "nine women, one man, and one 13 year old boy" (90). The major characters in this story first appear in *Journals* in a comic titled "The Smileys" (72). The comic recounts an earlier moment in Chuck's childhood. Like some of Cobain's signature songs, such as "Even in His Youth," Chuck's story is narrated in chronological order. But since the story, in contrast to Cobain's songs, is long and detailed, it provides an in-depth psychological profile of the principal character.

As also indicated in chapter 2, this particular entry stands out because of the explicit parallels that exist between Chuck and the historical Kurt Cobain, as he is captured in Cross's first biography, for example. They both are the "first grandson and nephew for both sides [of the family]" (*Journals,* 91), and both, as children, are loved and doted on by relatives. Chuck's childhood further resembles that of the real Cobain in that both have a younger sister and both are born to young, idealistic parents who love each other but who slowly settle into a dysfunctional relationship. As a child, Chuck, too, is medicated for hyperactivity and he also possesses a "bizarre but funny sense of humor" (95).

Mothers that Cobain represents as women, as female characters, do not appear prominently in his creative texts. Chuck Taylor's mother is a rare exception. Mary Taylor, who is loving but subservient and a victim of spousal abuse, arguably finds an analogue in Cobain's actual mother, the Wendy Cobain that some biographers depict.[14]

It is the portrait of the father and the relation between the father and son, however, that thematically link the serial killer's story more closely to Cobain's songwriting. Chuck's father, Joseph Taylor, comes across in the story as a monster who closely resembles the abusing husband/narrator in the song "Control." He stands also as another version of the abusing fathers in two other songs: "Laminated Effect" and "Even in His Youth." Joseph Taylor, however, takes his contemptible parenting to another level, one merely hinted at in Cobain's lyrics. He abuses his wife while forcing his son to watch, administering harsh corporal punishment if Chuck does not react appropriately. As the narrative makes clear, corporal punishment, exposed here as an especially sadistic form of "spanking," is designed to assure that the son will "grow up to be MAN . . . a winner" (93).

Just as in many of Cobain songs, the narrative perspective in this story also shifts. The episode begins as a third-person cautionary tale told by an omniscient narrator who is not a character in the story he is relating. But in the third paragraph, the perspective shifts to the first person; it is Chuck's sister, Jenny, who narrates. The story then shifts back abruptly and inexplicably to the perspective of a third-person, omniscient narrator. Further, through the technique of internal monologue, the narrator enters into the minds and hearts of both father and son, exposing their innermost thoughts and emotions.

The story reaches its midpoint with the following sentence, as the narrative reverts once again to the first-person perspective of the sister: "Chuck would never talk about it [his torture by father], when I questioned him I felt sorry for him [because he] must have felt this self-destructive need to put up with his abuse" (93). The shifting narrative perspective produces the same effect in this journal entry as in Cobain's songs. It conflates the narrator and the characters in such a profound way that it is not always easy to discern who is relating the story and, therefore, whose perspective is being presented. Father, mother, son, and daughter form a composite in effect, one that, just like in a song such as "In His Room," can be compared to the dynamics of a dream in which the dreamer is playing all of the constituent parts.

In other entries of various lengths, Cobain also concocts stories in which all the characters together make up a single persona, one who exhibits complex and contradictory characteristics. In this respect, his notebooks explicitly expose a feature of his literary technique that remains implicit between the lines of his lyrics. In listing the eight essential characteristics of his personality, the narrative voice Cobain takes on concludes the self-assessment with a remarkable assertion that speaks to his writing style: "I use bits and pieces of other's personalities to form my own" (105). Later in *Journals,* KurDt confirms this trait: "I have no opinions because I agree with everyone" (133).

In the narration of Chuck Taylor's comfortless life, just as in the song "Laminated Effect," it is the conflation of father and son that commands the reader's attention. Because of the way Cobain composes the story, the attitude and comportment of Chuck and those of his father, Joseph, elide in such a way that these two characters become virtually indistinguishable. With his actions, Joseph Taylor succeeds in reproducing his own monstrosity within his son. In doing so, he merely magnifies his son's already learned deviancy. The composing of the serial killer's biography in such extraordinary detail, therefore, allows Cobain to return to a theme that he rehearses over and over again: a son's anxiety that he is destined to turn into his father.

I comment on this particular story at length because it is emblematic of *Journals* as a whole in that it constitutes a text, like Cobain's lyrics, that succeeds in representing hegemonic masculinity as inescapably disturbed and disturbing. Also like Cobain's lyrics, this story presents the male body, literally and figuratively, as contaminated and in need of either a cleansing overhaul or a complete eradication. The male body functions in *Journals,* then, in the same way it does in Cobain's lyrics. In the central entry, for example, the narrator insists on "Bringing an everlasting, sterile and bacterial herbaceous and botanical and corporate cleansing for our ancestors to gaze in wonderment and awe" (178–79). As I have shown, readers encounter flashes of this image and flare-ups of these sentiments in several songs.

In another commanding entry partially cited above and that Cobain titles "The Late 1980's," the first-person narrator, who is a grunge musician, dreams of a disease named after him that will document and immortalize his corporeal debility. "Just let me have my very own unexplainable rare stomach disease named after me," he pleads. He insists further that this disease should constitute "the title of our next double album, 'Cobain's Disease,' a rock opera which is all about vomiting gastric juices [by] . . . a borderline anorexic Auzhwitz [*sic*]-Grunge Boy" (193). Just as in this entry, *Journals* as a whole, again like several of Cobain's signature songs, continually exposes an abject male body. *Journals*, too, also offers an ongoing critique of masculinist culture, described as a "society that has sucked and fucked itself into a rehashing value of greed" (5). In this way, Cobain's illustrated notebooks take on all the interconnecting themes that emerge in his songs: Masculine contamination, anxiety, guilt, self-criticism, and phantasies of emasculation, death, and suicide.

A White Boy Sings the Blues: Inscribing Race into Cobain's Personal Writings
As I have shown, one can read Cobain's lyrics and his published journals as complementary and, at times, as intersecting texts in terms of their themes, images, and literary techniques. In one significant aspect, however, Cobain's journal writings represent a radical departure from his lyrics. Whereas race as a social construct and an object of cultural analysis is absent, or more properly has been erased, from Cobain's lyrics, racial difference is explicitly reinscribed into his notebooks. That is, whereas masculinity is evoked as race-neutral or race-less in songs such as "Control" and "Laminated Effect," *Journals* suggests, both implicitly and explicitly, that masculinity has no meaning separate from the notion of race.

One can see a clear indication that Cobain has expunged race from his lyrics by comparing the different versions of two songs as they appear initially in *Journals* and then as they reappear in recorded form. The final version of "All Apologies," for example, contains the following lines: "What else could I write" / "I don't have the right." An earlier version of this song appears in *Journals* under the title "I Like Girls." This version contains these alternate lines: "What else could I write" / I'm sorry I'm *white*" (224, emphasis added). In effect, this refrain, in which the narrator expresses contrition for his whiteness, is repeated, both literally and metaphorically in various ways throughout the pages of *Journals*.

In a manner similar to the editing of "All Apologies," Cobain does not specify the race of the couple profiled in "Swap Meet" in the final, recorded version of the song. In this instance, however, the fact that Cobain does not specify the couple's race signifies that the couple is white. There is no need to designate the characters' race, since whiteness is posited as normal, the default position.

By contrast, an earlier version of this song appears in *Journals* under the title "Travelin' White Trash Couple." The original title, notwithstanding the problematic use of the qualifier "white," constitutes a clever play on words since "trash" designates the couple's class status as well as the nature and value of the merchandise in which they traffic. In this sense, *Journals* would seem to confirm Ryan Moore's contention that "Whiteness became visible in popular culture during the 1990s . . . especially in stereotypes about 'white trash' . . . in which peculiarities of white culture were exposed [and ridiculed] rather than idealized" (172). Moore's remarks are on point, but he, like the executives at Sub Pop discussed in chapter 2, also fails to completely unpack the expression "white trash." Cobain's use of the expression produces a particular effect.

Although the tone and tenor of the final version of what was to become "Swap Meet" remain consistent with the tone and tenor of "Travelin' White Trash Couple," the lyrics are completely different. Not only is the whiteness of the couple absent from "Swap Meet," the origin of their "trashiness" is not indicated. Only in the first version of the song does Cobain expose the root of the couple's ethical depravity. He underscores the fact that the man in this couple is challenged hygienically and that he is poisoned by his very hormonal makeup:

> He bathes [only] in gallons of men's cologne
> He's fill up full of testosterone
> . . .
> They rip you off and then they leave your town
> The local swap meet is their battle ground

The couple is unsavory and evil; however, as Cobain writes in the central entry, the "strong ox male is in charge. He decides" (177). In this song, Cobain represents white trashiness as an especially male trait. As he suggests elsewhere in his writings, white women are superior to white men.

In examining how Cobain edits these two songs for publication, one question that emerges, but that may remain unanswerable, is the following: What is the aesthetic and cultural logic of inscribing race in *Journals*? Or, put inversely, what is the logic of erasing whiteness from Cobain's lyrics, songs he characterizes in his notebooks as a rejection of, and an antidote to, the music performed by the "stupid heavy metal bands carrying on the legacy of sexism and homophobia in *white-boy* rock and roll" (261; emphasis added)? Although Justin Henderson is not responding to this specific question concerning race in Cobain's lyrics, he does offer an observation about Seattle's music history that problematizes the perception (and the reality) that independent rock music, as it evolved during 1980s and 90s, was naturally and obviously "color-free," as he describes the scene. "Not having witnessed grunge's early years," Henderson writes, "I can't speak from personal experience, but I feel compelled to wonder: Was there even one African-American on the grunge scene? Grunge may have been the whitest rock-and-roll movement in history" (13).

Besides song lyrics, race is also reinscribed in Cobain's notebooks in the way the text represents white supremacy as an extreme ideology and practice. As epitomized by its depiction of the KKK, *Journals* posits white supremacy as an aberration, a psychotic reaction to racial difference and to blackness specifically. This text also represents a less extreme but equally psychotic embodiment of white supremacy in a character Cobain describes as the "stump-dumb average Joe," a white man characterized by his "inability to comprehend [racial] injustice" (184). These men, Cobain specifies, are physically deficient. On top of, or because of, their befoulment by testosterone, they lack an "extra group of cells in the brain that welcomes a questioning consciousness" (184).

In addition to representing the Klan and other racists as pathological, *Journals* also evokes the normalcy of white supremacist ideology and practice by describing its less visibly violent and seemingly benign, everyday effects. These effects are manifest, as the text specifies, in the business model of the music industry, for example. They are also evident, as the text specifies further, in the practices of the cultural production industry in general. The cultural production industry includes the entertainment press along with institutions and arbiters of tastes like the Grammy awards: "The Afro-American invented rock and roll," KurDt protests, "yet he has ONLY been rewarded ←→ or awarded for their [*sic*] accomplishments when conforming to the white man's standards" (111).[15]

The critique of the KKK in *Journals* is expressed both visually and verbally. The text contains two sketches that include Klan members in full regalia. The first is a small drawing titled "Fig A" (145). It accompanies a narrative text already cited in the first section of this chapter. This entry constitutes an abbreviated version of the central entry in *Journals,* the one that denounces the "hairy, sweaty, macho, sexist Dickheads" who must be destroyed by their own sons. In this iteration of the central entry, the Klan drawing is just one among eight unrelated sketches that appear at the bottom of a single page. This image, however, constitutes the only one among the group that has a connection to the content of the written entry. The Dickheads and the Klan, the reader is to assume, are interchangeable; they are pursuing intersecting agendas.

The first Klan drawing depicts, in the upper right corner, a lone male figure on a rooftop. He is wearing what appears to be a helmet, and he is armed with an assault rifle (145). This figure constitutes a variation of a drawing that appears earlier in the text depicting a hanged football player–soldier who has either been executed or has committed suicide (116). The would-be assailant is aiming his weapon downward at five robed and hooded Klansmen who are parading on the ground below, unaware of his presence and their imminent danger.

The second Klan drawing, which appears forty pages later in *Journals,* is a variation of the first (162). It is a larger drawing with more details. In this version, it becomes clear that the rooftop assassin and the hanging football player–soldier do indeed represent the same figure. His military uniform now is more clearly drawn and his weapon is identical to that of the hanged man. Instead of five Klansmen, this version depicts seven parading members whose leader is carrying a placard displaying a swastika. And rather than being one of several images on a single page, this second Klan drawing is placed in the very center of the page. It is a single image that dominates a short, written entry whose connection to racial politics is tangential at best. In the paragraph below the image, the narrator applauds what he calls the "social changes of the 90s [that] brought the attainment of finally accepting various styles of music (and styles of dress)" (162). Eliminating the Klan, the image suggests, will facilitate the emergence of the young white punk musicians with whom Cobain's narrator identifies.

The two images offer slight variations on the same theme: That is, all Klan members must be executed, extra-judicially and presumably by the small group of white men who possess the "extra group of cells in the brain" that make them sensitive to racial injustice. In effect, the Klan drawings provide yet another image of self-destruction in *Journals.* All the men depicted in the two images are white. Given the way the persona Cobain adopts is revealed implicitly to be both antiracist and racist, the executioner and the executed in the drawings are the same white man.

The Klan, as the physical embodiment a particular kind of white man, and Klan ideology are referenced in six separate entries in Cobain's published journals (56, 74, 234, 243, 256, 273). Most pointedly, the terrorist group appears in the video proposal for "Heart Shaped Box." In the storyboard, Cobain's narrator imagines himself as his own young daughter in the process of being indoctrinated and physically contaminated by a racist father:

> 4 year old Aryan girl with bright blond hair [and] with vivid blue eyes in a Klu [*sic*] Klux Klan robe on [,] sitting in a small shack. The walls of the shack [are] covered with *stargazer lilies* with stems cut off and the butt end of the flower ~~and~~ glued everywhere on the walls . . . another shot of little girl holding hands with an elder. He squeezes her hand as if she could never escape. Bright red blood soaks from inside the girl's robe. (243)[16]

Given the way this image is repeated in *Journals,* it reconfirms Cobain's obsession with the theme of a child becoming corrupted by a reprehensible parent. The young white girl appears once again as Cobain's alter ego in a second journal entry titled "Technicolor effect for Film." This entry constitutes another variation of the storyboard for "Heart Shaped Box." Cobain presents these notations: "[D]uring solo. violin shots. Chris as New Wave keyboardist. And very quick edits of strobe light. Image of little 3 year old white arian [*sic*], blond girl in KKK outfit being led by the hand of a KKK parent" (256).

∞

Cobain's personal notebooks explicitly operate as a racialized space. In sum, the draft versions of "All Apologies" and "Swap Meet," as they appear in *Journals,* indicate that he has at least parenthesized if not completely erased race from his lyrics. Further, the evocative manner in which images of and comments on the Klan are represented in the text serve to underscore the role of whiteness in his journal writings and drawings. In addition, these same narratives and images serve to signal the role of fathers/men in the origin and perpetuation of racial injustice. These visual renderings and the comments on the Klan also signal, like the draft lyrics to "Swap Meet," the relation between whiteness and masculinity. But the most consequential inscription of race in Cobain's notebooks results from the way these entries are underwritten and seemingly haunted by the spirit of Lead Belly.[17]

Kurt Cobain's "Negro": The Ghost of Huddie William Ledbetter in *Journals*

Cobain employs four different terms in his notebooks to designate American blacks and black culture: "Afro-American," "Negro," "darkie," and "nigger." The two latter terms—as I indicate below in my reading of how Cobain commandeers the term "nigger"—are uttered by narrators as a way to condemn the contemporary KKK. These terms are also deployed to excoriate white supremacists from the past, such as "the majority of our so-called outlaw heroes of the Old West [who were] nothing but fucked up psychopaths ex-Confederate soldiers . . . killing every darkie they could find" (234).

As evident in the earlier citation above concerning the lack of recognition of black musical achievement, Cobain employs "Afro American," on one single occasion, to designate an entire generation of black songwriters, musicians, and performers from the past who "invented rock and roll" (111). He also employs the term to designate contemporary black musicians like NWA, as in the following entry: "I like the comfort of knowing that the Afro American has once again been the only race that has brought a new form of original music to this decade, i.e., hip hop/rap" (111). By contrast, Cobain seems to reserve "Negro" for Lead Belly and other *individual* male musicians within the blues tradition that would include Robert Johnson, John Lee Hooker, Muddy Waters, and Howling Wolf. He writes, for example, "I find a few things sacred such as the superiority of women and the Negro to art" (121). And by art, in this instance, Cobain means the art of composing, recording, and performing authentic music and lyrics.[18]

Record executives, historians, and music critics typically categorize Lead Belly as a "bluesman." They do so, for example, on the CD *Blues Masters: The Essential History of the Blues* and in the Richard Music Folios series: *Leadbelly: No Stranger to the Blues*. Some late twentieth-century biographies as well as recent online accounts of Lead Belly's life and music, however, have succeeded in capturing more fully the extent of his talents and his influence as a folk singer, songwriter, and song adaptor.[19] He had himself been influenced by spirituals and the music of the black church, as well as by children's songs and cowboy culture and mythology. Lead Belly adopted the twelve-string guitar as his instrument of choice; today he is identified with it. But he was also proficient on the accordion, piano, and the harmonica. His composition or adaptation of songs such as "Cotton Fields," "The Bourgeois Blues," "Good Night Irene," "Rock Island Line," and "Midnight Special" directly influenced the folk songwriters and performers of the 1940s, including Pete Seeger and Woody Guthrie. These songwriters and performers, in turn, helped to shape the folk revival and the development of rock music as these genres evolved in the 1950s and '60s.

Lead Belly is the only folk and blues artist to appear in Cobain's published journals on every list of his favorite musicians, albums, or songs. For the vast majority of Nirvana fans, his cover of "Where Did You Sleep Last Night?" would have been their introduction to Lead Belly. The song was regularly included on set lists. Cobain is said to have programmed this song, along with other covers, to mitigate the rowdiness and potential violence of certain young men in the audiences (Soulsby, *Dark Slivers*).

But it is the MTV Unplugged performance of "Where Did You Sleep Last Night?"—and the subsequent videos—that has played the greatest role in introducing Lead Belly to a mass pop and rock audience.[20] In 1989, before he achieved national and international prominence, Cobain had already covered another song that Lead Belly had adapted and recorded. In addition to "Where Did You Sleep Last Night?," he recorded "They Hung Him on a Cross" as a member of a tribute band, The Jury. The Jury featured Novoselic on bass and two members of Screaming Trees: Mark Lanegan on vocals and Mark Pickerel on drums. The tribute band also performed an instrumental version of Lead Belly's adaptation of "Grey Goose."

Judging from online comments, even when Nirvana fans are aware of Cobain's debt to Lead Belly in his MTV performance, they do not consider him to be performing the folk repertoire or appropriating black music. Judging from comments on YouTube specifically, fans consider him to be performing universal (white) music.[21] The very hybridity of rock would support such an observation and would argue against categorizing Cobain's covers as essentially white or black in terms of music structure and performance. An attentive reading of Cobain's personal writings, nevertheless, suggests a contradiction, or at least an ambivalence, in the homage to Lead Belly.

The narrator's embrace of the performer simply signals a desire to highlight his own difference from mainstream aesthetics. He identifies with and claims for himself the status of artist as melancholic outsider. The persona in which Cobain is so invested in his personal writings, however, just like the historical Kurt Cobain, makes no *explicit* or self-conscious claim to blackness in his aesthetic choices. As a result, Cobain writes in a naïve way that indicates he remains unaware of the implications of canonizing Lead Belly, even as the persona he takes on, KurDt, tacitly professes a certain knowledge of black political struggle for racial justice. In other words, the implicit and explicit political claims that *Journals* makes (in the voice of the persona Cobain creates) contrast with the ideological work that the text (written by the real Kurt Cobain) actually accomplishes.

As Bannister argues, along with Kier Keightley and other scholars, some rock practitioners resort to a cultural aesthetic and practice that essentialize black culture as the very definition of authenticity (27). They also perceive black music to constitute the epitome of "performance, immediacy, improvisation, and emotionality" (Negus, 101). As a result, these rockers succeed in associating their own music composition and performance with a marginalized group and thus with cultural and social resistance. Yet more often than not, they preclude themselves from engaging with black culture in a sustained and meaningful manner. Such an engagement would evince an awareness of the persistence of racialized phantasies; and it would pose a real challenge, rather than a merely symbolic one, to racial politics and hegemonic power dynamics.

A nuanced reading of *Journals* supports this contention. Cobain, as narrator and character in this text, takes his appreciation of Lead Belly and other black performers in and of itself to constitute a statement of political solidarity and proof of his status as an ally. His explicitly antiracist statements notwithstanding, there is no representation in these notebooks of an active engagement with African American culture. As Bannister suggests about white rockers in general, the narrator's embrace of Lead Belly signals not only a desire to highlight his own difference but also an existential *need* to identify with and claim for himself the status of artist as authentic and nonconformist.

Cobain's representation, or misrepresentation, as it were, of blackness does not occur in isolation, of course. His lyrics and journal writings must be inserted within the tradition of punk and postpunk, subcultures that entertain, at best, a problematic relation with racial difference. In his account of U.S. alternative music, Ryan Moore examines how the genre merged with political activism and social movements concerned with race and class politics; nevertheless, he still theorizes punk subcultural resistance as a quintessentially white phenomenon (67). On the contrary, "the racialization of the figure of the punk" (Nyong'o, "Punk'd Theory," 21) is a scholarly project that recent academics and activists have undertaken from different theoretical perspectives. An insightful account of the racial politics of punk appears in Duncombe and

Maxwell's *White Riot: Punk Rock and the Politics of Race*. And, in addition to Tavia Nyong'o's publications, critical works by political scientist Cathy Cohen and by gender theorist Judith Halberstam have problematized the privileging of the figure of the punk as white, male, and straight. As I indicate in the introduction to this book, these writers have done so in a manner that has influenced not only my reading of whiteness in Cobain's creative writings but my understanding of his representation of masculinity and straightness as well.

The homage to Lead Belly, explored further in part III of this study, in the end allows for a phantasied identification with a marginalized subject-position while inadvertently highlighting the narrator's own dominant identity and position of cultural power. In addition to the Lead Belly entries, Cobain's journal notations further underscore this dominant identity and position of power in another entry that includes the sketch of a proposed album cover for *Nevermind*. In the distinctive voice of the persona he consistently takes on, Cobain writes, "Thanks to ... the white macho American male for reminding the small percentage [of young white men] who are capable of recognizing [racial] injustice [,] to fight you and learn from your sick, sadistic instinctual ways" (165). His notebooks indicate that this minority of young white men are the heroes in this American story. They will, in effect, gallantly rid the culture of the scourge of racism.

But what an exquisite irony! The persona by which Cobain is so captivated—a young white man plagued by a chronic, debilitating stomach ailment—comes to identify so readily with an old black musician rumored to be physically tough and resilient enough to endure long stints in southern prisons. This performer's very stage name suggests a man with metal guts and thus impervious to such a feminizing physical condition. Although Cobain does make a point of mentioning other unknown or lesser-known musicians he admired, Lead Belly is the only noncontemporary performer whose work he attempts to canonize above all others. Within Cobain's phantasy world, it is important that Lead Belly be black, male, and dead. Although he mentions other black musicians, Cobain includes each of their names only once on lists presented simply as compilations of noteworthy musicians or songs.[22] Some of these musicians were alive at the time Cobain was writing (NWA [77], Johnny Mathis [80], Isaac Hayes [128], Bad Brains [259]; other predeceased him (Jimi Hendrix and Billie Holliday [128]). In the final section of this chapter, I return briefly to the significance, or rather the insignificance, of the inclusion of Billie Holliday, the sole black woman performer on Cobain's lists.[23]

Lead Belly, by contrast, is included on these special lists eleven times. His name appears on every list in the text, with one exception. The exception occurs near the end of *Journals* (251). This particular list is relatively short when compared to the others. It is limited to pop-rock musicians, some of whom exemplify the very mainstream that Cobain frequently rejects, such as Bay City Rollers, Terry Jacks, and Leo Sayer. In addition to appearing on every list, Lead Belly is also the only musician mentioned in two entries that are more than mere compilations. He is the sole musician to merit comment and analysis, if one excludes musicians Cobain knew personally and with whom he had performed: Buzz Osborne, Mark Lanegan, Eugene Kelly, and drummers Dale Crover and Dave Foster.

The first entry featuring Lead Belly that is not a mere list highlights several punk and postpunk groups (Sex Pistols, Pixies, the Vaselines, Young Marble Giants, Wipers, etc.), and the name of each group is accompanied by a brief notation. Lead Belly seems out of place among this particular group made up, in Cobain's own characterization, mostly of young *white-boy* musicians known for producing punk-inspired white noise. Such groups typically do not show a partiality for black musical forms. Nor, generally speaking, do they display in their music or lyrics any affinity, real or symbolic, to black political struggle.[24] The notation on Lead Belly in this first entry cites the name of a specific recording, followed by a random collage of impressions that are not concretely connected to the album cited. Nor are these notations tied to the musician in any way that is made evident. Rather, the collage returns to Cobain's ongoing obsession, found in his lyrics as well as in his notebooks, with the male body, health, hygiene, and gender. He writes the following lines: "Leadbelly's last sessions (Folkways) vol. 1—orgones, pyles, cells and he probably knew the difference between male and female hemp" (173). With the word "pyles," the line connects Lead Belly to the narrator's phantasy of being penetrated. I circle back to the implications of this phantasy below.

The second entry with Lead Belly casts the performer as a character in one of the elaborate phantasy scenes described in *Journals*. I have already cited, in a different context, a portion of this entry titled "WOMBan by KurDt Kobain." This typewritten entry is presented as an analysis, Cobain writes, of "the current state of the underground, youth culture." The entry also includes fragments of the storyboard for the "Heart Shaped Box" video. The fragments repeated here, like in the earlier video description, include another first-person account of the narrator's penetration and impregnation by a Burroughs-esque character. In this version, however, as a result of his mating with the "famous old [white] man" (196), the previously ailing narrator—hooked up to an IV and very near death—is immediately and completely restored to life. He becomes, in fact, miraculously imbued with a superhuman capacity. Although suggested in the earlier entries in which Burroughs and Lead Belly appear separately, it is in this entry that *Journals* establishes conclusively that these two men function as the young grunge musician's inspiration and as the putative godfathers of his lyrics and music. It bears repeating that one of these men is an old, gay, iconoclastic white man; the other an old, presumptively criminal black man.

Lead Belly and Burroughs, therefore, play analogous roles in Cobain's personal writings. Identification with this specific musician and with this specific writer reinforces the marginalized subject-position that Cobain's published journals construct as ideal for the persona he inhabits. This subject-position is anathema to the "stump-dumb Joe" character and the white masculine norm this character embodies. In a 1992 interview, while expressing his desire to hang out with Burroughs, Cobain, embracing fully his role as a humble, reluctant rock star but unabashed fanboy, confirms the importance he places on both Lead Belly and Burroughs: "Last time I was in Kansas, I wanted to try just to knock on his [Burroughs's] door, but I was too nervous. I had a Lead Belly record in my arm; I was ready to go.... Actually [,] Burroughs gave me a first edition of *Naked Lunch* signed" (Crotty and Lane, 363).

The young musician-songwriter is nourished by the life and literature of Burroughs, whom, in turn, he intends to compensate by sharing the life and music of Lead Belly. Cobain fancies himself a young apprentice who takes in the essence of the Beat writer by reading *Naked Lunch,* and he intends for Burroughs to incorporate Lead Belly's essence by taking in his authentic, arresting music. In a different entry earlier in *Journals,* Cobain's narrator has already confirmed a phantasied relation to marginalized men in general. He has already declared his utter dependence on the ingenious works of these men in order to function physically, mentally, and creatively. "I was once a magnet for attracting new offbeat personalities," he declares, "who would introduce me to music and books of the obscure and I would soak it into my system like a rabid sex [-] crazed junkie [or a] hyperactive mentally retarded toddler who just had her first taste of sugar" (199).

In addition to establishing a connection between Burroughs and Lead Belly, the entry titled "'WOMBan' by KurDt Kobain" also puts forth for the very first time the analogy that Cobain's notebooks establish between the idealized musician and Christ. Thus, later in *Journals* when Cobain sketches a Christ-inspired self-portrait, the image underscores the connections that the text implicitly establishes between the persona Cobain embraces, Christ, Burroughs, and Lead Belly:

[The old man] will die just as he comes inside of me and all of his orgones and bad thoughts and desires for truth will soak into the walls of my lower intestines. I will be re-fueled. So re-fueled as to work up the energy to run on foot to the grave of Leadbelly, dig up his corpse and put us on a one [-] way ticket to the Vatican. *I will nail the corpse of Huddie* in a corner of the ceiling, paint him white and decorate him with costume jewelry. (196; emphasis added)

As already asserted in a prior entry, Lead Belly, as a consummate but unappreciated black artist, must be rendered superficially white before he can take his place in this all-male pantheon. That is, as the text has already confirmed, Cobain regrets that even though black musicians "invented rock and roll," these progenitors of the genre must conform to white standards in order to be recognized for their talent and accomplishments (111).

Cobain's journal entries further underscore the fusion of Lead Belly, Burroughs, and Christ in the second, detailed video proposal for "Heart Shaped Box" (titled "Technicolor Effect for Film"), already cited in part. First, in the opening scene of this particular version, Cobain phantasizes himself as Burroughs, an "old weathered man in hospital bed." Then, in the closing scene, he phantasizes Burroughs (the Cobain persona) morphing into Christ: "Old weathered man in hospital bed with a rubber foetus in his IV bottle . . . [becomes an] old man *on a cross*. Old weathered [,] interesting looking man with black crows on his arms, pecking at his face—Scarecrow / Jesus" (243). I have already pointed out in my reading of the song "In His Room" in the previous chapter how the persona that Cobain curates has a connection to the Passion, the brief, final period in the life of Jesus.

As pointed out in chapter 3, an actual sketch for the proposed final scene for

"Heart Shaped Box" appears much earlier in *Journals* (127). When the drawing "Scarecrow / Jesus" initially appears in the text, the image seems displaced. The drawing does not include a title or any kind of description. But because it appears on a page that also displays, in addition to three sperm cells, three of Cobain's self-portraits, the image functions to identify the man on the cross as Nirvana's front man himself. Cobain draws three promotional Nirvana T-shirts that encircle the emaciated, Christ-looking figure on the cross. The self-portraits are emblazoned on the T-shirts with "NIRVANA" at the top. One shirt displays a full-body image of the group's lead singer on a cross, another displays a full-body portrait but without a cross, and the third depicts a closeup of the singer's face. As they are represented on this single page, the self-portraits are superposable and interchangeable with the drawing of Christ on the cross. Given that the content of Cobain's written journal entries establishes a connection between Christ, Burroughs, and Lead Belly, this particular visual rendering reinforces Cobain's imagined identification with the writer and the musician.[25]

∞

When one considers the nature of Cobain's phantasy identification with a black musician from an earlier period, the grunge musician is not, in one important respect, an exception. Rather, he exemplifies the rule that leads to white boys singing the blues. Among historians of rock, there has been a robust discussion about the role of race in the birth and evolution of the genre. This history is nuanced and has been refined, especially over the past two decades, as historicist scholarship has become increasingly informed by critical race theories.[26] Notwithstanding this scholarship, Michael Bane's *White Boy Singin' the Blues* presents, in its most unadulterated form, the principal thesis concerning white rock and roll's debt to black culture. Bane's 1982 book presents the history of this debt also in a surprisingly entertaining manner, even though his very accessible account is not nuanced at all. *White Boy Singin' the Blues* accomplishes a fair amount of cultural work. The book's explicitly stated objective is to "set the record straight" concerning the birth and evolution of rock. In documenting how white performers exploited black music and texts, however, Bane emphasizes the personal actions of individual white men, while ignoring altogether the social and institutional practices that sanction their actions. Consequently, his book avoids a critical analysis of systemic racism and the privilege and power of white men as a group.

Nevertheless, as Bane's account reconfirms, it is not unusual that a white rock musician of the late twentieth century would draw real or symbolic inspiration from, would idolize, and would perhaps even imitate or appropriate the music and lyrics of a legendary bluesman, one resembling Chuck Berry's "Johnny B. Goode."[27] "Black masculinity is usually represented as having some kind of parental role in the production of white rock: 'Buried deep in the collective unconscious of rock and roll there's a simple figure drawn from real life: One man, one guitar, singing the blues. But he is not any man. He is black, Southern, poor, and . . . dreaming'" (Bannister, 33, citing Marsh). Bannister's observation does not suggest that the "collective unconscious" of rock is based upon anything other than a phantasied blackness, a misrepresentation of black culture, a notion that reveals more about the white rocker than it does about any individual musician or about black culture overall.[28]

The "Nigger" and the "Fag" in Cobain's Notebooks

In spite of Cobain's posturing, ambivalence, and self-contradictions, *Journals* appears to privilege gender over racial, affectional, and generational differences. In other words, the persona Cobain is so intent on assuming is represented as male first and secondarily as white, heterosexual, and young. It is particularly difficult to pinpoint and then make complete sense of what accounts for Cobain's representation of whiteness as an identity. The specific mechanisms of KurDt's white identity are not immediately evident. In particular, the reader is left to decipher what being white means beyond simply an opposition to a presumptive blackness. The attentive reader suspects that since the persona Cobain embraces claims an affinity to black culture, the blackness in question is necessarily abject.

The suspicion is borne out by the problematic presence of Lead Belly, "the Negro," as a discursive object in *Journals,* that is, as the topic of a diffused philosophical and political reflection and as an object of identification. This suspicion is also borne out by the narrator's sense of empowerment and his palpable pleasure in appropriating and redeploying the invective "nigger" in two revealing entries in the text. Given the commensurate gay-male identification to which KurDt also stakes a claim, the reader would expect the "Gay Man" to emerge in Cobain's notebooks also as an object of discourse and identification. Further, one would anticipate KurDt's appropriation of an equally charged invective, "fag"/"faggot," to designate an abject homosexuality. This appropriation does indeed occur in two additional and equally revealing entries.

There is a significant difference, however, between the way the two invectives are employed as ideological constructs and as discursive tools in *Journals*. With one exception found at the beginning of *Journals* (26), "nigger" invariably describes a *white* male subject who is the antithesis of the antiracist persona that Cobain's notebooks bring to life.[29] Cobain writes, for example, that "The KKK are the only niggers" (5) and "The Imperial Wizard of the KKK is a nigger" (74). By contrast, he employs "faggot"/"fag" in a manner commensurate with the cultural politics of the persona his notebooks succeed in constructing. For example, the text merrily evokes a "Euro disco *fag* bar" (65) as a venue that will be receptive to and enhance the cultural capital of the kind of music that the narrator prefers to listen to and that he also creates.

Moreover, in a letter to the readers of *The Advocate* (280–82), a national gay magazine, the narrator begins by saluting his "fellow Advocatees." He then expresses contentment and a sense of superiority for having granted an interview to this magazine because of, or in spite of, its primarily gay readership. He concludes this letter to the editor in a manner that indicates he considers himself an honorary "fag" at least. "Thank you," he writes, "I'll always be an Advocate for you fags. I love you and appreciate your gracious compliments. Love Kurdt. Stay Gay all the way" (282).

With the difference in the way the epithets for black men and for gay men are appropriated and redeployed, the persona Cobain at times blithely assumes cannot be an honorary "nigger." His notebooks inadvertently reveals what Seshadri-Crooks describes as "the deep relation between whiteness and the unconscious" (358). As a result of this relation, a white identity, real or imaginary, functions as a condition, a prerequisite, to assuming any other dominant subject-position, such as masculinity or heterosexuality. The presumptive naturalness and superiority of masculinity and heterosexuality evolve—and cannot be disentangled—from the inadvertent representation of whiteness as *the* core, defining identity-position in Cobain's phantasy universe. It is for this reason that the role of whiteness in his representation of identity is not self-evident. Nevertheless, one sees how skin color is valued in Cobain's notebooks in the unintended way that heterosexual masculinity gets conflated with whiteness. This conflation becomes even more evident, as I have revealed, when Cobain's personal writings are read specifically as a run-through for the composition of particular songs.

But even in the central entry in *Journals,* where race is mentioned only parenthetically ("white, corporate male"), all the men are white and presumptively heterosexual, not only the "macho, strong ox male," the football players, the Wall Streeters, and "corporate dickheads;" but also "the alternative thinking bands" and "the young, gullible fifteen-year old boys" as well (177–79). Therefore, the overvaluation of skin color is revealed in the elliptic way that whiteness also gets conflated in the text with both authenticity and creativity (playing punk guitar) and with inauthenticity and lack of creativity (producing corporate music). In this sense, the central entry mimics the drawings of the Klan, images in which all the actors—both the good and the evil—are also white men.

To the degree that Cobain, as the narrator/protagonist in *Journals,* is conscious of his own color, he is both relieved and perturbed that he experiences his whiteness, unlike his maleness and his straightness, as indelible and immutable. Even though the character KurDt appears to live his gender, race, and sexual orientation as overlapping and inextricable, he bemoans his whiteness. Yet he does not explicitly and consistently contest his color to the same degree as he does his maleness or his straightness. For example, throughout this text, KurDt consistently feminizes his body (as passive, anorexic, and penetrated), just as on occasion when assuming his onstage persona, Cobain appropriates feminine dress and makeup. In this respect, of course, the persona Cobain takes on in *Journals* and on stage is not exceptional because this kind of self-feminization is well within a certain tradition of pop and rock performance (Zaplana). Yet the persona that emerges in *Journals* does constitute an exception because of the particular way Cobain's narrator phantasizes his body as possessing female parts.

Just as the persona Cobain cultivates in his creative writings contests his maleness, he also calls into question his straightness. He persists in queering his body. That is, not only does KurDt desire a body with female parts, he desires to be penetrated and impregnated by other men. Yet even a certain degree of queering, according to Alexander Doty, also characterizes performances of masculinity in contemporary popular culture in North America.[30] But the way the persona Cobain constructs identifies with gayness corresponds to the way some participants in the alternative rock subcultures succeed in contesting and resisting gender and sexual conventions. Mimi Schippers documents, for example, how some musicians and their fans (who were part of the alternative scene in Chicago during the 1990s) succeeded, by way of their attitude and their actions, in contesting, blurring, and stepping outside of the "hierarchical sexual identities that define individuals as homosexual or heterosexual" (131).

Particular fragments in Cobain's notebooks, like the attitudes and actions of these Chicago rockers, also operate to call into question not only the bifurcation of gender into male and female but also the very logic of the hierarchical division of sexual identities into the two categories of hetero and homo. In ascribing same-sex desire to heterosexual musicians and actors—including KurDt himself—Cobain's notebooks represent "gayness" as specific practices and, therefore, as something that a person *does*. Gayness, in the universe Cobain creates, is not an identity; it does not specify who *one is*. Thus, detailed scenes of sexual activity in *Journals* can be read in a way that aligns with the call of some queer activists to disrupt the heterosexism of our current sexual order by refusing to define sexuality as particular categories of men and women.

The narrator and characters that Cobain creates are not "gay" because, the reader is to assume, they do not limit their erotic practices to gay sex. Their erotic desire just happens to be open to men. The intragender sexual activity of a Michael J. Fox or a Bruce Springsteen does not reflect some unchangeable essence of their being. They remain true to their authentic selves. Further, when Cobain writes in his notebooks, "I'm not gay although I wish I were, to piss off the homophobes" (192), he is inhabiting the persona of a young artist who rejects homophobia and heterosexism. Yet as Schippers reveals to be the case for the participants in the Chicago alternative scene, Cobain's notebooks, too, conflate gender and sexuality. By representing sexuality as fluid while at the same time collapsing "penetrating" and "penetrated" into masculine and feminine respectively, *Journals* comes to represent sexuality in a complicated manner. In Cobain's universe, hegemonic and counterhegemonic attitudes toward sexuality are operative concurrently.

Compared to an explicit identification with a feminine subject-position and with a gay-male subject-position, the persona Cobain assumes is circumspect and seemingly conflicted when it comes to a potential black identification. Whereas Cobain's notebooks represent gayness as what a man does, they represent race as *who a man is*. In this sense, gayness constitutes an identification whereas whiteness and blackness constitute an identity. In particular, Cobain constructs blackness in a way that his alter ego simultaneously rejects ("nigger") and embraces ("Negro"). Further, as I suggest, the "Grunge-Boy-Musician" role Cobain takes on does not appear, upon first blush, to resort to a metaphoric blackface by *consciously* appropriating stereotyped black idioms and poses.[31]

As indicated, KurDt ends up acquiescing to his color, even as he refuses to assent to the limitations of his gender and his orientation. This difference confirms, as Seshadri-Crooks indicates (when she opens up psychoanalytic theories of subjectivity to the contingency of race), "the particularity of 'whiteness' as an ideological structure" (357) and how white identity operates unconsciously in our culture. This particularity of whiteness is evident in the circuitous, unintentional way KurDt's white racial identity, in spite of his assertions to the contrary, emerges within the pages of *Journals* as the very core of his being. Cobain's notebooks prove Seshadri-Crooks' thesis: Racial identity in a race-conscious culture functions to structure gender and sexual identities. In psychoanalytic terms, gender and sexuality, as they appear both in Cobain's writings and with our culture, lean on race to a significant degree.

In addition, Cobain's notebooks represent an ill-defined and irresolute experience of race that is contingent both on the abjection of whiteness as "white trash" and the construction of an abject blackness. In the confused and confusing universe Cobain creates, however, abject blackness is revealed to be just another form of a reprobate whiteness, as seen in his characterization of the KKK as "niggers." Cobain, as KurDt and narrator/protagonist in *Journals,* is explicitly antiracist. But this text illustrates that Kurt Cobain, as writer of the text, may not be completely aware of his own problematic convergence with African American history and music culture.

For example, the writer produces an extended lyrical and narrative text that puts forth "the superiority of women and the Negro to art." In doing so, Cobain seems unaware that he reduces African Americans to black *men* and that he then conflates black men with white women, rendering women of color altogether invisible and insignificant within the subculture to which he pledges allegiance. As a result, Cobain's journal entries idealize underground women musicians who are white, like the members of the punk group Bikini Kill. But these entries remain silent on the women of color, like Billie Holliday and Sister Rosetta Tharpe, who are integral to the artistic tradition and music lineage that the persona he inhabits reveres and claims as his very own.

In sum, Cobain approaches his notebooks as a creative space in which to reflect on his *masculine* identity. It is because of the specific way whiteness operates in our culture to inflect gender and sexuality, however, that he unwittingly succeeds in privileging race over gender, sexual, and generational differences. In putting forth masculinity as the dominant identity of the persona he constructs, Cobain inevitably foregrounds the whiteness of this character. But the antiracist discourse that Cobain inscribes in his journal entries functions to undermine the very whiteness that the text itself constructs. As a result, and as opposed to his lyrics, the writing and the illustrations in his notebooks do not silence race; rather, they speak out loudly and in a critical but equivocal voice.

The persona and principal subject-position Cobain adopts in all his written texts, his lyrics as well as his personal writings, is constructed in a confounding and at times seemingly unintelligible manner. With specific texts, like the song "Travelin' White Trash Couple" or like the journal entries describing the narrator's impregnation by William Burroughs, readers find it challenging to identify precisely what kind of young man this is. The mode of masculinity that Cobain's creative writings represent as superior, if not ideal, is antiphallic and antimacho. This phantasied gender mode can also be characterized as "feminized" or "hysterical." I define this mode, rather, as testerical in order to underscore its connection to an equally phantasied male body. As I now explore, this testerical mode, with its *masochistic* and *melancholic* propensities, proves to be just as problematic for any subject who identifies as masculine and heterosexual but who exists within a misogynist and homophobic culture.

THEORIES

MASOCHISM AND MELANCHOLY

5 POWER, PLEASURE, AND PAIN
Creating a Masochistic Persona

Masochism is a powerful diagnostic tool. Usually understood as a desire to abdicate control in exchange for sensation—pleasure, pain, or a combination thereof—it is a site where bodies, power and society come together in multiple ways. . . . As such, masochism allows us to probe different ways of experiencing power. Masochism's rich analytic possibilities stem from its ability to speak across theory and practice, disciplines, and identities.
—AMBER JAMILLA MUSSER, *Sensational Flesh* (1)

Masochism has a distinctive history, and the manner in which analysts and cultural critics theorize the concept gives it enormous interpretive potential for an analysis of Cobain's creative writings. The interpretive value of masochism for an interrogation of the content and the structuring of his lyrics and journal entries is especially evident because of the singular way his texts create a persona structured around representations of a white male body engaged in experiences of pleasure, pain, and power. Near the end of the twentieth century, "Self-Defeating Personality Disorder" was proposed, but ultimately rejected, as the official diagnosis for masochism (Glick and Meyers). Specific Cobain lyrics, like "In His Room," and specific journal entries, like "Triple Suicide," bear witness to the wisdom of this proposal.

In Cobain's creative writings, a masochistic desire to take on physical and psychical pain serves to ensure the defeat, if not the eventual death, of the self. Some of Cobain's texts succeed in creating captivating narrators and characters who seek pleasure in pain, powerlessness, and humiliation. Further, these texts, by way of ingenious literary devices, constrain readers to identify with these self-destructive narrators and characters. Therefore, we can understand some of the stories Cobain attempts to tell and many of the images he produces by understanding how these stories and images function as a masochistic phantasy.

Beyond the narrow definition of masochism (as erotic desire) within sexology, this so-called perversion has been redefined within various disciplines such as film, literary, and queer studies. Within these very different disciplines, scholars retheorize masochism as a particular interrelation of power in general, rather than exclusively as gender and sexual power relations (Tobin). This retheorizing facilitates an understanding of how power comes to be inscribed on the bodies and within the psyches of individual subjects, such as the narrator in "Heart Shaped Box" and the serial killer in "Chuck Taylor."

Also within these distinct disciplines, descriptions of masochism are informed, to varying degrees, by psychoanalytic theory because the theory provides an effective way to understand how phantasy works. Therefore, certain aspects of film, literary, and queer studies are especially helpful in mapping the themes and diagramming the aesthetics of Cobain's writings because of the singular way his texts represent gender and racial identities as resulting from a *phantasmatic* process. Through this process, desire and anxiety find corporeal expressions. As I demonstrate in part II of this book, Cobain's lyrics and journal entries come to posit masculine subject-positions and white subject-positions as coincidental phantasies. Further, his creative texts represent gendered and racialized subjectivities in ways that are also revelatory of how heterosexuality, as an institution and as a discourse of power and coercion, also relies on a phantasy construct. Since some of Cobain's texts—like the twentieth-century novels and films David Savran examines in his cultural analysis of masochism—take on themes and images of self-destructive male narrators and characters, his texts constitute "sites in which and through which [white heterosexual] masculinities are regulated, iterated, and performed" (6).

If theories of masochism can facilitate a reading of Cobain's creative writings, some of his texts, in turn, can help theorists unravel the knotted workings of masochistic desire and their relation to hegemonic performances of masculinity. A careful examination of the masochistic persona that Cobain takes on, in other words, assists readers in recognizing the ideological and cultural structures that undergird masculinity and heterosexuality to the extent that these structures are transgressable. And the manner in which these hegemonic identifications are transgressed in Cobain's writings parallels how masochism, within psychoanalytic theory, violates the dictates of conventional masculinity. Put simply, the way the persona Cobain inhabits disrupts the norms of phallic and heterosexual behavior—in texts such as "Beeswax" and "WOMBan"—parallels the way masochism within Freud's theory calls into question normative gender and sexual identities.

Because masochism is linked inextricably to melancholy—in both psychoanalytic theory and in certain works of literature—understanding masochistic subjectivity becomes important for understanding the nature of Cobain's creativity. Melancholy, of course, can be seen to underwrite his ingenuity. In addition, melancholy, as I explore in the next chapter, constitutes another psychoanalytic concept that has been retheorized within other disciplines in ways that make it remarkably applicative for deciphering how certain films, paintings, and works of literature operate to produce meaning. I return to the linkage between masochism and melancholy in Cobain's writings at the conclusion of this study. I concentrate presently on masochism because the concept broadens our appreciation of the function of phantasy within his writings. The concept also illuminates the relation that exists between power-pleasure-pain on the one hand and, on the other, music performance, understood specifically as an all-male activity.

The following journal entry, for example, illustrates how the phantasy of a music performance, as an implicitly homosocial activity, interlaces pleasure and pain to reveal the narrator's masochistic propensity. Live performance, amid the bleeding, wounding, and self-wounding, is represented as the ultimate ecstasy. It emerges in Cobain's notebooks as the narrator's most intense physical and emotional activity. He is creating art in the form of authentic music, and he is doing so with the young men to whom he is the most profoundly attached emotionally. The entry appears to have no beginning, as Cobain is in the middle of describing the tension that exists between the "crowd" and the band because of the aggression of the beer-swigging, entranced attendees. After describing the futile efforts of the roadies to prevent the audience from assaulting the band, Cobain describes in detail how the members are injured and how they injure themselves during the performance. He does so in a manner that confirms the inextricability of playing music and experiences of pain and pleasure:

Kurdt the vocalist & guitarist screamed his last scream to the 2nd song then BAM[!] and then the crowd smacked the mike into his mouth. Blood oozed from his lip but they instantly started "Floyd the Barber." After wiping Kurdt's face, Chris the bass player accidentally hit Kurdt in the eye with his bass headstock [,] it wasn't too deep at first until Kurdt rammed his [own] head into the wall next to him ... So Kurdt took his guitar & hit Chris straight in the mouth causing a big cut lip. By now they were pretty bloody ... They were obviously becoming dizzy and were in pain, but proceeded to play the set quite out of tune. (*Journals,* 10)

MASOCHISM IN HISTORY, LITERATURE, PHANTASY, AND THEORY

The authoritative history of masochism began at the end of the nineteenth century. As is well known, Krafft-Ebing first used the word to describe sexual practices during which the subject experiences pleasure from pain or from being abused and humiliated by a partner. As is also well known, the sexologist drew inspiration from novelist Leopold van Sacher-Masoch's *Venus in Furs* (1870). From the very beginning, then, masochism has been linked to literature and fiction. Krafft-Ebing theorized, as Freud would later reiterate, that masochism need not lead to actual sexual acts. Both men considered it to be, first and foremost, a phantasy and a phantasmatic process. In addition, when compared to the other perversions, Krafft-Ebing and Freud both suggest that masochism is by far the most spectacular and theatrical. Masochism is most prone to stage and to overdramatize its "symptoms."[1] Masochism thus always consists of a story, a scenario with a cast of characters and a specific plot made up of a beginning, a development, and a deferred dénouement. This story, in its structure and its contents, resembles the overall story that Cobain's lyrics and journal entries are struggling mightily to tell.

The theorizing of masochism, as opposed to its history, began in earnest with Freud. After Freud, the psychoanalytical understanding of masochism as erotic practice (in the lives of individual, adult participants) has evolved significantly. For example, theorists and practitioners have come increasingly to conclude that it may be humiliation more so than pain that the masochist seeks (André). In addition, most experts contend that masochism is never a simple matter of pain or torture in general (M'Uzan). Rather, a masochist seeks a specific kind of excruciation, a precise and exquisite pain that is, in some significant way, unique to that particular individual, as one witnesses with the characters "Kurdt" and "Chris" in the journal entry cited above.

As I indicate, it is the way that masochism has been retheorized outside of psychoanalysis proper and within other disciplines that is especially helpful in understanding how Cobain's writings succeed so deftly in creating a masochistic persona. These disciplines, in addition to film, literary, and queer studies, also include cultural studies and feminist scholarship. It is especially scholarship within cultural studies that has forced us to understand "masochism as a relational, contingent term that describes a plethora of relationships" (Musser, *Sensational Flesh,* 21). These relationships can exist among individuals and between individuals and institutions of power. Thus the theorizing of masochism within cultural studies has social and cultural implications, which explains why "masochism now names a recognizable subgenre in mainstream literary and film culture" (Finke, 13).

Masochism, in the specific sense that I use the concept as an analytic to read Cobain's texts, must be understood as a particular way of experiencing the body as an instrument or as a casualty of power.[2] Given the distinction that I make between Cobain the person and the persona he takes on, however, it should be clear that I am not invoking masochism to describe any aspect of the historical Kurt Cobain's real sexual history or libidinal interests. Instead, I am referring to the specific narrators and characters he creates in his written texts.

If scholarship within cultural studies has forced us to understand masochism as a cultural phenomenon rather than a clinical one, feminist theory confirms more specifically that masochism entertains a particular and particularly involuted relation to *masculine* modes of existing within patriarchal culture. Freud initially attempts to explain this relationship in 1905 in *Three Essays on the Theory of Sexuality.* But it is Kaja Silverman's rereading of Freud—by way of Lacan and from an explicitly feminist perspective—that specifies the intricate relation that exists between masochism and masculine subjectivities. In *Male Subjectivity at the Margins,* Silverman describes this relation in a manner that illuminates how the persona Cobain takes on engages in acts of self-emasculation and self-destruction as a means to cope with anxiety. Silverman writes about and theorizes "deviant" experiences of masculinity, by which she means "masculinities whose defining desires and identifications are 'perverse' with respect not so much to a moral as to a phallic standard" (1). That is, she equates perverse with nonphallic.

As explored in chapters 3 and 4, specific texts written by Cobain reveal that certain male narrators and characters do indeed undermine normative masculine identity and sexuality because these writings operate to impeach the very notion of the bifurcation of gender into a masculine and a feminine modality.

For example, in a song like "Beeswax" or in a journal entry like the first story-board fragment for "Heart Shaped Box" (196), Cobain adopts a perspective that belies the logic of a gender binary. In these texts, a male narrator proudly represents his body as penetrated and/or impregnated. Lyrics and journal entries like these dramatize testerical men who incorporate feminine modalities into their thinking and behavior. Put another way, Cobain's texts highlights a particular kind of man, one who fervently takes on penetration and castration, or a sense of lack and inadequacy, as endemic to his identity.[3] The persona Cobain assumes constitutes precisely the kind of man Silverman designates as existing "at the margins" of conventional masculinity. Certain Cobain texts—those that represent male corporeality and masculinity as diseased and corrupting—operate invariably to embrace alienation and abjection. These texts also include songs like "Mexican Seafood" and the central entry in *Journals*.

Before proceeding with my analysis of the construction of a masochistic persona in Cobain's writings, it would be useful to open a brief parenthesis in order to recall some remarks from part I of this study concerning the logic and the implications of my appropriation of psychoanalytic aesthetics. As I indicate, I use the psychoanalytic paradigm as a methodology that serves to give voice to the silences within Cobain's creative texts and, therefore, that serves to flesh out the persona in which Cobain is so manifestly invested. I continue throughout this chapter to highlight how representations of the male body function within his creative writings. I analyze what I identify as the autofictional KurDt's desire to "cure" his male body by assuming a feminine cultural and social position, as if he were "a man lying in a gynecological chair with legs up in sturrops [*sic*]" (*Journals*, 279).

At various times offstage as well as during his stage performance, Cobain explicitly appropriates cultural signs of femininity, like wearing makeup and dresses. In this chapter, however, when I refer to a desire on the part of Cobain's narrators to assume a feminine position, I am speaking metaphorically. I am referring to the desire to abdicate power, to assume a subordinate position, to identify as nonphallic. Nevertheless, notwithstanding the literal meaning of certain utterances in Cobain's writings, like the imperative "Let me grow breasts" (*Journals*, 224), I do not interpret a desire for femininity to mean a desire to become a woman or to impersonate one. Therefore, I use "masculinity" and "femininity" in this chapter more often to designate psychical experiences and identifications rather than merely corporeal realities, properly speaking. In a similar manner, in this chapter—and again notwithstanding a literal reading of some of Cobain's texts—by "castration" I do not mean simply the excision of male genitalia. I also mean an experience of hurt and deprivation. In Cobain's lyrics and published journals, a desire for castration signals a masochistic need to experience pain and loss; it also signals a need to mourn.

Men "Under Construction": From Freud to Cobain / Exposing Masculinity as a Problematic Process

All accounts of masochism subsequent to Freud's begin with his descriptions. Freud develops and systematically revises his ideas in three principal texts separated by nearly twenty years: *Three Essays* (1905), "A Child Is Being Beaten" (1919), and "The Economic Problem of Masochism" (1925). We can read Freud writings on masochism and Cobain's creative texts in tandem because both writers conceive of masculinity in similar ways. They both posit masculinity as a fraught process rather than a stable identity. In *Three Essays,* Freud proposes that masochism and sadism always operate together in a complicated way. He later revises this idea by positing the notion of primary masochism as a standalone desire. In spite of his frequent revisions, however, Freud never alters his belief that masochistic desire signals a passive attitude and comportment on the part of the subject in question. In "A Child Is Being Beaten," he proposes the notion of a universal "beating phantasy" on the part of all subjects, whether or not they seek therapy. He then introduces the question of gender and how manifestations of masochism, whether in phantasy or in practice, differ for male and female subjects. For the male subject, a woman plays the role of the sadist and the subject himself assumes a role considered "inimical to that of a man." That is, Freud writes, "the masochistic attitude coincides with a feminine one" ("A Child Is Being Beaten," 197).

Freud reveals, however, that we learn from a close analysis of these subjects that the seemingly crucial role played by the woman in male masochistic desire is belied by the central role that the father actually plays in this beating phantasy. It is the father who carries out the beating. The son submits to the father's power. Freud theorizes further that the beating phantasy not only emanates from "a feminine attitude toward the father ... [it] *has its origin in an incestuous attachment to the father"* ("A Child Is Being Beaten," 198). Freud comes to the conclusion that because of a passive attitude toward the father, the masochistic male subject's gender identification is complicated. Freud means, of course, and certain of Cobain's texts such as "Laminated Effect" bear this out, that it is the normative, heterosexual identity of the subject that is complicated.

Given the importance Freud places on the father and the son in the oedipal triangle, masculine heterosexual identity within his theory is predicated on a homosocial, if not homoerotic, relationship between these two actors. And according to his initial insights into masochism, Freud postulates that there is a necessary relationship between male masochism and a disavowed homosexual desire on the part of the heterosexual subject. Cobain's creative writings also suggest that father-son relationships are determinant for the male subject's desire and his sense of self. Specific Cobain lyrics and journal entries, like Freud's theory, also reveal that masochism exists in a dialectical relation with homosexual desire.

In texts like "Even in His Youth," in addition to "Laminated Effect," homosexual desire, however, is not disavowed, though it does complicate the relationship between father and son and clouds the son's future. For Freud and Cobain alike, identity, and life itself, is indeed *all about men*. Even in "Chuck Taylor," where a sister and mother play seemingly crucial roles, it is the relationship between father and son—especially the father's verbal and physical abuse—that provides the objective of the narrative, the reason it is told in such detail, and the lesson it is designed to impart.

Other theorists, after Freud, have refined Freud's intuition that descriptions of masochism and portraits of masochistic male subjects, whether fictional or real, confirm that male homosexual desire and its disavowal constitute a prominent feature of *one form* of masochism. Savran, for example, concludes that since, for the male subject, masochism signals a problematic relation to the father, "It represents no more and no less than a scandalous eroticization of patriarchal relations, a desire for the father that is transformed into a desire to submit to the cruelty of the father's will" (32). On this point, Savran concurs with Judith Butler, who also points out that Freud invariably links "the evasion of homosexuality with an admission of the homoerotic character of heterosexual identity" (*Gender Trouble*, 77). Musser goes further. In her reading of masochism, by way of Deleuze, she concludes that the masochist is a particular type of queer subject ("Masochism").

Indeed, most cultural theorists whose writings are informed by psychoanalysis also conclude that patriarchal culture constitutes "an affair between men," with "affair" taking on the meaning of both a "business" and an "intimate

relationship." The culture writ large is structured around power relations between men; it depends upon, but disavows, the eroticizing of these relations.
The principal story that Cobain's creative writings labors to tell confirms this
definition of patriarchal culture. One has to look no further than the central
entry in *Journals,* a long fragment that describes a battle royale between men,
"old dickheads" versus "young punks," for the future of rock music. The entry
constitutes a premier episode in which men "beat" each other up and women
exist merely as passive bystanders.

In a third essay on masochism, "The Economic Problem of Masochism,"
Freud explores this desire in relation to the pleasure principle. In this paper,
he distinguishes three iterations of masochism that he labels "feminine," "ero-
togenic," and "moral." These distinctions, I argue, help to decode the specific
manner in which a masochistic phantasy underpins some of Cobain's most
expressive texts:

> Freud defines erotogenic masochism as receiving *pleasure from physical pain*
> and feminine masochism as a practice that relies on *the fantasy of submission* in
> which *male* actors gain pleasure through the adoption of the feminine role and
> the performance of submission. Moral masochism . . . is an unconscious *desire*
> *for punishment* that manifests itself clinically as almost paralyzing feelings of
> guilt. (Musser, *Sensational Flesh,* 7–8, emphasis added)

To varying degrees and in various ways, Cobain's signature texts put on stage
narrators and characters who exhibit these three characteristics: They are
seekers of pleasure in pain; they phantasize submission; they are overwhelmed
with guilt and a desire to be punished.

It is Freud's conception of feminine masochism (a desire for submission
on the part of male subjects) and moral masochism (a desire for punishment)
that is particularly germane to my discussion of Cobain's creative writings. In
addition, Cobain's writings, in turn, are helpful in illuminating some of the gaps
and contradictions in the psychoanalytic understanding of these two forms
of masochistic desire. Cobain's texts respond to the principal questions that
Freud either leaves unanswered or refuses even to pose concerning the origin,
symptoms, and apparent incurability of masochism. Cobain's writings, as I
explore them as representations of a self-defeating persona, help readers to
understand why certain male subjects find pleasure in suffering.

Before publishing the third foundational text on masochism ("Economic Problem"), Freud published *Beyond the Pleasure Principle* (1920). In this book, he seems to come to a different understanding—or at least he puts forth a more comprehensive explanation—of the etiology of masochism. He proposes a fuller account after his exploration of the death instinct (or drive), which he puts forth as a countermand to the pleasure principle (eros).[4] Freud's expanded understanding of masochism in this text makes his theorizing even more applicative to a reading of Cobain because of the way that self-recision, a desire to censure and punish the self, undergirds so many of his lyrics and journal fragments. It is the instinctual death drive, Freud reveals, that propels the organism to self-annihilate. He postulates that the libido counteracts the death drive by redirecting it toward external objects. This redirection produces several results, one of which is the sexual function. The sexual function emerges as sadism, that is, *activity* as distinct from *passivity*. The active and passive positions, within Freud's paradigm, get conflated with masculinity and femininity respectively. It is this very conflation, and the reduction of gender to binary opposites, that specific Cobain texts call into question by representing male bodies as passive, pliable, and penetrable and by representing male desire as fluid.

When Freud links masochism to the death instinct, only then does he describe a primary masochism, one that is not the inverse of sadism and that does not need a prior sadistic instinct to emerge. He specifies that a death instinct (that is sexualized and internalized by the subject) expresses itself invariably in phantasies of being castrated, being beaten, and experiencing the anus and buttocks as erogenous zones. The way Freud's theory links masochism to the death drive makes this aspect of the theory, once again, especially relevant to my reading of a signature Cobain text such as the different versions of the storyboard for "Heart Shaped Box." As I have shown, several themes and images re-emerge invariably in all these narratives: namely, sexual submission via a penetrated male body and representations of violence, pain, pleasure, death, and rebirth-creativity. These themes and images recall Freud's conclusions concerning the phantasies associated with primary male masochism.

Compared to Krafft-Ebing's descriptions, Freud's psychoanalytic model transforms masochism from a simple sexual practice into a way to characterize a mode of being and acting in the world. This mode of being and acting comports with the psychology and the actions of the persona Cobain assumes in his written texts. The emotions and behavior of the Cobain persona are characterized by a persistent "negativity, in the form of guilt, shame, and a desire for death" (Musser, *Sensational Flesh,* 8). Musser is not writing about Cobain specifically; she is describing the masochistic male subject in general. Yet her description captures perfectly the themes in the lyrics to "All Apologies" and "Negative Creep" and in the journal entry "A Leonard Cohen Afterworld" (191).

It is not Freud but Leo Bersani who theorizes masochism in a way that more clearly implicates Cobain's writings to the extent that his lyrics and his journal writings represent pain and death as pleasure. As Musser also indicates, Bersani "articulates a vision of sadomasochism [understood] as a form of 'nonsuicidal disappearance of the subject'" (*Sensational Flesh,* 15). An alienated subject can cease to exist, eliminate his alienation, without doing himself in. Bersani views sadomasochism as the fusing together of desire and the death drive that results in the dissolution and subsequent *recreation* of the subject. Masochism, from Bersani's perspective, represents the promise of immeasurable pleasure (jouissance). It provides a means for the subject to come undone, to have the boundaries of the ego—the subject's very identity—broken down. This dissolution results in the merging of masculine and feminine, gay and straight, self and other into an indivisible composite. And, as I have already suggested and as I now explore further, the whole of the Cobainian creative enterprise consists of representing the masculine subject in the process of coming undone and attempting to come to pleasure, re-emerging as whole. Indeed, Cobain creates the persona of a young man hopelessly seeking a superior, if not ideal, self.

∞

To summarize, when Freud's writings are considered in their totality, they represent normative masculinity as an ambivalent and vulnerable construction, in part because masculine identity is predicated on an experience of lack, anxiety, and disavowal. His theorizing specifically of masochism aligns with a major thrust within Cobain's creative writings. This thrust gives rise to the creation of a resisting, nonconforming persona overwhelmed with disquiet and possessing a marginal, complicated gender and sexual identity. In addition, Cobain's texts, like Freud's theory, take masochism out of the realm of sexual perversion to make it a constituent component of heterosexual masculine identity and its inherent experiences of anxiety and guilt.

Cobain's lyrics and journal entries further mimic Freud's writings in two important ways. First, both writers, ultimately and obsessively, represent heterosexual masculine subjectivity as the norm from which women and nonheterosexual men deviate. Second, Cobain's and Freud's representations of masculinity are ambivalent because these representations give legitimacy to masculine power and privilege while simultaneously exposing the vulnerability of masculine subjectivity. Cobain depicts this vulnerability as a particular kind of *agony*.[5] As I indicate in chapter 2, I do not entirely buy into some of the assumptions within Freud's writings. Yet I do find that his theorizing of masochism—by exposing fortuitously the illogic and the vulnerable underbelly of masculine identity and, implicitly by extension, of the entire patriarchal order—provides a useful vocabulary to talk about the obsessive themes and the recurring images in Cobain's creative writings. But Cobain does Freud one better: He introduces race into the equation by exposing how normative masculinity in our culture is coextensive with whiteness.

In *The Acoustic Mirror,* Silverman makes evident how psychoanalysis postulates that lack is at the origin of all subjectivity. She also demonstrates how the theory then goes to great discursive lengths to displace lack onto female subjects. "Freud's discussion of . . . castration anxiety serves as a prime example of how this displacement" influences the way our culture represents gender differences (Brintnall, "Masculinity, Masochism and the Crucifixion," 22). Further, Silverman reconfirms how psychoanalytic theory ascribes power, plenitude, and privilege to the male subject and the social consequences of this ascription for the way that certain subjects, like the persona Cobain projects, come to identify as masculine.

Cobain's writings, I argue, operate on one level, precisely, to belie the privilege, plenitude, and authority of the masculine subject by ascribing to him the very lack that psychoanalytic theory displaces onto the female subject. As I indicate, castration is not disavowed in Cobain's writings. On the contrary, castration is embraced because the persona that Cobain projects, an invertible masochist but a masochist nonetheless, is enamored with his own lack and subjugation. In addition, he derives pleasure in not living up to the phallic, heterosexual model, as when he gleefully describes himself as lacking a penis.

Whereas the male subject, as conceived within psychoanalytic discourse, attempts to counteract anxiety and alienation by projecting lack onto the female subject, Cobain's writings expose the utter failure of such an attempt. Further, the male subject that psychoanalytic theory describes "is symbolically and imaginatively constructed in closer alignment with the phallus [than the female subject]; the phallus as privileged signifier, [then], ascribes both *being* and *meaning* to the male subject" (Brintnall, "Masculinity, Masochism and the Crucifixion," 13, emphasis added). It distinguishes him physically from the female subject, and it endows him with an inherent value. But, once again, an examination of specific themes within Cobain's lyrical production in particular confirms that his writings problematize the very value and privilege ascribed to masculinity. As I first establish in chapter 3 and in more detail later, even with its focus on the male body, neither Cobain's lyrics nor his journals, when it comes to evoking a nonconforming masculine subject, equate the penis with power, authority, or pleasure. It is in this way that his creative writings call normative masculinity into question by broadcasting the utter nonalignment of phallus and penis.

Within this context, the phallus is understood, in the broadest sense, as the symbolic nature of power, whereas the penis is understood as power's real and material effect on individuals.[6] For the idealized persona Cobain consistently tries on, male corporeality is not commensurate with power and does not necessarily signify complicity with social and cultural authority. In other words, Cobain's writings, and some of his visual art as well, compel readers and viewers to see masculinity for the socially constructed phenomenon that it is.

The fiction, or constructedness, of masculinity is made manifest, for example, in the central entry in *Journals*. As mentioned, the narrator in this entry proposes to put an end to "macho-dickheaded-ness" by using punk music to seduce the "young, gullable 15 year old Boys" who have not been fully indoctrinated into "what they've been told a man is supposed to be" (177). Masculinity is also presented as a learned behavior in the "Mr. Moustache" comic. This brief comic, like the extended central entry, leads readers to conclude that what we think of as "natural" masculinity is merely an ideological construct, a trait that men can acquire. Like a moustache, it can be cultivated, but it can be easily shorn. Both texts also suggest that a form of masochistic self-destruction, in the form of self-abortion, can function as a preventive measure against the malignancy of conventional masculinity.

The "Mr. Moustache" comic (26) appears, inauspiciously, as the very first one in *Journals*. Cobain composes it in four exquisitely drawn panels displayed in two columns. As usual, he exhibits an expert eye for detail, from the floral pattern of the woman character's dress, for example, to the décor of the couple's living room that prominently displays the male character's assault rifle. This same weapon will reappear in the Klan images and in the image of the hanged man. In the first panel, Mr. Moustache, a soon-to-be father—depicted as a macho, mustachioed, young white man—puts his ear to the woman's stomach in order to surveil his unborn child. Holding a can of beer and exposing his hairy, tattooed arm, he appears content, convinced that he is having a son. "MY SON!" He croons admiringly. "Boy, he's gonna be quite a man, listen to the power in those little strong legs! He's gonna be a football player!" Of course, it is only much later in Cobain's journals that the reader will learn the likely, and likely deserved, fate of this baby as he grows up into young adulthood and resurfaces as an executed, or more likely, a self-murdered football player-soldier.

The second panel, in contrast to the first, depicts only a close-up of Mr. Moustache's face; he now wears an expression of both anger and anxiety. "This kid," he warns, while shaking his finger at the woman's stomach and, simultaneously, at the viewer/reader, "better not be a lousy little girl. I want my very own honest, hard working, jew, spick, nigger, and faggot hatin' 100% pure beef *AMERICAN MALE!* I'll *teach him* how to work on cars and exploit women" (emphasis added). As I previewed in the previous chapter, this comic constitutes the only occasion where Cobain does not employ "nigger" to designate a psychotic, racist white man; rather he employs the adjective "nigger-hatin'" as coming from the mouth of what is presented as a typical, "red-blooded," white American man.

The third panel of the drawing finds the would-be father back in the same position as in the first: his ear is pressed gently against the mother's stomach. Now with eyes closed, he is once again content, at peace: "AHH, Listen to those strong little kicks," he repeats. It is in the final panel, to be sure, that Cobain delivers the punch line, or in this case, the "kick" line. As Mr. Moustache continues surveilling him, the gestating child violently kicks through its mother's stomach. The blow succeeds in smashing through the skull of his controlling, putative father, ostensibly murdering him. The word "KICK" appears in large block letters at the bottom of the panel. The word offers a stark contrast to the tiny signature, "Kurdt Kobain," that is barely legible in the far-right corner of the panel. The artist's name is adorned with the floral pattern from the woman's dress. This final visual cue in the comic confirms that Kurdt identifies masochistically with the pregnant, passive, and silent woman in this scenario.

The comic puts forth a two-pronged message. First, Cobain ingeniously reveals that whereas violence may be a natural masculine trait, like the ability to grow a moustache, misogyny and sexism, like auto mechanics, have to be taught and learned. Second, he suggests just as cleverly that there exists only one sure way to prevent this boy from growing up and perpetuating the evils of the father. Even if the father is murdered, the son is doomed to take his place. To avoid this fatality, this comic, and Cobain's writings overall, prescribes a masochistic, pre-emptive solution on the part of the child: self-abortion.

THE COBAIN PERSONA AND THE MALE-BODY-IN-PAIN:
TAKING IT LIKE A WOMAN

Cobain's creative productions can be read as confirming and, simultaneously, contradicting the underlying thesis within the works of two scholars: David Savran's *Taking It Like a Man* and Kent L. Brintnall's "Masculinity, Masochism, and the Crucifixion: The Male-Body-in-Pain as Redemptive Figure."[7] These two writers build upon Silverman's insights, though they also critique her analysis and conclusions. As opposed to the seemingly ahistorical claims of classic psychoanalysis, Savran historicizes masochistic subjectivity. He posits masochism as endemic to "the very structures of male subjectivity as it was consolidated in Western Europe during the early modern period" (10), that is, from the end of the Middle Ages to the beginning of the Industrial Revolution.

In addition, Savran reads contemporary white American masculinities, as seen in late twentieth-century film and fiction, as inescapably masochistic in the way men in these cultural productions valorize submission and victimization. Because post-1950 film and fiction represent white male characters as victims, other critics, like Sally Robinson in *Marked Men,* also describe contemporary white men as assuming, at least temporarily and strategically, subject-positions culturally marked as feminine. Savran in particular makes expert use of psychoanalytic logic and its vocabulary to analyze all the different ways in twentieth-century fiction and cinema in which white male characters masochistically adopt a feminine identification, as does the "artist" in the "Mr. Moustache" comic. He traces how this identification has adapted and continues to adapt to historical and cultural changes from the 1950s onward.

Savran analyzes mid- to late twentieth-century cultural productions, including writings like Jack Kerouac's *On the Road* (1957) and Norman Mailer's "The White Negro" (1957) and films such as *Forrest Gump* (1994) and *Regarding Henry* (1991). He theorizes that in addition to being feminized, contemporary masochistic white masculinity is also "blackened." In these writings and films, Savran finds evidence that "for a white male subject living in a pervasively racist and misogynist culture, a black [social and cultural] position can function analogously to a feminine one insofar as both represent positions of abjection" (33). In other words, although blackness and femininity are not structurally identical, they become perfectly analogous, if not interchangeable, within the masochistic phantasy. In fact, the phantasy itself is attractive to certain white male subjects, both psychically and socially, because it allows for the easy overlaying of racial and sexual differences.

The phantasy becomes a convenient way for certain white male subjects to assume the role of victim by identifying with a marginalized position, a feminized or blackened position. As demonstrated, it is this dynamic that propels the narrator in *Journals* to identify with "women and the Negro" and, in particular, to overidentify with Lead Belly. The position of victim also allows the hegemonic white male subject in general to be *queered* as well, as *Journals* also attests in the way this text conflates KurDt Kobain not only with Lead Belly but also with William Burroughs, as demonstrated in chapter 4.

From the historicist perspective that Savran outlines, we can understand the mid-twentieth century as a period that witnesses the emergence, in real and fictional men, of what Freud would label feminine masochism (a desire for submission on the part of male subjects). More specifically for my reading of Cobain, Savran traces a particular iteration of the "fantasy of the white [masochistic] male-as-victim, beginning with his appearance on the U.S. cultural scene in the 1950s and ending with his transformation into a number of disparate but related [male] figures, both fictional and non-fictional" (4) well into the twenty-first century. The 1950s were profoundly marked, of course, by the lives and the writings of the Beats. The template of masculinity inaugurated by the most influential Beat writers, like Burroughs and Ginsberg in addition to Kerouac, evolved in North America during the 1960s and 1970s. This model of masculinity finds echoes and inflections in writings like Ken Kesey's *One Flew Over the Cuckoo's Nest* (1962), Hunter S. Thompson's *Hell's Angels* (1967), and Tom Wolfe's *The Electric Kool-Aid Acid Test* (1968).[8] As Simon Warner documents, the Beats also had an impact on poets-musicians like Jim Morrison in *The Lords and the New Creatures* (1969) and Leonard Cohen in *The Spice-Box of the Earth* (1961).

Further, from Savran's historicist perspective, we can understand the second half of the twentieth century in general as the period when what Freud labels moral masochism (a desire for punishment)—and some critics like Silverman label "Christian masochism"—came to dominate the representation of masculinity in literature and film. More precisely, we can understand the transition from the 1950s and 1960s to the 1970s as a shift to what Freud labels "reflexive sadomasochism," a subjectivity manifested as a split between, on the one hand, a passive, feminine, and masochistic component, and, on the other, an active, masculine, and sadistic component. The end result of this ingenious and self-serving scission is that it provides the male subject with the opportunity to prove his manhood, that is, that he can be beaten mercilessly but can "take it like a man."

Typically within the masochistic phantasy, as found in action films, the male subject might flirt strategically with victimhood (subjugation, femininity, blackness, or queerness), but he does so all the while confirming his unshakable belief in a hypermasculine, heteronormative, white manhood. After enduring the perils and pain of a Rambo or Rocky, for example, the subject rises up and proves his natural worth. This kind of masculine subject temporarily assumes the position of an abused, or self-abusing, victim only to resume his heroic role with even more legitimacy and authority.[9] It is for this reason that a masochistic identification can be considered a kind of ruse, since in those cultural productions where it is manifest and where a white male character initially seems totally defeated, the stories all end with normative, phallic masculinity restored to its position of dominance.

The major thrust within Cobain's writings, however, operates to subvert this dynamic within the phantasy. His creative texts put forth narrators and characters who embrace victimhood as a *permanent* status. Yet, as I shall explore, his lyrics and journals also operate at times to reaffirm heteronormative, white manhood, but in a different way. That is, notwithstanding the progressive thrust within Cobain's writings, his texts reconfirm, as recent analysis of masculinity and whiteness bear out, that the cultural hegemony is uncannily resilient. White men are ingenious in transforming their circumstances and finding ways to retain, reinforce, and solidify their position of power, whether in politics, economics, or culture in general. Sally Robinson, for example, uses fiction, nonfiction, and film from the last decades of the twentieth century to illustrate this thesis concerning the resilience of white masculinity.

Cobain's signature lyrics and some of his most affecting journal entries reject and, at the same time, reaffirm white, heteronormative masculinity. Over the remainder of this chapter and the next, I explore how this tension within Cobain's writings either plays itself out or is forestalled in specific songs and journal fragments. One determinant question will anchor my reading of these texts: Is phallic masculinity "rescued" in any way in the masochistic phantasy found in Cobain's written texts?

In contrast to Savran's materialist account and his historicizing of the emergence of white masochistic masculinities within American culture, Kent Brintnall aligns more with Silverman, for whom "materialist accounts of ideology are incomplete because it is fantasy [or] the realm of imagination . . . [that] makes a particular ideological construction seem real to the subject" ("Masculinity, Masochism, and the Crucifixion," 32). Brintnall uses the trope of the "male-body-in-pain" as his point of departure to explore the relation between masochism and masculinity as represented in literature, photography, painting, and cinema. He does so in a manner that parenthesizes historical processes proper. Brintnall examines the commonalities between Hollywood action films, paintings by Francis Bacon, and photographs by Robert Mapplethorpe as a way also to explore the psychical, social, and political dynamics underlying representations of the crucifixion of Christ.

Brintnall draws significantly from Silverman's core notion that masochistic masculinities deviate from the phallic modality. As does Savran, however, he also emphasizes that representations and performances of masochism are ambivalent. He argues, for example, that although images of an afflicted male body can undermine the presumptive power and privilege of hegemonic masculinity, these images can at the same time reaffirm and reproduce phallicism and expand hegemonic power and privilege. Specifically, Brintnall argues that "the figure of the male-body-in-pain enables a reading of the crucifixion of Christ as a repudiation [of conventional notions] of masculine subjectivity." Yet he maintains that since Christ's resurrection represents "a moment in which the suffering body is restored to wholeness" ("Masculinity, Masochism and the Crucifixion," 12), this rebirth presents an image of this body that contradicts the way the crucifixion itself undermines the notion of masculinity as invulnerable. The resurrection has points of intersection with the revenge scene in action films. In this sense, Brintnall's analysis coincides with Savran's. Both see the submission/defeat of the male subject as provisional. The masochistic persona that Cobain takes on would seem, therefore, to contradict the theories of these two writers since, in his writings, there appears to be no revenge or resurrection on the part of the masochistic characters he creates. There is nothing within a text like "In His Room" or "WOMBan" that can be clearly interpreted as a resurgence.

Nevertheless, Brintnall has theorized the notion of the male-body-in-pain in a way that allows for an understanding of the logic of the masochistic persona that Cobain assumes. But it is Sally Robinson's analysis of the writings of white male novelists and essayists from the final quarter of the twentieth century that demonstrates the most conclusively that it is through a wounded body that white men invariably represent themselves as disempowered and as victims of the power of specific others or of cultural power in general. Therefore, her analysis provides another effective key to understanding the logic of Cobain's representation of the suffering male body. She examines the fiction and nonfiction of writers like John Updike, Michael Crichton, Alan Bloom, Philip Roth, and Stephen King.

Yet, just like Savran's and Brintnall's view of the masochistic white male subject, Robinson, too, understands this self-representation of corporeal assault and wounding—which is prevalent especially in fiction produced in the United States after the 1970s—as constituting a "strategy through which white men [can] negotiate the wide-spread critique of their power and privilege" (6). Sensing that their power and privilege are imperiled, these men respond by representing different forms of assault to the male body. Robinson analyzes this strategy in popular novels like Roth's *My Life as a Man* (1974), Irving's *The World According to Garp* (1978), and King's *Misery* (1987). For example, she proposes that we read King's *Misery* exactly for what it is, namely, a novel in which a male character who is a writer emerges hobbled, but still triumphant, after undergoing the most excruciating torture at the hands of a psychotic woman. Therefore, Robinson concludes, we must read the novel "as King's staging of male masochism, put on for readers who are primarily male" (124).

In the end, both Savran and Brintnall, in contrast to Silverman and Robinson, put greater emphasis on the ambiguity posed by male masochism rather than on its disruptive and "perverse" potential. It is the disruptive effect of masochism, however, that constitutes *the* defining feature within Cobain's writings. Still, all four critics apply the concept of masochism to written texts, films, and other visual images. Whether they are writing about the Beat writers of the 1950s, the emergent countercultural masculinities of the 1960s, or the newer hegemonic forms of masculinities that presented themselves at the end of the twentieth century, Savran, Brintnall, Silverman, and Robinson all confirm two important phenomena. First, masochistic phantasy plays a significant role in determining the content and general aesthetics of the fiction, films, and artwork that these American men authors, cinematographers, and artists produce. And second, masochistic phantasy also plays a symbolic role in many of the real-life experiences of these men and of many other American men as well. Although I do not undertake a reading of Cobain's biography, his life story is also indicative of the symbolic role of masochism to the extent that his creative writings so irreversibly conflate autobiography and phantasy.

It is because masochism within cultural studies has come to designate a particular structure and dynamic within culture and society as a whole that there has arisen, along with what might be termed *social* or *cultural* masochism, the notion of a "masochist text" as a specific genre. I follow the tradition of other writers, such as Sander Gilman and Michael Finke, in using "masochist" as an adjective only when designating this genre of writing. It is a genre to which many of Cobain's writings seem to belong. Gilles Deleuze's critical studies are especially revelatory in this respect because of the way he explores masochism by returning to literature and, specifically, to texts written by the Marquis de Sade and Leopold von Sacher-Masoch. In doing so, Deleuze explores masochism not in order to explain it as a clinical condition but to interrogate how it functions as a literary structure and theatrical event (Thanem and Wallenberg, 2).

As the literary and cultural analyses put forth by Savran, Brintnall, Silverman, and Robinson suggest, the masochist text, though drawing significantly from particular thematic developments concerning physical pain, is not limited to these themes. This kind of writing can develop themes that, on the surface, might not appear connected to the body. In Cobain's journals, for example, writing itself, and composing lyrics specifically, is represented as a masochistic act. Emotionally, writing is excruciatingly painful, but it provides a source of immeasurable pleasure (*Journals,* 33). Further, beyond any particular theme, any text that presents itself as marginal, minority, or as somehow oppositional to the cultural hegemony possesses the potentiality of a masochist text. Going against the odds and the powers that be, as do punk rockers, is inherently masochistic. In this sense, Cobain's antiracist drawings in the Klan images operate as a masochist text, one in which the disappearance of the racist subject is a form of self-destruction since the executed racist and his executioner must be the same white man.

Even though what one can identify as masochism within this genre might have only a metaphorical relation to *individual* psychology, self-abnegation, or self-punishment, the masochist genre does define itself, I argue, by exhibiting a specific relationship between textuality and corporeality, between the written text and living flesh. The body is the engine that propels the masochist text. A critical reading, in particular of Cobain's journal entries, confirms Deleuze's intuition that "the writer's body . . . comes to be an extension of the imagined body of the father" (Gilman, v). Deleuze departs from Freud since he does not envision the father as the father in the oedipal scene, that is, the aggressor who has the potential to overwhelm the son. He is not the imagined father poised to destroy the son, to "castrate, imbue [him] with lack, and turn him into a woman like his mother" (Thanem and Wallenberg, 2). In addition, for Deleuze, the son is not the victim in the male beating phantasy. Rather, the father is the one being beaten. Deleuze asks rhetorically: Is it not the image of the father, which the son recognizes in *himself,* "that is manipulated, beaten, ridiculed, and humiliated? The sin or malefaction that the [masochistic] subject atones for is his resemblance to the father [;] . . . the formula of masochism is the humiliated father" (Deleuze and Sacher-Masoch, 60–61), rendered in the guise of a self-humiliation.

Indeed, at specific junctures, narrators and characters in key entries in Cobain's journals and in some of his lyrics, similar to the prototypical masochistic subject in the Deleuzian sense, experience a specific anxiety, the fear of turning into the father. In addition to representing this fear explicitly in a journal entry such as "Chuck Taylor" and in a song such as "Even in His Youth," the anxiety of turning into the father is merely hinted at in other lyrics and journal fragments as well, including the "Mr. Moustache" comic. As I have demonstrated, this fear is also implicit in the central entry in *Journals.* It is in the first "chorus" of this long entry, we recall, that the father figure is scorned as an old reprobate who is doomed to extermination by his own progeny in a "pool of razor blades and sperm." The entry goes on to suggest, however, that the sons will simply take the place of the fathers to perpetuate the current system of abusive power.[10]

Nevertheless, in Cobain's writings, as is true for most other masochist texts, one must not be too literal. One must not focus exclusively on the thematic, surface structure of the text, just as one must not resort inevitably to biography. With this kind of writing, because one is in the realm of phantasy, one must consider the imaginary realm where subtext and unconscious dynamics predominate. The masochist text, as I define it, signals, foremost and invariably, a divided, conflicted, vulnerable subject, the very essence of the masochistic persona Cobain wishes to inhabit. But instead of exhibiting a masculine fortitude in the face of unbearable pain, and instead of "taking it like a man," the persona Cobain embraces "takes it like a woman." "I parade [my children/my suffering] around in peacock victory and maternal pride," Cobain writes, "like a whore relieved from the duties of repeated rape and torture" (189).

Without exception, however, and as Cobain's writings further attest, the masochist text functions to stage what Sander Gilman terms "the inevitability of decay" that narrators and characters undergo (iv). The nature of this decaying is such that the fading away of the subject, in some form or fashion, constitutes the ultimate storyline that the masochist text attempts to put into motion. "Oh, yeah," writes Cobain in "Critic Goes God," "I've decided to eventually become a H [heroin] addict and slowly decay on the streets" (87). I have argued earlier that the male body constitutes a defining theme in Cobain's writings. I now explore further, and in *theoretical* rather than thematic terms, how and why the male body figures at the very center of Cobain's artistic enterprise and his creation of a masochistic persona. Not only do his creative writings confirm that the genre compulsively deconstructs the male body by representing it in the process of decay, his lyrics and journals frequently suggest that this body is, as I indicate, in the process of "self-aborting."

Masochism and the Male Body in Cobain's Writings: "Abort Christ!"

"Abort Christ" is a provocative graffiti that Cobain allegedly spray-painted on buildings. The slogan does appear strategically in two entries in *Journals* (56, 110). The imperative to eliminate Christ before his birth does not constitute so much a comment on Christianity, or on religious practice in general, as it points to a certain conception of male corporeality. The corporeal disintegration of the body appears more strikingly evident in some of Cobain's drawings and sketches, as apparent in the image of Crybaby Jenkins being dissected, cooked, eaten, digested, and excreted, as discussed in chapter 4. But throughout Cobain's written works as well, the persona he creates is compulsively returning to his own experience of a debilitated, prostrated body.

I allude to some of Cobain's visual art as found in his notebooks and on album covers. But I concentrate in this chapter on his written texts in order to explore not only how the narrators and characters he invents understand their physical pain and psychical suffering, but also how they endeavor to *name* their distress and discomfort. Although the aesthetics and politics within Cobain's writings are structured around representations of the male body, the very nature of these representations confirm that this body is not conceived as an object that is purely biologically determined. The body Cobain represents is culturally and historically specific (white, male, heterosexual, American, late twentieth-century), but his lyrics and journals put forth a body that is not static. Rather, it is malleable.[11]

Not only is the male body within Cobain's texts explicitly represented as coming undone, it is represented metaphorically as devolving into its origins as "a waste of sperm and egg." In addition to writing this expression in his journals, Cobain repeats it in the liner notes to *Incesticide* to describe a certain kind of young white man attracted to Nirvana's music.[12] As a close reading of *Journals* makes clear, the masculine identity of the persona Cobain wishes to appropriate is rooted in an irrepressible sense of alienation from his own physical being. KurDt resists his own corporeality. It is in this sense that he inhabits the body of a masochist, deriving pleasure from his corporeal weakness and pain.

Though more manifest in certain journal entries, in his lyrics as well, Cobain's creative talent seems to burst forth from an existential need that is both spiritual/intellectual and physiological, as in "Spank Thru." This need is represented as an inscription on and in the body; it is evoked as an excruciating wounding, a kind of aching void, as if his narrators and characters were missing a limb. In the journal fragment immediately preceding "Triple Suicide," Cobain writes, in the afflicted voice of KurDt, "I can't speak, I can only feel. Maybe someday I'll turn myself into Hellen [*sic*] Keller by puncturing my ears with a knife, then cutting my voice box out" (125). Crybaby Jenkins, as I suggest, embodies the ultimate example of a character who is completely dispossessed of all of his body parts and functions.

If fans read Cobain's lyrics and journals as autobiographical, in the strict sense, then they will come to an inevitable conclusion: The texts Cobain writes or the images he draws do not meet the need or heal the wounding his writings so eerily evoke. On the contrary, in his effort to understand his psychical suffering and to alleviate his physical pain, Cobain ends up producing writings and drawings that increase his affliction (Hervey and Higgins, 39), assuming, of course, that Cobain's person and his persona can be made to seamlessly coincide.[13] It is evident from certain journal entries, like "A Leonard Cohen Afterworld" (191) and from certain lyrics like "Pennyroyal Tea," how these texts do not compensate for Cobain's lack, a void that both causes his wounding and results from it. Rather, Cobain's texts reopen and probe his wound more deeply:

> Sit and drink Pennyroyal Tea
> Distill the life that's inside of me
> . . .
> I'm anemic royalty
> Give me a Leonard Cohen afterworld
> So I can sigh eternally

The persona that Cobain creates, in his lyrics overall, represents his body as the locus and the very essence of his being. But it is indeed in his journals, most noticeably, that his body is evoked as especially debilitated, that is, emaciated and chronically in pain. Cobain writes, for example, of his "enemic [sic], rodent-like body" (72), and he phantasizes about returning to an elusive home where, giving in completely to his malnourishment, he can savor suffering.

Cobain's representation of the male body, like representations of the suffering male body in general as Brintnall theorizes it, constructs meaning in a complicated, often contradictory way. Within contemporary Western culture—given the impact of Christianity—one cannot entirely separate representations in general of male bodies in pain, as found in Hollywood action films for example, from representations of Christ's crucified body. Contemporary representations of the suffering male body, as Brintnall confirms, signify in the same way as does the body executed at Calvary. Therefore, Cobain's lyrical and narrative representations of the male body, taken as a composite, can be examined on one level as an analogue of the representations of the crucified body of Christ, as it appears within certain theological discourses and iconography.

The Christian masochist, observes Silverman, "seeks to remake himself . . . according to the model of the suffering Christ, the very picture of earthly divestiture and loss. Insofar as such an identification implies the complete and [seemingly] definitive negation of all phallic values, Christian masochism has radically emasculating implications" (198). Cobain's written and visual texts, however, confirm Brintnall's conclusion that the cultural and ideological meanings of images of the male-body-in-pain are not necessarily self-evident, coherent, or unchanging. In representing the male-body-in-pain in a complex manner, Cobain's creative writings are often opaque and self-contradicting lyrical and narrative fragments.

If the crucified body of Christ represents the ultimate image of bloody, suffering flesh, then it is worth underscoring the obvious: "The body on the cross is a *male* body. It figures a decidedly *failed* masculinity" (Brintnall, "Masculinity, Masochism and the Crucifixion,"1, emphasis added). Within Christian discourse and ethics, however, Christ's wounded body is presented as one to be admired and emulated, even though it contradicts the phantasied strong, impenetrable body of patriarchy. Therefore, Christianity writ large has a curious— if not immediately obvious—parallel to the cultural and philosophical discussions, as well as to some of the images, in Cobain's journals. As I have suggested in chapters 3 and 4, Cobain seems to have been captivated if not by the image then by the very notion of Christ. We see signs of this fascination in the lyrics to "In His Room" and "Been a Son," in the storyboards for the "Heart Shaped Box" video, and in his covers of the Vaselines' "Jesus Don't Want Me for a Sunbeam" and Lead Belly's version of "They Hung Him on a Cross." Lead Belly's song, for example, contains the following lines that underscore the symbolic function of the abused body of Christ: "They whooped him up the hill" / "They bit him in the side" / "They hung him on the cross" / "He hung his head and died. *For me*" (emphasis added).[14]

The last line of "They Hung Him on a Cross," as revealed later in chapter 6, finds echoes in the postscript to Cobain's suicide letter. This letter, too, presents death as a self-sacrifice—in the guise of an execution—motivated by a divine love for followers. Finally, "Abort Christ" is the implicit message embedded within the "Chuck Taylor" entry in *Journals*. In writing the serial killer's biography, Cobain creates his own Kafkaesque version of the holy family. Chuck begins his life, after all, as the infant son of Mary and Joseph (Taylor); he is the Christ child that should have been aborted.

In addition to the infamous "Abort Christ" slogan, Cobain's investment in the body of Christ becomes even more manifest when one examines specific features of some of his unpublished visual art. According to Charles Cross, Cobain not only stole crucifixes to provide materials for his multidimensional art, he also produced images in a way that signals that he was both enamored and disdainful of hangings and crucifixions in general (*Cobain Unseen*, 9, 19). This fascination and disdain are evident, as revealed in chapter 4, in several images in *Journals*, including some very Christ-like self-portraits. Whatever the context of these specific images, Cobain seems fixated on producing images of men or boys, like the narrator in "Sliver," under duress or coming undone. The back cover of *In Utero* also reveals this fixation. Cobain has described the cover as "sex and woman and In Utero and vaginas and birth and death" (Gerber). But the collage actually depicts a jumble of umbilical cords and placentas, drawing attention to a confused mass of putatively male fetuses/infants captured in various stages of incompleteness. The cover constitutes an image for which it is unclear if the collage represents a fetus that is evolving into a child or devolving into its constituent components of sperm and egg. For many of Cobain's images, the body on the cross could have served as an inspiration to the extent that his images, too, often foreground the male body either in pain or fading away, becoming dematerialized.

Since the masculinity of Christ is put forth as willfully self-sacrificing, it must be read as masochistic. Yet, as I indicate, most representations of masochistic phantasy according to Silverman, Savran, and Brintnall invariably end up reinventing or reinforcing phallicism and hegemonic masculinity. This kind of return to phallicism, as Brintnall makes clear, is most evident in the very notion of the resurrection of Christ, just as in the Hollywood action film this return to a phallic modality surfaces in the revenge and rebirth scenarios of the masochistic hero that Rambo or Rocky embodies. Although the masochistic phantasy that Cobain's texts enact does not appear to return to or to reinforce phallicism, his texts do retain, nonetheless, the potential to valorize patriarchal values in another way.

Even though the persona Cobain takes on appropriates a feminine cultural and social position, his texts marginalize women as characters, as in the "Mr. Moustache" comic. His signature lyrics and journals invariably reduce the world to fathers and sons.[15] Most significantly, in the production, distribution, and preservation of punk rock—which is represented as the defining mission of the persona in which Cobain seems to lose himself—all the principal players are men. In spite of a professed love and reverence for women, Cobain's signature texts, just like his suicide letter, represent girlfriends, wives, sisters, and mothers as passive observers of a masculine performance. His signature texts represent the circumscription of women in this manner, even while his creative writings, overall, represent the contagion and the iniquity of conventional masculinity.

But in spite of the way Cobain's writings reinforce patriarchal values by marginalizing women protagonists, his lyrics and journals still allow readers to recognize and then analyze the literary text as a creative site of masculine self-rescission and self-effacement. Some of Cobain's journal entries as well as some of his songs, like "Been a Son," demonstrate, in addition, how certain representations of masculinity expose the illogic and the tragedy of the cultural consequences of gender difference:

> She should have stayed away from friends
> She should have had more time to spend
> She should have died when she was born
> She should have worn the crown of thorns

Considered as an ensemble, it is these Cobain texts that prompt readers to question notions of male superiority as well as myths of masculine plenitude and self-sufficiency. In this way, Cobain's texts function, both overtly and covertly, to belie three defining features of patriarchal culture: (1) That there are only two genders that are distinct and counterposed, (2) that masculinity is characterized by mental fortitude and by corporeal strength, durability, and reliability, and (3) that heterosexuality is the only natural and valid form of desire. Consequently, the texts Cobain pens do not merely embrace castration, androgyny, and queer sexuality, they do so with varying degrees of exultant defiance. Thus, the masochistic elements in Cobain's writings confirm Brintnall's conclusion that every male masochistic phantasy that one finds in literary and cinematic texts "serve to expose the illusion that [patriarchal culture] . . . sustains" ("Masculinity, Masochism and the Crucifixion," 40) concerning the naturalness and superiority of heteromasculinity. Cobain's texts expose this illusion, as do the masochist texts and images Brintnall describes, by severing what seems to be the inherent and indivisible bond that links penis and phallus together, that binds the symbolic (ideology) and the real (actions).

Within Cobain's oeuvre, this disjoining of penis and phallus is not necessarily intentional, even though the persona Cobain insistently takes on seems to be acutely attuned to the ramifications of this decoupling when he is presenting his verbal and visual self-portraits. Cobain's alter ego seems especially sensitive to the difference between the penis and phallus in those lyrics and journal entries in which he longs for his own castration, whether represented as real, as in "Spank Thru," or as symbolic, as in "In His Room." Cobain's lyrics and journal entries, overall, expose the phallus to be what Ellie Ragland, a scholar of English literature and Lacanian psychoanalysis, describes as "a mask." And his texts expose "normative sexual prescriptions . . . as a comic masquerade" (4). Ragland, who draws from Lacan's theory of gender identification, does not write about Cobain but about the camouflaging nature of masculine identity within patriarchal culture in general.

Masochism and the Invisibility of the Penis in *Journals*

After Cobain's death, fans on line frequently speculated about the size of his penis, how he used it, and the gender of his partners. His widow is the source of some of the mythology surrounding Cobain's "member," most conspicuously perhaps in a 2011 interview she gave *GQ* magazine. *GQ*'s objective was to celebrate the twentieth anniversary of the release of *Nevermind.* In responding to a question about her late husband's legacy as a musician, Courtney Love offers this simple, though somewhat perplexing, assessment: "Kurt had more presence and more beauty than Brad Pitt—who wanted to play Kurt, by the way. He was a leader, he was strong, in fact he was well fucking hung, if you really want to know" (Goodwyn). The quote incited hundreds of posts and articles on social media with titles such as "Just in Case You Wanted to Know about Cobain's Junk"; "Kurt Cobain Had a Giant Penis"; "Kurt Cobain's Beautiful Soul and Sizeable Dick," etc.

The *GQ* interview was not the first time Love had made a reference to her husband's anatomy, his sexual prowess, and their conjugal activities. However, it is this 2011 interview that seems to have first generated so many online comments about Cobain's "manhood." The interest in, and one might say the obsession with, Cobain's penis may have peaked with the brouhaha surrounding a YouTube video that allegedly shows Cobain exposing himself during a performance. Different versions of this video, titled "Kurt Cobain Shows His Dick," had been viewed tens of thousands of times between 2014 and 2018. Viewers have engaged in a spirited debate concerning whether or not the organ is actually visible in the clip and, if so, the specifics of its girth, length, and overall significance for Cobain's masculinity and his legacy within American popular culture.[16]

I have already examined in chapter 3 how possession of the penis emerges as problematic within Cobain's lyrics. I have also mentioned the one visual depiction of the penis in *Journals*. It is beyond the scope of this book to present a detailed examination of Cobain's multidimensional art, his drawings, sketches, and paintings. It is worth noting, though, that in addition to representing the male body as diseased, deformed, disarticulated, and in the process of decaying, Cobain's visual art also frequently depicts male genitalia as troublesome. Two online images attributed to Cobain are suggestive of how his artwork conceives of the penis as vexatious and the male body, as a whole, as unremittingly unsavory.[17]

Reminiscent of the "Crybaby Jenkins" comic, one painting features a collage composed of a fetus, a human face, and an image of what appear to be several other detached body parts, including the outline of a male-appearing face, a head in profile, and an erect penis. A second painting, inscribed with the names of bodily deformations and afflictions ("fistula," "rectal abscess," "spinabiffida" [*sic*]), also features, among other images, the outline of a male form and two humanoid-marionettes with detachable limbs. One of the marionettes possesses a protruding appendage that could be an outsized but unformed fetal penis. In addition to these images, Cross writes about allegedly lost or privately held paintings, possibly from Cobain's early to middle adolescence, that include several images of Satan displaying a huge, erect penis (*Cobain Unseen,* 94). In these images, Satan's erection would seem to symbolize the same venality that phallic masculinity represents in Cobain's written texts.

However, Cobain's most arresting images, as they appear in his published journals, show covered male bodies. But since he set outs explicitly in his overall creative writings to problematize hegemonic masculinity and patriarchal privilege, the absence of any explicit discourse on the penis, in this expansive text specifically, seems surprising and contradictory. Unlike in his lyrics, there is no slang for the male organ, which is virtually invisible as an object of reflection in his published notebooks. The word "penis" appears as a near-afterthought in four entries. The first two instances are connected thematically, though separated by thirty pages. In each instance, the word surfaces in an isolated, parenthetical, and puzzling manner: "John lennons [sic] Penis" (3) and "Penis balloon insertion for everyone" (31). Though occurring at different points in the text, these two references are describing scenes from an amateur movie, as the text specifies, filmed by KurDt and some unnamed friends:

> in Tacoma at NEVER NEVERLAND. it's a surrealistic fantasy story book place for kids. And we made Shelli wear a mask of Cher's head and dance around by big mushrooms and butt fuck the wolf bending over to blow down the three little pigs house. Other stars included Rick Derringer and John lennons Penis. (3)

In these entries, the emphasis is not on the penis as a penetrating organ, but rather on the rectum as an orifice to be penetrated. The limited visibility of the penis thus raises an intriguing question: What might account for the constrained visibility and the absence of any explicit discourse on the male organ in Cobain's notebooks?[18]

Within patriarchal culture, the mystique of the phallus, as Susan Bordo reveals in *The Male Body,* both results from and depends on the penis remaining invisible. The phallus retains its power because its emblem and its double, the penis, is kept hidden. It is especially the tumescent organ—the state that exposes symbolically the inconstancy and the vulnerability of hegemonic masculinity—that must remain hidden. Cobain's lyrics, as opposed to his journals, do indeed counter the power and mystique of the phallus. In this sense, the message in a song like "Spank Thru"—which contains lyrics that expose and ridicule the penis—would appear to countermand the subtending message in Cobain's journals as they were first published in 2002. Because the penis is inconspicuous in the written entries in this text, Cobain would seem to be unwittingly complicit with the very ideology that he sets out insistently and explicitly in his lyrics to undermine.

In *Bad Objects,* Naomi Schor echoes Bordo. She also argues that "to subject the penis to representation is to strip the phallus of its empowering veil . . . [because] while the phallus can be said to draw its symbolic power from the *visibility of the penis,* [actual] phallic power derives precisely from the phallus's inaccessibility to representation" (112). In *Running Scared,* Peter Lehman also points out that to represent the penis is to erode the mystique of the phallus because "in patriarchal culture, where the penis is hidden, it is centered. To show, write, or talk about the penis creates the potential to demystify it and thus decenter it" (28). In *The Shock of Men*, Lawrence Schehr builds upon Shor's and Lehman's arguments to conclude that it is not fortuitous that "the penis has been the most hidden of male body parts because of the ideological . . . temptation to turn the penis into its evil twin brother, the phallus" (16).

Yet a significant portion of Cobain's discursive enterprise, in representing masculinity as corrupt and corrupting, is predicated implicitly on demystifying the phallus. Ordinarily, then, the progressive, cultural politics found in his writings would require exposing the penis as often as possible as a vulnerable organ rather than a powerful weapon. As I indicate, this tactic is precisely the one Cobain takes in his lyrics. In spite of the seeming contradiction, however, he also employs this tactic implicitly when writing his journals. Because Cobain's writings expose masculinity as a problematic process, the testerical features within his journals, just as in his lyrics, stem in part from an absolute refusal to equate penis and phallus in the first place. Although articulated explicitly in his lyrics, Cobain's journal entries—in putting forth a masochistic subject—also refuse to equate the organ with its emblem. In the brief instances where the penis appears within his notebooks, in addition to the organ's penetrative potential being called into question, it is the receptive eventuality of male orifices that comes to define the essence of masculinity. In this sense, Love's assertion in *GQ* goes counter to the very nonphallic core of Cobain's own carefully cultivated persona.

It is precisely because Cobain's notebooks represent masculinity as testerical and *masochistic* that these fragments refrain from conflating penis and phallus. Again, as in his lyrics but taking a different tactic, Cobain's journals put forth subjugated or masochistic narrators and characters who do not return to a phallic mode as their natural state. By representing a perversion of gender and sexual norms, the ensemble of Cobain's writings demonstrates how masochism and testeria can function as a social and political critique, one that calls into question not only conventional masculine behavior but also the very nature of the male body.

One can argue that Cobain's creative texts narrate a specific kind of crucifixion, a self-crucifixion, but one that affirms that no resurrection is forthcoming. His journal entries as well as his lyrics operate necessarily to problematize the resurrection/erection that defines the crucified or self-crucifying masochistic hero.[19] The persona Cobain insists on projecting appears to eschew the possibility of a return to a phallic mode, to some kind of heroism that characterizes the typical masochistic phantasy as it plays itself out most auspiciously in contemporary American film and fiction. It is in this way that his texts operate to erode "the banks of the masculine self" (Brintnall, "Masculinity, Masochism and the Crucifixion," 41) and, therein, that they function, in spite of their contradictions, as a sustained critique of conventional masculinity and patriarchal culture.

When considered as an ensemble, Cobain's creative texts operate as an imaginative, creative space in which the writer—by way of the white, hetero-masculine persona he adopts—reveals his external dangers and his inherent vulnerabilities. These texts constitute a privileged space in which the writer can examine, from the safe distance of a carefully crafted persona, his problematic relation to normative masculinity and thus his relation to cultural authority and power. He can safely assume a feminine position, seemingly without beating a hasty retreat to a heroic, phallic stance that reaffirms masculine unity and completeness. Still, one might be tempted to read the *phantasy of suicide,* as represented in Cobain's lyrics and journals, as a phallic gesture, a desire to return to a conventional masculine mode of strength and control. Thus one might be tempted to read these texts themselves, like "Triple Suicide," as ultimate signs of a phallic discourse.

But one can argue just as convincingly against this interpretation of suicide as phallic and as a heroic act for two principal reasons. First, such an interpretation runs counter to the profile, the strategy, and the aesthetics of the masochistic persona as he is represented within Cobain's writings. In his texts, the masochistic persona he creates is arrantly nonphallic and manifestly testerical in his abnegation of traditional masculine thinking and behavior. Second, interpreting suicide as a recourse to phallic values complicates, if it does not completely negate, the profile of the male masochist as psychoanalytic theory describes him. This theory establishes that the true masochist is not suicidal at all. In fact, recent theorizing on the subject leads to the conclusion that although masochism and suicidality (suicidal thoughts, plans, and attempts) may be related because both involve self-attack, they follow two distinct trajectories (Loewenstein).

As Mark Goldblatt confirms in "Suicide and Masochism," there can be "a complex interplay between masochism and suicide because they can co-exist as a narcissistically stable structure" (97). They can lean on each other. Masochism, however, does not lead to suicide, but functions rather to protect against it. And, as Cobain's masochistic narrators and characters reveal, in a text like "In His Room," three features must be operative if the suicidal wish is to be fulfilled: not only the wish to kill (sadism) and the wish to be killed (masochism), but also, and most crucially, the wish to die and to be seen dead. The masochist wishes to hurt himself, to debase or humiliate himself, but he does not wish to die. He wishes to suffer and to be seen suffering. Masochism is defensive because it works to preserve both the subject's self-esteem and his life (Bieber).

As I shall explore when examining the Cobain persona as a *melancholic* subject, the wish to die, as opposed to a desire to suffer, enters into the equation when masochism shifts, so to speak, into depression and a loss of self-esteem ensues. The masochist, however, remains hopeful; he endures the pain and suffering because he wishes to perform, to be seen—and to see himself—performing. "Self-attack serves to restore a [delusional] sense of competence and the capacity to cope" (Goldblatt, 98). Self-attack does not signal total resignation, capitulation. Although the masochistic persona Cobain appropriates might be Christ-like in his suffering—which he takes on in order to transform the world in which he lives—his punishment by others and his self-punishment are for naught, even though they do give hope and preserve his self-regard. Generally, the masochistic subject, just like the Cobain persona, functions to expose the culture's abuse and oppression for the world to contemplate. He gives in, necessarily, to this oppression and abuse. That is, the masochist does challenge power, the status quo, but he is an incompetent challenger. He is, especially like the persona Cobain creates in his journals, physically frail ("an underdeveloped spaz" [112]). He recasts himself as a perpetual victim ("strung up by the balls" [145]), rather than a wielder of patriarchal power. He cherishes the spectacle of his crucifixion, but he must remain alive in order to continually enact it.

∞

When considered as an eclectic ensemble of narrative and lyrical texts that represent masculine subjectivity, the discourse within Cobain's journal entries and lyrics—texts that function invariably to subvert phallic law and to challenge the logic of heteronormativity—is clearly predicated on a masochistic subject-position. Not only, however, do Cobain's creative writings buy into patriarchal ethics by marginalizing women, these texts, in zeroing in on hegemonic masculinity as a target to be critiqued and censured, confirm the very power of the hegemony. Texts like the lyrics to "Beeswax" or like the "Chuck Taylor" entry in *Journals* accomplish two contradictory results: they confirm that masochism can subvert phallic masculinity and, at the same time, they reconfirm the centrality and the dominance of this mode of masculinity and the "macho dickheads" who embody it. Everything begins with him; he constitutes the point of reference, the degree zero. Cobain offers a remarkably telling confirmation in the central entry in *Journals*. "At the top of the food chain," KurDt intones in this letter to a girlfriend, "is still the white, corporate, macho, strong ox male.... He's in charge. He decides" (177).

What's a Straight White Man to Do? / Experiencing Heteromasculinity as Oppositional

Cobain's masochist texts succeed partially in destabilizing the strict borders and the binary oppositions that undergird hegemonic culture and via which it operates: sex and gender; masculine and feminine; powerful and powerless; and heterosexual and homosexual. As a result, the persona Cobain creates in these texts is *queer*. Even though he takes on the persona of a straight man who is open to gay possibilities, I am defining "queer" in this instance not in reference to erotic object choice, but as any person or discourse that exposes and then attempts to disrupt or completely dismantle the very logic and privileges of heteronormativity.[20]

Cobain's queer discourse clearly and cleverly relies on masochism for its articulation. But this discourse, notwithstanding its progressive intent and its actual effect, still does not move *beyond* masochism—and phantasies of submission and punishment—in order to reach a more critical and progressive discourse and practice. Such a discourse and practice would put forth a more nuanced critique of heterosexual masculinity. But what else, indeed, is a straight white man to do when he is committed to a profeminist and gay-affirmative politics? Further, if this straight white man is also committed to an antiracist practice, as is the persona Cobain adopts, then he finds himself in a particular quandary.

As I have demonstrated, several of Cobain's journal entries and illustrations do speak to the scourge of racial violence and injustice. That these texts, though, do not appear to operate quite as successfully in destabilizing the border between white and black (as they do other hegemonic oppositions) makes his writings also less effective in offering a critique of whiteness that gets beyond a sentimental, phantasy identification with blackness and that gets beyond guilt: "I'm sorry I'm white." Therefore, one could lodge against Cobain's racial politics, as they emerge within his written texts, the same concern that scholars have raised about the first publications to appear within whiteness studies. The pioneering essays in this field, too, did not initially move beyond "positions of guilt or resentment [and] towards a more critical whiteness studies that would provide a more 'nuanced, dialectical, and layered account of whiteness'" (Huq, 136–37, citing Giroux).

I take my subtitle above—"What's a straight white man to do?"—from George Yudice's 1995 essay. He published the provocative, seemingly plaintive piece in a collection of well-intentioned essays titled *Constructing Masculinity*. The collection attempts in various ways to respond to this fundamental question. Some of the more compelling essays in the collection are literary analyses that examine the political strategies and cultural aesthetics of straight white male characters and narrators as they appear in late twentieth-century American films and fiction. This manifestly perplexing question is the very one that is posed implicitly between the lines of nearly every Cobain text that presents itself as the articulation of a resisting cultural and political ideology within what is presented as a heterosexist, sexist, and racist social order.

Unsurprisingly, Cobain's writings do not present a straightforward, definitive response to the question posed to and by some straight white men. Even though his texts put forth only the beginnings of a critique of whiteness, specific songs, like "Laminated Effects" and "Even in His Youth," and specific journal entries, like the "Heart Shaped Box" storyboards, do invite, on the contrary, a specific kind of queer *reading* and thus a more sustained critique of heterosexuality. In the preface to *Straight Writ Queer: Non-Normative Expressions of Heterosexuality in Literature,* Richard Fantina convincingly argues that there are ways presumptively "straight" texts can incorporate a queer, heterosexual critique of heteronormativity. This critique necessarily points to a theory of gender and sexual identity as fluid. Although none of the essays in Fantina's collection takes on Cobain, his lyrics and journals, nevertheless, constitute a critique of heterosexuality, one that presupposes a fluid gender and sexuality.

Still, the major thrust within Cobain's aesthetics and cultural politics compels us to ask what has become, in some recent scholarship on men and masculinities, another vexing question: Given the way that power and privilege operate, can heterosexual men ever pursue a credible and sustainable opposition to the masculinist social and cultural hegemony, an order from which they inevitably benefit?[21] Like other progressive texts, Cobain's creative writings—as evident, for example, in his unsent letter to *The Advocate*—envisions queerness as the logical site for opposition and disruption to heteronormativity. The persona that Cobain envisions, however, identifies as straight, even though he then leans into a self-queering.

As a result, Cobain's queer discourse suggests that heteromasculinity itself possesses progressive, if not radical potential. His texts do not represent straight identity as an unchanging and unchangeable monolith. That is, by embracing his heterosexual experience and psychical makeup, the persona with which Cobain is so enamored—and thus Cobain's queer discourse—refuses to conflate heteromasculinity with hetero*normativity*, homophobia, or misogyny. His writings suggest that in an ideal world, heteromasculinity can and ought to be a site of social change. The persona Cobain takes on would seem to experience his sexuality as being at variance with the norm, but not necessarily as its obverse. In this same sense, KurDt's actions allow for what Chris Beasley proposes, in his critique of heterosexual orthodoxy, as "a politics of the personal; that is, a deviation from the heteromasculine norm that is transgressive, even if it is not radical and part of a social movement" (136).

A close examination of the gender performance of Cobain's alter ego indicates that heterosexuality is indeed represented as plural, such that it can be innovative and disruptive by being indiscreet, mischievous, and offensive in order "to piss off the homophobes" (*Journals,* 192). In this sense, a progressive, heterosexual subject can be, as the title of Ann Powers's essay suggests and as the slogan goes, *"gay in the streets, straight in the sheets."* The persona Cobain so meticulously constructs would be part of a small subgroup known during the 1990s as "queer straights." Ron Becker includes the real Kurt Cobain in this small group of musicians and actors that includes Madonna, Sharon Stone, and Sandra Bernhard. These performers, Becker argues, "continued to have heterosexual sex in the bedroom but cultivated a public image of gender and sexual ambiguity" (132). This group also includes certain noncelebrities and academics like Judith Butler and Eve Kosofsky Sedgwick, all of whom, like Cobain's alter ego, have sought at various times and in various ways to distance themselves from heterosexuality as an oppressive institution and practice.

They have sought, again like the narrator in *Journals,* to forge instead a new, flexible gender and sexual identity.[22]

Therefore, even though the defiant persona Cobain takes to heart ("I wish I were gay" [*Journals,* 192]) and the resisting subject-position found in his signature texts can be considered queer simply because they embrace intragender sexuality, they can also be considered queer in another way and for another reason. Since the very inception of queer theory, scholars have theorized the possibility of the queer straight man. That is, queer theory has always made allowances for nonnormative modes and practices of heterosexuality because the theory calls into question any natural or facile conflation of erotic phantasy and practice, on the one hand, and identity on the other.[23] Scholars and activists problematize this conflation in such a way that queer theory precludes the notion that eroticism might reveal an essential "truth" about an individual. As I have also shown, in Cobain's creative texts, "gay" describes what a narrator or character does; it does not define who they are.

In the case of the alter ego that Cobain projects, as Calvin Thomas writes about the disruptive potential of heterosexual practice in general, "queer" can be taken to designate not an alternative identity, "but an alternative *to* identity, 'less an identity than a *critique* of identity'; as an 'anti-identitarian identity'" ("Foreword," 3).[24] Not only Cobain's creative productions specifically, but popular music studies in general, because of the very nature of the object of study, would be significantly advanced by calling upon the interpretive potential of queer theory. It is "the *homosocial* dimension of popular music culture," attests Warren Zanes, that "requires the introduction of queer theory" (306). Moreover, Cobain's creative texts confirm that it is imperative that all of popular music scholarship mobilize queer theory precisely because of the way that the theory itself has mobilized psychoanalysis. The queer critique and critical appropriation of psychoanalytic aesthetics, as found in the works of scholar-activists like Edelman, Bersani, and Butler, prove that the interpretive value of queer theory extends beyond the study of queer creative productions, acts, and audiences, as narrowly defined.

A careful reading of Cobain's creative writings confirms that even though the creation of a masochistic persona might not mean a *conscious,* complete, and continuous subversion of gender and sexual norms, this creation does always point to, and is underpinned by, representations of a problematic masculine identity. I shall suggest one cause, as well as a direct consequence, of this troublesome identity when I explore in detail the role of melancholy as a theme and as a topic of reflection within Cobain's writings. As indicated in part I of this study, there is a relationship between masochism and melancholy in Cobain's lyrics and journals. Masochism in his creative writings modulates into melancholy in the same way a song might shift from a major to a minor key. One hears a single note of this modulation, for example, in the following sentence, a revealing snippet that is inserted into an otherwise opaque, rambling, disjointed, 450-word journal entry titled "Censorship is VERY American": "I am now in my *sad* style, before it was naïve [self-] *hate*" (112, emphasis added). It is, however, in other discrete texts that Cobain composes—including his suicide letter—that his writing can be heard the most clearly in the process of shifting from a major to a minor key.

6 THE PLEASURES OF DEATH
Creating a Melancholic Persona

As my analysis of the Cobain persona as masochistic reveals, masochism in the grunge musician's creative writings logically leads to a conceptual analysis and to the posing of specific theoretical questions. These questions concern the acquisition and exercise of cultural power in relation to experiences of the male body and masculinity. But, as suggested at the conclusion of the previous chapter, getting at the dynamics that structure the representation of masculinity in Cobain's writings requires an investigation into how masochism in his texts modulates into and alternates with melancholy. The difference between songs like "Drain You" and "Milk Me," on the one hand, and "Spank Thru" and "Beeswax," on the other, reflects the way the persona that Cobain takes on vacillates between masochism and melancholy and between mania and depression. The perspective in these songs shifts from a male subject who is seeking a seamless, euphoric fusion with a female self/other—in order to reclaim his femininity— to a subject who is seeking, disconsolately, to excise the very emblems of his maleness and masculinity.

Freud clearly establishes that there is, necessarily, an observable degree of masochism in melancholy. In "melancholia," he writes, there is a lowering of the subject's self-esteem that brings on masochistic self-reproaches and a self-reviling, resulting "in a delusional expectation of punishment" ("Mourning and Melancholia," 252).[1] In addition, as Mark Quellette observes, "As the internalization of grief, melancholia has a masochistic component" (202). The subject takes his own failings and the woes of world upon himself. As with the masochist, with the melancholic, too, one observes a subject who is harshly judging and severely disciplining himself. Readers encounter just such a self-judgmental and self-disciplinary role on the part of narrators and characters in many of Cobain's lyrics and journal entries.

Merely characterizing the linkage between melancholy and masochism in this manner already illuminates a key feature of Cobain's writings. He produces texts that evoke the complex interrelations between anxiety ("What else can I do?"); depression ("Look on the bright side, there's suicide"); guilt ("It's all my fault"); mourning ("Here I am . . . I have died"); *and* aggression ("Kill the homophobes!"). All these lyrics and journal fragments point inexorably to a conflicted and self-defeating masculine persona. Because aggression is turned inward, the self-berating melancholic resembles the self-torturing masochist in key ways that become evident in Cobain's texts. Both the melancholic and the masochist operate according to the same psychical mechanism. Both are keenly attuned to their problematic relation to alterity, including the outside world and their own bodies, and both ascribe to an ideal which they fail to live up to. Like the very essence of the masochistic persona Cobain so fervently takes on, the melancholic persona he embraces is also endlessly regretting and mourning an ideal, unified self that never existed.

It is precisely because melancholy, more so than masochism, involves a complex overlay of grief and anxiety with aggression that the melancholic subject sets out, in the end, to annihilate himself. He is bereft and overwhelmed with disquietude. The evident overlaying of masochism and melancholy, however, does not mean that the one can be unproblematically collapsed into the other. An inescapable tension exists between the two conditions. Through a reading of Cobain's masochist texts in the previous chapter, I have shown why scholars like Silverman, Deleuze, and Ryalls are correct to theorize masochism primarily in terms of desire, pleasure, and power. I will now explore, in a recapitulation of the major themes and the unique structuring of Cobain's signature texts, how melancholy can be theorized more pointedly in terms of identity and alterity, self and other. The persona of which Cobain seems so enamored displays "symptoms" of both conditions.

As I explore how melancholy appears conceptually and rhetorically in Cobain's creative writings, my objective in this chapter is twofold. In the first section, I demonstrate why, for a fuller understanding of melancholy, one must consider the insights of Melanie Klein and of certain theorists within gender and feminist studies. These insights help identify how melancholy functions in Cobain's texts specifically as a *gendered* performance of grief. Further, in calling attention to the relationship that exists between melancholy and clinical depression, I explore how melancholy, in cultural history as well as in psychoanalytic theory, has been characterized predominantly as a masculine form of expression. I go on to demonstrate how this same tradition of melancholy as masculine is manifested or contradicted in Cobain writings.

In the second section of the chapter, I draw from the writings of French feminist writers, in particular from Julia Kristeva's theory of melancholy and her literary analysis of French Romantic poetry, in order to explore how melancholy in Cobain's writings operates in a dual manner. I demonstrate how grieving functions, in the first instance, as a catalyst for the creation of poetry and poetic prose, and, in the second, as confirmation that death by suicide is idealized as the ultimate act of resistance on the part of a specific kind of dispossessed and bereft young man.

THE COBAIN PERSONA, MELANCHOLY, AND REPRESENTING POSTMODERN MASCULINITY

I begin my exploration of the melancholic persona that Cobain's lyrics and journals construct by identifying the four categories of theory scholars have advanced over the centuries to explain how melancholy and melancholic personalities emerge. A summary account of these theories illuminates the distinct manner in which Cobain's lyrics and journal fragments, as an ensemble, constitute a textual production of melancholy. This summary also reveals how Cobain's texts represent a psychical and a corporeal reaction to loss.

Historians and theorists have accounted for melancholy in four principal ways. First, they have proposed biological theories that explain melancholy as an imbalance in bodily humors or as a disturbance in brain chemistry. Second, writers have resorted to astrological and cosmological theories wherein melancholics either are born under the sign of Saturn, they lack sufficient religious faith, or they are possessed by the devil. Third, experts have relied on theories of loss that posit melancholy as a condition resulting from impossible mourning for a personal, unconscious, and unconscionable loss. And, fourth, observers have put forth cultural causation theories that explain melancholy as resulting from socialization (including experiences of gender), cultural traumas, or social losses.

Notwithstanding the different theories put forth by writers over the years, every Cobain biographer draws attention to his melancholy, including

Azerrad, Stanford, True, and Cross in particular. They take pains to document his apparent, episodic, and seemingly inexplicable bouts of depression and his overall depressive personality. In addition, as noted in part I of this study, most of the critical essays on Cobain's music and lyrics identify melancholy as an inspiration for his songs, if not as the very root of his creative genius. Soulsby, for example, writes of the incessant "venting spleen that runs throughout [Cobain's] lyrical output" (*Dark Slivers,* chap. 3). In fact, music historians and journalists often characterize the entire grunge scene, like Seattle and the Pacific Northwest in general, as infused with a palpable gloom and melancholy. Justin Henderson writes of "the sense of desperation expressed by many of the bands on the scene" (8). Citing graphic designer Art Chantry, Henderson paints a clichéd, Goth-inspired picture of the region, a version of which appears in nearly every description of Seattle in general, but especially during the grunge years:

We have more unsolved serial killings here [in the Northwest] than any other place in the United States. I mean the Manson family used to vacation up this way. This place is weird—a lot of occult stuff. All this stuff is a factor in what happened in the music. Toss in soft gray unrelenting rain, add a shot of end-of-the continent isolation, stir in the countless other ingredients . . . that make rock-and-roll re-invent itself every few years, and you have a moment. (8)

Finally, Cobain himself writes poignantly about melancholic symptoms and episodes, even though, as I suggest below, he frequently misidentifies sadness as anger and aggression. Still, he accurately captures the essence of melancholy when he imagines himself in his published journals, for example, as "a manic depressive on smack" (114). He does so again when, in KurDt's distinctive voice, Cobain concludes the central entry in this text by linking depression to the weather and to the physical condition of his body. "I can't wait to be back home," KurDt laments, "(wherever that is) in bed, neurotic and malnourished and complaining how the weather sucks and it's the whole reason for my misery" (182). In addition, Cobain subtly evokes a melancholic sensibility in several songs, as he does forthrightly in other songs like "Lithium": "I'm so lonely / That's okay, I shaved my head / And I'm not sad." Therefore, in any sustained analysis of his written texts, one is called upon to pay attention to this particular affect, that is to say, to the melancholic emotions and structures of feelings that his writings represent on the part of the narrators and characters he creates. As Jennifer Radden specifies, however:

> To ask about a person's [or a character's] emotional functioning . . . is to ask as many as six questions, not just one. What types of feelings are these? Which kinds of situations elicit these feelings? What do the feelings signify for those experiencing them? What rules of appropriateness guide the expression or display of these feelings? When they are not expressed or displayed, how are these feelings "handled"? Emotions have meaning. To understand a person's emotional life, it is necessary to engage in a conceptual analysis. (51)

According to psychoanalytic theory writ large—and as articulated specifically by Freud in "Mourning and Melancholia"—a venerated love object that has been lost sets both mourning and melancholy in motion. Both mourning and melancholy entail a narcissistic identification with the lost object. Whereas mourning is an external process and condition, melancholy functions internally. "Melancholia's internal functioning reflects a situation in which the missing [and cherished] object is something lacking in the melancholic person him[self]" (Quellette, 202). The melancholic feels responsible for this loss, which explains why he attempts to alleviate his guilt by attacking and punishing himself. Further, mourning, according to Freud, is a normal reaction to a real, concrete loss; it signals that the process is successful. Melancholy, by contrast, is a pathological reaction, a fixation on the loss of something that may have been possessed only in phantasy. Melancholy signals that mourning has failed.

Within the fields of literary and cultural studies, Freud's writings have been enormously influential in shaping current views on melancholy and its relation to identity, alterity, and loss. Although he was not the first to link melancholy to loss, in portraying melancholy as a narcissistic disorder of loss that is intricately tied to notions of identity and otherness, Freud was laying out a substantially new theory with enormous explicative potential. The major change he instantiates, by tying experiences of loss to a disorder of self and self-identity, operated to further shift the meaning of melancholy from earlier understandings of it. Melancholy ceased to constitute a simple mood of dejection and disquiet to become a complex and fixed disposition, a permanent process of grieving. It became a way of existing in and experiencing the world, an existence characterized most fundamentally not only by a lack of something (experienced as a "loss"), but also by harsh self-criticisms.

In Cobain's texts, too, melancholy is represented as more than an emotion. It is put forth, as I have explored, as a particular way of being masculine and heterosexual in a misogynist and homophobic social and cultural order. The combination of the loss of a part of the self and the loss of self-regard emerges implicitly as a theme in several of Cobain's lyrics, like "All Apologies." And this theme emerges beguilingly in the following journal entry: "I started it first. It was me. I'm the one. I was the originator. I'll take the blame. I was doing it long before anyone. . . . I'll take full responsibility. . . . Blame me. Point the finger at me. Here's my receipt. Where do I sign? Give me whats [*sic*] rightfully mine, give me what I deserve" (130).

In spite of the importance of Freud's thinking on my reading of Cobain's texts as literary representations of melancholy, his theory has limitations in its capacity to serve as a template for diagramming how Cobain's grunge writings represent melancholy thematically and textually through the use of specific literary techniques. The limits of Freud's theory explain in part why literary critics have felt obliged to modify his theory in their examination of literary representations of loss and grieving during different historical periods.[2] When one considers the constraints of Freudian theory for an analysis of Cobain's writings, Freud's assumption of a normative, masculine model of subjectivity makes his theorizing less apt to account for some of the nuances found in the representations of the persona Cobain works overtime to embrace. For example, Freud's theory does not lead to an understanding of how Cobain's texts represent the process of mourning specifically as performances of a *failed* masculinity, or how his texts shift between representations of masochism and representations of melancholy. Freud neglects, in fact, to make explicit the gender implications of his description of mourning.

In addition, Freud parenthesizes the social implication of melancholy, that is, the degree to which melancholy, though intensely personal, also manifests a social and political dimension, since the condition tells us something significant about the subject's relationship to social and political norms. In this respect also, Freud's descriptions are less likely to illuminate some of the subtle ways Cobain's texts represent the actions and attitudes of the male narrators and characters he invents. For example, the persona Cobain assumes as the narrator in the central entry in his published journals is depicted as single-minded in his desire to transform society and its unjust institutions, including the music industry. He has no other purpose. "We can pose as the enemy," he insists, in order "to infiltrate the mechanics of the system to start its rot from the inside. Sabotage the empire by pretending to play their game" (178).

Therefore, without minimizing the interpretive value of Freud's insights, it is by moving beyond his writings on mourning and by considering how post-Freudians and contemporary, politically progressive scholars have understood melancholy that I bring the discussion back squarely to the function of loss and grieving in Cobain's creative productions. All the contemporary scholars whose writings I draw upon—Judith Butler, Leo Bersani, Jennifer Radden, Juliana Shiesari, Hélène Cixous, and Julia Kristeva—have been influenced, either directly or indirectly, by Melanie Klein's theories. It is Klein's view of subject formation, and in particular the role of unconscious phantasy in the development of subjectivity, that presents an illustrative model for interrogating how masculine identity is represented in Cobain's writings as inherently melancholic. As explored in chapter 4, Klein's notion of unconscious phantasy confirms that phantasy is directly related to the mitigation of anxiety and to how subjects conceive of and experience the body as gendered. One can anticipate, then, that melancholy in Cobain's writings will appear unfailingly as a corporeal manifestation, as embodied.

In these Kleinian-inspired writings, one confronts not only the gender of grieving but also the politics of melancholy, the very features that are under-developed in Freud. Writings on melancholy specifically by Butler, Bersani, and Kristeva pave the way for a more comprehensive understanding of how melancholy in Cobain's texts signals more than a self-defeating retreat from the world. Melancholic actions and reactions invariably appear in Cobain's texts, as evident in the central journal entry, as a mode of cultural and political resistance, not only to the reality of hegemonic power (the military, political institutions) but also to its symbolic effects. These symbolic effects are manifest, for example, in the way certain young men use words to produce rock lyrics and instruments to produce authentic music that will bring about the collapse of the corporate music industry. Cobain's writings confirm that the melancholic can be a hero in the precise manner of the young "punk" narrator in his published journals.

The theories elaborated by the scholars cited above have forced a rethinking not only of the gender and the politics of melancholy, but also a re-examination of how melancholy functions to produce a particular kind of written text in terms of its form. Scholarship by Kristeva and Cixous, for example, helps readers to come to terms with what I identify as the melancholic "structuring" of Cobain's lyrics and journals, including their frequent opacity and the circularity of their internal logic. Kristeva's and Cixous's work helps to draw attention, therefore, to the way the Cobainian text attempts to represent an expressly postmodern experience of masculinity. In particular, this scholarship facilitates an understanding of how Cobain's literary texts have recourse to the techniques of fragmentation and montage. As I have illustrated in examining Cobain's journals in particular, he employs these literary techniques in a way that problematizes the very nature of representation itself, including the limits of writing as a form of communication, one of the hallmarks of the postmodern text.

I argue that Cobain's lyrics and journals entries, taken as a whole, are nonlinear. As a result, they do not necessarily succeed in telling a coherent or cogent story. Rather than assuming the form of a linear narrative, his songs and notebook writings are more frequently circular and mimetic in that they do succeed foremost in evoking emotions. Of all the emotions that his texts elicit, a devastating—even if seemingly inexpressible—perception of inadequacy and loss oftentimes dominates. Recall from my analysis in chapter 4, for example, the way "Emergence of a Pedophile" (*Journals,* 124) functions as a lyrical text that presents an impressionistic, discomfiting portrait of a narrator and character. Or recall, from my comments in chapter 3, the way the song "I Hate Myself" fails to tell any story at all but succeeds merely in evoking an experience of desolation and resignation.

In another text, the suicide letter as I examine it below, the melancholic narrator's actions—just as in the central entry—are also represented as heroic. Consistent with Cobain's melancholy lyrics and journal fragments, this letter, too, must be understood as a performance of gender in the guise of a personal confession *and* in the form of a critique of the structure and rules of society. The letter constitutes the dramatic staging of a self-serving self-sacrifice. In other words, as Jean Gillibert has concluded, not only can the melancholic be heroic and "the redeemer of a race" through his self-sacrifice, he can also satisfy his own narcissistic ideal of himself by taking his own life, thereby assuring his very legacy (Sánchez-Pardo, 52).

In a similar fashion, Leo Bersani in *The Freudian Body,* via a queer-inflected reading of Freud (*Civilization and Its Discontents*), underscores how the opposition between the individual and society can be characterized as a melancholic protest. For Bersani, the queer subject is a particular kind of subject. Just like the persona Cobain inhabits, the queer subject calls into question the social proscription of nonheterosexual practices of sexual pleasure. In challenging these sexual prohibitions, the queer subject, like the resisting punk persona that Cobain takes on, is engaging in a melancholic resistance to society in the name of individual freedom and contentment.

Loss of a Feminine Self / Loss of a Masculine Self in Cobain's Texts

As I have explored in part II of this study, KurDt's *testerical* experience of lack and inadequacy results from what he perceives to be the loss of a determinant, feminine self/other. The persona Cobain takes to heart mourns this loss while phantasizing an ideal, unified self that is both masculine and feminine. He longs to be a male giving birth and lactating, for example. In this chapter, on the contrary, I argue instead that it is the very loss of *phallic* masculinity that KurDt *fails to mourn* and that provokes his melancholy and his depressive personality. He fails to mourn the loss of phallic masculinity either because he misrecognizes the loss or he is unconscious of it.[3]

In the Cobainian text, phallic masculinity is depicted explicitly as negative, as physically diseased, morally reprehensible, corrupted, and corrupting. Cobain appropriates the persona of a young man who incessantly condemns, abnegates, and attempts to destroy this mode of masculine being in the world by attempting first to destroy it masochistically in himself. Externally, he targets this mode of masculinity, for example, by attacking the "dickheaded-ness" that is manifest in a certain type of male consumer of rock music that is excoriated on the *Incesticide* sleeve for being racist, sexist, or homophobic. This kind of male fan is the same one that the narrator exposes in "In Bloom," as the one "who likes all our pretty songs, who likes to sing along . . . but he don't know what it means."

In spite of his abnegation and condemnation of conventional masculinity, the persona Cobain adopts is a young musician who still acquiesces to certain "manly" or phallic notions, evident in several of his attitudes and actions. As indicated in chapter 1, while on stage and in full grunge-rock character, Cobain was known on occasion to antagonize and even to provoke physical altercations with macho or merely obnoxious young men attending Nirvana's concerts. In addition, the persona Cobain embraces, as he appears in certain lyrics and journal fragments, implicitly valorizes a hegemonic masculine comportment. A closer examination of some of the images and ideas expressed in his writings reveals that phallicism constitutes even a kind of ideal, a negative one to be sure, but an ideal nonetheless. In the central entry in *Journals,* the abnegated phallic mode constitutes the very strategy that the narrator envisions in order to confront and destroy the corporate ogres who are subverting authentic rock music. Revealingly, he pledges to annihilate these men, as the text reiterates, in "pools of razor blades and sperm." As I also specify in chapter 4, the narrator does not recognize that in destroying the "dickhead" corporate executives, he is, in effect, destroying himself, his future self. Elsewhere in Cobain's published journals, in addition to the central entry, the recourse to phallic aggression is posited as the solution to an intractable problem, namely the annihilation of the Klan in order to eliminate racial injustice.

When I suggest that the loss of the phallic masculine mode is unconscious or misrecognized on the part of the persona Cobain is cultivating, I mean that compared to the loss of femininity, the separation from the masculine mode is not experienced or "registered" consciously as a personal loss. Readers encounter this unconscious experience of loss in "Spank Thru" and "Beeswax," for example, two songs that explore masturbation and castration. Also in other lyrics and journal entries in which the narrator prescribes his own emasculation, he relinquishes his phallic potential with enthusiasm and jubilation. He experiences what Joan Oluchi Lee describes as "the joy of the castrated boy." The narrator implicates himself in his own castration precisely because he does not and cannot envision the nature or the scope of his loss. This very feature accounts for the fact that mourning is incomplete and that it fails.

There is a degree to which the persona that Cobain takes on does not think about or "know" the loss of his phallic capability. He remains unaware of its significance to him. Although this experience is more evident in lyrics that explicitly represent a desire for emasculation, it is also evoked in lyrics and in fragments in Cobain's journals in which the narrator's desire for emasculation is implicit. In these texts, the desire for emasculation is represented as acts of self-deprecation, as in "Scoff" and "Blew." In each text in which self-diminishment emerges as the underlying theme, the narrator does not conjure up the breadth or the depth of his impending depravation.

The nature and scope of the loss remain hidden from and unknown to him.

Or, if this loss is known, as Stefan Polatinsky writes about representations of grief in certain literary and philosophical works, it does not appear in the text as an explicit "object of representation; [it appears] rather as a recurrent experience of being, an existential as opposed to a representational knowing" (12). Although it is unthought, an affect like melancholy can, nonetheless, be known. Thus, phallic loss for Cobain's most fully realized first-person narrators, as found in the central entry in *Journals,* might be considered an "unthought known." Christopher Bollas explores in depth the notion of "unthought known," defining it as certain instances of human experiences of the self when one knows without thinking; when one knows without necessarily knowing that one knows.

Although phallic masculinity constitutes a way for Cobain, by way of the persona he adopts, to think about his identity and his relation to his body and the outside world, this mode of being masculine in the world is *psychically* abandoned (lost) by him. At the same time, however, this mode of masculinity is *physically* omnipresent and impossible to relinquish to the extent that KurDt acknowledges, even though he does not fully embrace, his own maleness. That is, he is resigned to the reality of his male body parts and functions: "Don't touch my balls / I got a dick, dick," he intones regretfully in "Beeswax." The result is an untenable contradiction: acknowledging the physical possession of the penis/phallus while psychically denying its possession and concomitant power. The result of this contradiction is an unmistakably melancholic torment brought on by an unrealized and unrealizable desire to be definitively divested of the phallus: "I got my diddly spayed" ("Beeswax") is repeated twenty times in one text alone. It is in this sense, more precisely, that I argue that the persona Cobain is so intent on "fleshing out" is incapable of mourning the loss of his phallic potential. He is incapable precisely because he does not experience alienation from the masculine mode in the same way as he does his separation from the feminine mode. He experiences masculinity merely as a current liability.

Even while appearing to be proclaiming and celebrating the nondesirability and the nonviability of phallic masculinity—whether embodied as football player, soldier, macho father, Klan member, record company executive, or misguided heteromasculine Nirvana fan—the young man Cobain phantasizes himself to be still identifies with this masculine mode. It is this very identification that intensifies his conflicted feelings of guilt. In spite of his protest, phallicism is a constituent part of KurDt's identity, an undesirable part, but a component nonetheless. In fact, Cobain's creative writings confirm the following psycho-analytic tenet: to respond melancholically to loss means precisely to be unable to undertake the "work of mourning," and to arrive at a resolution, because of the very nature of the attachment.

In "Spank Thru," for example, the narrator's attachment to his phallic potential is such that what he loses but cannot mourn is, in actuality, his un-acknowledged *emotional* attachment to this mode of being. As his desire for castration reveals, he is not attached whatsoever to any body part. From his perspective, the male body consists of burdensome appendages, fleshly reali-ties that he would willingly excise. Nevertheless, some of Cobain's texts, includ-ing, again, the central entry in his published journals, are themselves covertly phallic, at the very least, in that they valorize a certain aggressive, masculine comportment. Try as he may, in other words, Cobain's alter ego—as he emerges explicitly as the rescuer of authentic rock music and as an ally of women and of gay and black men—cannot completely escape either his corporeal destiny or his psychical, hegemonic enculturation as a straight white man.

Therefore, whereas I argue in the previous chapter against considering sui-cide as a phallic act on the part of the *masochistic* persona Cobain inhabits, I argue presently that self-murder can represent a phallic gesture for the *melan-cholic* persona he embraces. Failure to mourn the loss of the phallic self leads, ironically, to what could be considered the ultimate phallic act. By contrast, because the loss of the feminine self in the Cobainian text is acknowledged and mourned, this loss does not lead to suicide on the part of the masochistic subject. As I have specified, the masochistic persona Cobain projects clings to hope. Suicide does not present an optimal solution to his predicament, since the act would entail him losing his most beloved victim. But because the loss of the masculine component is not acknowledged or recognized as a *subjective* loss, one that is costly and personal, it leads precisely to melancholy and the desire to valiantly do away with himself.

I shall now explore how the ensemble of Cobain's creative writings, includ-ing his suicide letter—considered together as a collage of lyrical and narrative texts—buys into what Juliana Schiesari describes as "the masculine myth of melancholic genius." I examine also how recognizing the presumptive gender of melancholy assists readers in understanding how melancholy appears themat-ically in Cobain's texts specifically as an unsuccessful, heteromasculine form of resistance. Calling attention to the presumptive gender of melancholy also brings into clearer focus how melancholy functions discursively in Cobain's writings to tell us something further about the relationship between experiences of loss, a failed masculinity, and creativity.

THE COBAIN PERSONA: THE GENDER OF MELANCHOLY, THE STAGING OF GRIEF

Rather than referring to Cobain's "melancholy" when writing about his affective state and his overall approach to life, his biographers more frequently refer to his gloom, his darkness, and his addictive, depressive personality. In fact, clinical depression, as understood today, is remarkably similar in some significant ways to melancholy and its effects, as the notion of melancholy has evolved since the writings of the ancient Greeks. Discourses on melancholy and its consequences can be found in texts written during the Renaissance, the Enlightenment, the Romantic period, and up to the present day in writings within the fields of sociology, anthropology, philosophy, psychiatry, and psychoanalysis in ways that reveal the links between melancholy and depression. Like Jennifer Radden writing in *The Nature of Melancholy,* I am not suggesting that melancholy and depression are perfectly congruent or that the notion of melancholy itself has remained unchanged over the course of its long history. On the contrary. The changing and sometimes contradictory meanings of melancholy and its relation to clinical depression are relevant to any examination of Cobain's creative works because of the way that melancholy, as opposed to depression, has persisted for a long time in being associated disproportionately with men.

Further, given Cobain's interest in and, one might say, his obsession with bodily functions and fluids, including the status he assigns to sperm as both an arm of patriarchy and a weapon for its destruction, it is entirely appropriate to insist on the term melancholy in discussing his writings. Aristotle links melancholy to "froth" (*aphros*) and to sperm. *Aphros* was thought to countermand the gloom and despondency of black bile (*melania khole*) with jubilation and euphoria. For Aristotle, *aphros* designates, more precisely, "a white mixture of air ... and liquid that brings out froth in the sea, wine, as well as in the sperm of man" (Kristeva, *Black Sun,* 7). Although the meaning of melancholy has changed over the centuries of its history and theorizing, a kernel of indices or "symptoms" has remained fixed. This kernel also characterizes one of the organizing dynamics and one of the principal themes within Cobain's creative writings: representations and evocations of sadness, self-loathing, and a sorrowful withdrawal unto the self that can be not only psychically crippling but also physically self-destructive. With this characterization, we are approaching the very essence of clinical depression, as the condition is commonly understood.

Radden provides a detailed history of the different discourses on melancholy and its relation to depression. She organizes her account around several themes, three of which are especially pertinent for illuminating how melancholy functions in Cobain's writings as an ideological construct and as a rhetorical device. In addition to an account of how melancholy and depression intersect, Radden examines the following concepts: the role of gender and the significance of loss in the development of melancholic temperaments, and the linking of melancholy to intellectual energy and acuity and to creativity.[4]

Cobain's creative productions, to the extent they constitute performances of grief, fit neatly into this history, especially as Radden has charted it from the Renaissance to today's postmodern creative and theoretical writings. Like the Hippocratic writings, Cobain's lyrics and journals present melancholy as a recognizable disease with a distinct set of physical symptoms ("'Cobain's Disease' . . . which is all about vomiting gastric juices [by] . . . a borderline anorexic Auzhwitz [*sic*]-Grunge Boy" [*Journals,* 193]). For these early writers, the disease results from an imbalance of the four humors: black bile, yellow bile, phlegm, and blood. For Cobain, it results from a gender imbalance. His writings, like the ancient texts, also suggest that this imbalance and the physiological disorders it engenders induce, in turn, a complex system of mental conditions and character traits. Cobain writes of "a notoriously fucked up heroine [*sic*] addict, alcoholic, self [-] destructive, yet overly sensitive, frail, fragile, soft[-] spoken, narcoleptic, *neurotic,* little piss ant" (*Journals,* 191). In this sense, he follows in the tradition of Renaissance writers who, as Schiesari documents, revived and relaunched Greek melancholy. Cobain also follows in the tradition of the Romantics and Decadents who embraced and ennobled melancholy before it was theorized by the newly minted psychoanalysts.

There was a significant shift in the description and the theorizing of melancholy at the end of the nineteenth century. Up to that point, the condition had been conceived of as manifesting both positive (creative) as well as negative (debilitating) effects, for certain men in particular. And it was considered to be quite distinct from depression in terms of its diagnosis and prognosis. Depression, as opposed to melancholy, was being characterized as devoid of redeeming or compensatory effects.[5] In addition, depression, as an observable pathology, was coming to be associated principally with women. As Radden explains, this separation of depression from melancholy is evident in English, in part, in a corresponding lexical change. *Melancholy,* whether chronic and severe or whether episodic and mild, came to designate more or less a normal emotional condition, whereas *melancholia* came to designate an aberration, a diagnosable disease.

Theorists and clinicians came to use "depression" more frequently to designate abnormal melancholy; and the term began to signify a different set of dispositions and actions. When considered a disease, as Radden explains further, melancholia/depression begins to be described more consistently as a behavior with outward symptoms that a third party could discern, rather than as a subjective manifestation that can, in actuality, only be truly known by the subject in question. In one sense, a subjective, psychical distress and suffering stood in contradistinction to a bodily distress and suffering. Melancholy continued to be valued, praised, and to be considered "a condition of poets, artists, and men, and as part of normal human experience" (Radden, 48). Since Freud's influential writings, it has *not* been melancholy but rather clinical depression that medicine and the social sciences have researched and written about.

Within the psychoanalytic tradition, Melanie Klein explicates and expands Freud's theory in ways that make it even more evident that what we now call clinical depression stands in an ambivalent and complicated relation to melancholy.[6] This same relationship, I contend, is also evoked within Cobain's writings. As I have indicated, melancholy in Cobain's texts is represented recurrently and cannily as both a psychical *and* a corporeal reality, as both an outwardly observable symptom and as an inner process of the grieving of loss. Just as there is a connection between melancholy as psychical distress and as bodily symptom in "Lithium," Cobain's journal entries also link melancholy inextricably to bodily afflictions. This link is expressly articulated in the central entry (179–82), as well as in the two fragments cited above (191, 193). In many of Cobain's texts, the male body emerges as both cause and effect.

In addition, understanding the connection between melancholy as psychical suffering and as a corporeal scarring assists in deciphering some of Cobain's most expressive but enigmatic texts, like the nearly nine-hundred-word letter to Mark Lanegan (*Journals,* 19–23). As discussed in chapter 4, the letter begins as a brief note to a dear friend in which a masochistic KurDt compliments Lanegan on his current music project. He then extends an invitation to Lanegan to collaborate on a future project. We recall that, after the first four hundred words, the letter subtly shifts into a melancholic meditation on the mind-body continuum. In this meditation, a body part the narrator refers to as his "conjunctiva" (the mucous membrane lining his eyelids), sets in motion, and cannot be distinguished from, his "semi-hypnotic state of sub-conciousness" [sic] and his "daydreaming" (19). This entry reconfirms that specific body parts and body functions set the narrator's sadness in motion. His sadness, in turn, contaminates his body externally and internally.

Making Melancholy Masculine and Gay

In the wake of extensive feminist scholarship undertaken during the latter part of the twentieth century, the role of gender and the cultural causation of depression and melancholic temperaments came into focus in both empirical and theoretical research. Given the dominant themes within Cobain's creative writings, this scholarship proves to be especially valuable in making further sense out of the structuring and the content of his written texts. Within feminist scholarship informed to different degrees by psychoanalysis, theorists like Butler, Cixous, and Kristeva have explored, in a more comprehensive manner than Freud, the role of gender and sexuality in experiences of melancholy. They have also explored the connection between melancholy and creativity. It is Kristeva and Cixous who have written the most compellingly about the connections between melancholy and literary genius in particular.

For her part, Butler in "Melancholy Gender" argues that compulsory heterosexuality makes melancholic subjects of us all because of a disavowed (or lost) same-sex attachment. Particular fragments in Cobain's journals and some of his lyrics, like "Laminated Effect" and "Even in His Youth," would seem to bear out this conclusion. Butler reasons that heterosexist culture facilitates us becoming gendered and sexed subjects by means of two taboos: incest and homosexuality. Prohibited from loving sexually our mother and father, we experience the result of the taboo as a loss that cannot be completely known or successfully mourned. Psychoanalyst Darian Leader also reveals how "the very process by which Freud characterizes melancholic identification . . . [he] later uses to describe the actual constitution of the human self" (55) in every instance and without exception. In other words, Freud theorizes, our egos are formed from the traces of our imagined and real losses. Cobain's journals in particular would seem to underwrite this aspect of the theory.

As for Klein, in addition to her writings on melancholy and depression, she wrote an insightful essay that establishes a relation between melancholy and sexuality, an essay she titles "The Effects of Early Anxiety-Situations on the Sexual Development of the Boy."[7] In this text, she posits a connection between melancholy and male homosexuality in a way that also recalls how gay male sex functions in "Laminated Effect" and "Even in His Youth." In Cobain's lyrics, gay sexual desire does indeed end up constituting a melancholic resistance to paternal authority specifically and to heterosexist norms in general. This same kind of resistance, Bersani postulates, is the very one that the queer subject in our culture undertakes. The connection that Klein theorizes between melancholy and male homosexuality also recalls how gay male sex functions in certain of Cobain's journal entries, specifically those fragments that describe sexual intercourse, either between Cobain's first-person narrator and William Burroughs (256), or those entries describing the penetration of American actors, musicians, and television characters (5, 78).

Whereas the Kleinian-influenced writings of Kristeva and Cixous have described melancholy in *theoretical* terms as a particular experience of gender, it is Schiesari who lays out most persuasively how and why melancholy has been gendered *historically*. She does so by interrogating "the masculine myth of melancholic genius," which, as she writes, "constitutes one of the effects" of how a male-dominated, heterosexist culture determines not only our actions, but the very way we think and the way we determine what is real, true, and ingenious (x). The linking of melancholy to intellectual brilliance and creative energy on the part of certain men, like its connection to sperm, also begins, ostensibly, with Aristotle, who asks rhetorically, "Why is it that all men who have become outstanding in philosophy, statesmanship, poetry, or the arts are melancholic, or are infected by diseases from black bile?" (57). During the Renaissance, the Italian philosopher and theologian Marsilio Ficino (1433–1499) posited a connection between this Aristotelian insight and Plato's idea of divine madness, a condition that was thought to produce everything that enhances our human existence, from love to the sciences, philosophy, and the arts (Farndell). It was Robert Burton (1577–1640), because of the numerous republications and translations of his *Anatomy of Melancholy* (1621), who was chiefly responsible for spreading throughout Europe this idea of melancholy as a masculine virtue.

The Renaissance notion of the artist as melancholic is consonant with the notion of the persona that Cobain has so thoroughly absorbed. He is a subject suspended within a prolonged, interminable process of grief for an unrealizable ideal of completeness and absolute contentment. And because Cobain's alter ego, like the Renaissance artist and intellectual, is defined by "an insuperable desire for an ontological and epistemological certitude that cannot be had" (Schiesari, 19), he, too, mourns this loss by internalizing the ideal of completeness and eternal bliss into his phantasy of an inerrant self. At its most basic level, as Cobain's sometimes inscrutable texts confirm, this desire for ontological and epistemological wholeness betrays a deeper desire to deny sexual difference. The desire propels Cobain's narrators and characters toward displays of melancholy and toward a specific aesthetic and cultural practice, as I have outlined it in chapter 2.

It is also Schiesari who reveals the most clearly why melancholy must be considered just as much a cultural category as a clinical and medical one. Her insights also make it evident why melancholy has become virtually a genre within Western literature, one that includes writers such as Italian poet Torquato Tasso (1544–1595) and French writers Jean-Jacques Rousseau (1712–1778), François René de Chateaubriand (1768–1848), and Gérard de Nerval (1808–1855), among others. The melancholy canon, which intersects with other genres like Gothic literature, has tended to systematically exclude women who have been relegated in many instances, as Schiesari also indicates, to an experience of loss considered inferior to melancholy: mourning. Mourning is dismissed as quotidian; it lacks melancholy's nobility. It is considered simply a way to grieve. Mourning is seen as a mere ritual, as opposed to a stimulant for ingenuity and a portal to creativity.

In other words, melancholy provides, presumptively to certain men, an inspired and inspiring way to express sorrow. The notion of melancholy as ennobling and poetic came, at the end of the eighteenth century, to overshadow the earlier notion of the condition as a disease. Goethe's character Werther in *The Sorrows of Young Werther* (1774) came to embody a melancholic subjectivity par excellence. But beyond an emphasis on the actions and disposition of a man of inordinate feelings and sensibility, melancholy came to be understood as a specific kind of *written text* that represents masculine subjectivity. It came to be understood as an account of how exceptional men rise to their destiny and the extraordinary thinking and actions that define them as great. It is because of melancholy, the theory goes, that we have not only great literature but also great cultural and political institutions.

Even up to the time that Freud was first writing on the subject, historians and philosophers conceived of melancholy as a potential mode of masculine creativity. As I have specified, Freud himself postulates that the melancholic suffers from the sense that something once possessed, or believed to be possessed, that had special meaning and that provided a sense of completeness and plenitude, has been lost. The *privileged* subject, however, could succeed in transforming this bereft sense of a deficient subjectivity and inadequate agency into a creative artifact.[8] Even though Freud does not address the significance of gender in his theory of mourning, the privileged subject he describes is presumptively male because, throughout his writings, he puts forth a masculine model of subjectivity as the default. Even as the suffering man laments his abject inability to make himself whole and to transcend his lack, as does the narrator in a text like Cobain's suicide letter, he is unusually contemplative and endowed with the expressive eloquence of a Hamlet, for example.

Although Freud and Ficino are separated by centuries, and while they differ in the nature and scope of their thinking and understanding of melancholy, both contend that for a subject in the melancholic state, the experience of loss becomes more significant than the lost object itself. Cobain's texts, as I explore further below, certainly substantiate this observation. Freud's alignment with Ficino means that Freud's theorizing owes a debt to Renaissance thinking, a legacy that would seem to account in part for the empirical and conceptual limits of his seminal essay on mourning and loss. Notwithstanding these limitations, later theorists, including Klein, Kristeva, and Cixous, have relied upon Freud's original insights. Yet they have critiqued and refined many of his discoveries. They have done so in ways that bring into sharper focus how Cobain's creative writings operate to suggest the confluence of melancholy, creativity, and a desire to self-destruct.

THE COBAINIAN TEXT, LOSS, AND THE "WORK" OF ART

If loss, mourning, and absence set the imaginary act in motion and permanently fuel it as much as they menace and undermine it, it is also undeniable that the fetish of the work of art is erected in disavowal of this mobilizing affliction. The artist [is] Melancholy's most intimate witness and the fiercest fighter against the symbolic abdication enveloping him—until death strikes and suicide imposes its triumphant conclusion upon the void of the lost object.
—JULIA KRISTEVA, "On the Melancholic Imaginary" (6)

I am using "work" in the above subtitle in the sense that psychoanalysts refer to the "work of mourning," as a process set in motion by an experience of loss. The reason Kristeva's writings on melancholy inhere especially for my reading of Cobain's creative texts is distilled in this epigraph. She concludes that experiences of loss and mourning give birth to and nourish the capacity to create; but these afflictions also work to stifle creativity, if not to abort it altogether. By "symbolic abdication," I take Kristeva to mean the madness that can overtake the melancholic subject, including an inability to create or understand symbols.[9]

In formulating her overall conceptual framework, Kristeva is inspired not only by Freud and Klein; she builds also on insights from Lacan. In her theoretical writings on melancholy, and as a result of her incisive literary analysis of the Romantic poetry and the letters of Gérard de Nerval, Kristeva confirms that there exists, inescapably, a relation between melancholic loss and access to language and the symbolic order. Lacan defines "the symbolic order" as "the social world of linguistic communication, inter-subjective relations, knowledge of ideological conventions, and the acceptance of the law" (Felluga). The symbolic order encompasses the ways we use language and nonverbal communication in our social and political interactions as well as in our interpersonal relations. It signals that subjects accept the conventions that make these communications and interactions possible. It is because of the connection between melancholy and participation in the symbolic order, Kristeva makes clear, that there is a relationship between melancholy and literary creation, the capacity to create symbols, to communicate.

As indicated in the introduction, Cobain as a mythologized rock hero can be read within the context of the French poetic tradition that Nerval has come to exemplify, in part, because of the emphasis that the European Romantic conventions placed on the connection between authentic art and the premature death of the artist.[10] The persona that emerges from Cobain's texts closely resembles the profile of the Romantic hero. Like the Romantic hero, he embodies a subject who, against all odds and in the name of authenticity, pits himself against the norms of society. Except for the fact that both Nerval and Cobain were writers who committed suicide, their actual lives have little in common. But in spite of the enormous differences between when, where, and how they lived, Cobain and Nerval, as writers, would appear indeed to be embedded within a continuing aesthetic tradition that spans at least three centuries. They both write a kind of autobiographical fiction that fuses phantasy and reality, the past and present, poetry and prose. And the two men write about loss and melancholy in a way that suggests a relationship between madness and literary creativity.

In encountering a Cobain text such as "Triple Suicide" (*Journals,* 191)—in which the narrator longs for a redundant death, a particularly gruesome demise—readers can sense his melancholic madness. Or, even more uncannily, listeners of the song "Come As You Are" can sense the acuity of the narrator's mental derangement and disconsolation—this almost palpable, emotional reality—merely in the plaintive repetition of the word "memoria" in the chorus. With all of Cobain's melancholy texts, readers and listeners often cannot really *know* this sorrow intimately because the melancholy that these texts are pointing to seems to be resisting semiotic expression. The reader, or writer, for that matter, may not be certain what specifically any particular song like "I Hate Myself" or "Come As You Are" is about. Yet as indirect representations, they operate in such a way that the reader still has access to the color, complexity, and confusion of a melancholic experience.

From this perspective, Cobain's journal entries in particular, as a semiotic system, function to register the effects of what Kristeva labels "a melancholic imaginary" (*l'imaginaire mélancholique*). It is precisely because these literary fragments do not succeed in elaborating melancholy that they can merely register its effects, point to its existence. In fact, neither Cobain's lyrics nor his journal entries constitute an elaboration of melancholy since they do not and cannot expose explicitly or comprehensively the causes of the psychical pain brought on by the loss of a testerical or a phallic self.

If Kristeva, along with Klein, is correct, however, these writings do provide a kind of tonic for the writer of the text. And because writing can provide remediation for the grieving subject, Kristeva, like other thinkers centuries before her, concludes that aesthetic practices, including above all others literary creation, can function to rechannel the madness of melancholy. Literary creation is a privileged mode of expression because of its recourse to the creation of characters, symbols, and plots. In this sense, Kristeva's formulations echo those of Robert Burton, first published nearly four centuries ago. Burton also proposes that writing about melancholy serves as a kind of prophylaxis. He concludes that the melancholic subject, more so than any other, may be perfectly positioned to undertake a life of the mind; and if a person is debilitated by the condition, writing about it, he insists, can have meaning and consequences.

Literary creation, according to Kristevian and Kleinian psychoanalytic aesthetics, does provide not only a palliative but also a cathartic experience for the afflicted subject. And, once again, the dominant themes and images in Cobain's writings seem to bear out this insight: "HERE I am," writes Cobain in the wretched voice of KurDt, "inspired to write because I'm pissed off. I don't feel as bitter as I want to be" (*Journals,* 135). One does not have to be able to read between the lines to ascertain that when Cobain writes about anger, he is, invariably, writing about sadness and pain. He does so, for example, when he writes, again in a deeply afflicted voice, about destroying the "Right Wing control freaks" and their "fucking . . . macho, sadistic, sick Right Wing, religiously abusive opinions" (*Journals,* 121). He seeks to decimate the religious right in order to preserve freedom of artistic expression in the United States. Beyond the sadistic furor expressed in this entry, it is the pending loss of his own right to create "authentic" music that the narrator is grieving. "Art is expression," he wails. "In expression, you need 100% full freedom and our freedom to express our art is seriously being fucked with" (120).

Given the relationship that exists between loss and creativity, and given the curative and cathartic potential of literary creation, all writing, Kristeva asserts, points to loss, to desire; and all psychical dispositions are, either manifestly or covertly, melancholic ("On the Melancholic Imaginary," 15). Precisely as Kristeva postulates, Cobain's collective works seem to substantiate her contention that the artist is a particular kind of subject, one who is overwhelmed but still unerringly inspired by loss. Cobain writes, "An artist is in need of constant tragedy to fully express their work" (120). In her theoretical writings, a crucial question remains for Kristeva, as it does for psychoanalytic theory overall: Why exactly is mourning sometimes "impossible"? Why precisely does grieving fail or is it expressly blocked? As with Freud's unanswered or unasked questions about masochism, it is, once again, Cobain's writings that point us in a productive direction, even if his texts do not suggest a universal or definitive answer.

Even if one does not subscribe to the universality and the transhistorical nature of Kristeva's or Klein's models of melancholy, it is clear that, for Cobain's writings, their theories possess explicative power. Even if his writings do not elaborate, cure, or provide a prophylaxis for melancholy, they appear to serve an important psychical function. Cobain seems to be acknowledging this function during interviews when, once again dutifully playing his role as rock star, he characterizes writing, as do many other authors, as an "escape" into another, more comfortable reality (Spiccia, 210). In his journals as well, Cobain suggests that writing functions as a kind of drug and that it constitutes an inescapable process, one that can be neither mastered nor completely understood:

> I need to relearn the english language. I seem insincere because I can't choose or decide fast enough. My penmanship seems scatological because of my lack of personality, or excess of personality. I am obsessed with the fact that I am skinny and stupid. [. . .] These past 23 years have served a sterile bacterial success. ~~I've been to a lot of bad poetry readings~~ . . . chemicals are the thing of today, today i'll take as many chemicals as I can get my greasy paws on . . . in my place of recovery. the place where I've crawled off to die like a cat under a house after he's been hit. lying around waiting. I don't invent subjects of interest for conversations. I don't have anything to say or ask, I just play along. I'm a reactionary in a way. I just react to what others say. I don't think & when I do I forget. give me a leonard cohen afterworld. (134–35)

In spite of their limitations as a possible universal template, Cobain's writings can help readers to approach the bleakness of depression and to begin to understand the operation of a melancholic disposition. His texts suggest why and how melancholy can inspire both writer and reader.

From Discourse to Imagined Act: Writing and Reading a Suicide Letter

Although I argue that the representation of melancholy in Cobain's lyrics and journals manifests specific meanings having to do with afflictions of the male body and a masculine performance of disconsolation, I do not, as I indicated at the beginning of this study, attempt to identify the actual causes of grieving in Kurt Cobain's life. I maintain rather that readers can identify with the persona Cobain projects, and they can then come to understand themes of melancholy within his writings: sorrow, despondency, suicidal fantasies. Readers can understand these themes, and even *experience* these emotions vicariously, without necessarily having to identify the putative events and circumstances in Cobain's real life that might have brought on these complex emotions. For this reason, in part II of this study, I have analyzed the theme of suicide in his lyrics and journals as *literary representations* and as examples of a discursive strategy, that is, as a way to reflect on and write about loss, inadequacy, and comfortlessness.

As a kind of manifesto, discursive suicide in Cobain's writings takes two forms. Sometimes it appears as mere evocations, without elaboration, as in "A Leonard Cohen Afterworld"; other times it appears in the form of detailed, complicated narratives, as in "Chuck Taylor." In both instances, discursive suicide, independently of the real events in Cobain's life, displays an internal logic. As a result, these imagined events make sense in and of themselves. These lyrical and narrative representations of self-mutilation and self-annihilation exhibit a coherent aesthetic. They also display a specific philosophy and a politics of masculine subjectivity and agency.

These representations always return, sometimes in indirect and confusing ways, to themes and images that underscore the challenges of existing as an antiracist, gay-affirmative, woman-positive, and profeminist man. It is in this sense that Cobain's melancholy songs and journal entries do not set out necessarily and specifically to communicate sadness to readers. Cobain's texts, like *The Sorrows of Young Werther*, oftentimes do operate instead as indirect representations. These indirect representations, by way of a fictionalized universe, give readers access to the overall involution and discomfiture of a particular subjective experience. It is within this same perspective that I read Cobain's suicide letter as a tactical maneuver and as a specific discursive strategy. I read it as literature, a form of fiction:[11]

To Boddah
Speaking from the tongue of an experienced simpleton who obviously would rather be an emasculated, infantile complain-ee. This note should be pretty easy to understand.
All the warnings from the punk rock 101 courses over the years, since my first introduction to the, shall we say, ethics involved with independence and the embracement of your community has [sic] proven to be very true. I haven't felt the excitement of listening to as well as creating music along with reading and writing for too many years now. I feel guilty beyond words about these things.
. . .
The worst crime I can think of would be to rip people off by faking it and pretending as if I'm having 100% fun. . . . I've tried everything within my power to appreciate [entertaining you] (and I do, God, believe me I do, but it's not enough). I appreciate the fact that I and we have affected and entertained a lot of people. I must be one of those narcissists who only appreciate things when

they're gone. I'm too sensitive. I need to be slightly numb in order to regain the enthusiasms I once had as a child.

. . .

There's good in all of us and I think I simply love people too much, so much that it makes me feel too fucking sad. The sad little, sensitive, unappreciative, Pisces, Jesus man. Why don't you just enjoy it? I don't know!

I have a goddess of a wife who sweats ambition and empathy and a daughter who reminds me too much of what i used to be, full of love and joy. . . . And that terrifies me to the point to where I can barely function. I can't stand the thought of Frances becoming the miserable, self-destructive, death rocker that I've become.

. . .

Thank you all from the pit of my burning, nauseous stomach for your letters and concern during the past years. I'm too much of an erratic, moody baby! I don't have the passion anymore, and so remember, it's better to burn out than to fade away.

Peace, love, empathy.

Kurt Cobain

Frances and Courtney, I'll be at your altar.

Please keep going Courtney, for Frances.

For her life, which will be so much happier without me.

I LOVE YOU, I LOVE YOU!

Given the letter's content and form, and in spite of the signature—"Kurt" versus "KurDt"—it could be seamlessly inserted into Cobain's journals as another example of discursive suicide. In this instance, however, the act itself is not narrated, as it is in other texts like "Triple Suicide." Since the act is not described, the letter can only constitute the prelude to an imagined, future event. Although journalists and biographers usually conclude that this 1994 letter is addressed to Cobain's fans, wife, and daughter, the text is composed, ultimately, as an open letter, like the other open and unsent letters in *Journals*. One could superpose this missive with the letter to the editors of *The Advocate* (280–82), or with the letter to Mark Lanegan (19–23), for example. It does not matter if the message is read by its ostensible recipient. The letter is written foremost to and for the letter writer himself.

In this specific instance, the narrator represents himself explicitly as the letter's addressee in the guise of an imaginary, childhood friend ("Boddah"). That is, just as in many of Cobain's lyrics and journal entries, the narrator conflates himself with his addressee in the sense that Boddah is a younger version of himself. Therefore, the central question posed in the letter is purely rhetorical: "[L]istening to as well as creating music along with reading and writing. . . . Why don't *you* just enjoy it?" I have underscored "you" in this passage, but the narrative voice in the letter shifts almost imperceptibly between the first and second persons, just as it does in songs like "Scoff" and "Frances Farmer." Courtney Love and Frances Bean Cobain, as addressees properly speaking, are reduced in fact to a mere afterthought, appearing as *recipients* only in the postscript to the letter. As such, they function as characters, in the same way as Boddah, in the story the narrator wishes to relate. Wife and daughter serve to advance the story the narrator is intent on telling. They also function, then, as characters in the same way that Frances Farmer does in Cobain's lyrics. Courtney and Frances Bean, in fact, permit the recounting of an alternate version of Frances Farmer's story, yet another one of Cobain's narratives whose ultimate objective is to insinuate the pleasures of death and dying.

More significantly, when it comes to representing a masculine subjectivity and agency, a specific way of identifying oneself and existing and acting in the world, the self-portrait that the narrator presents in the letter corresponds in every significant detail to the portrait that emerges elsewhere in Cobain's creative writings. The self-portrait in all these texts consists of five distinct features or symptoms. For example, the letter focuses, first, on the narrator's experience of profound loss ("I don't have the passion anymore") and on his failing efforts to recover from it ("I need to be slightly numb in order to regain the enthusiasms I once had as a child"). Second, the narrator presents himself as a weak, masochistic subject who is burdened by an overwhelming sense of guilt ("I feel guilty beyond words") and who seeks or phantasizes punishment in the form of emasculation ("an emasculated, infantile complain-ee"). At the moment of writing the letter, he emerges as a feminine and a moral, or Christlike, masochist, to return to Freud's terminology, just as he does in other texts like "All Apologies," "Beeswax," and "Triple Suicide."

Third, after confirming his masochistic propensity, the narrator proceeds to profile himself as a melancholic subject ("The sad little, sensitive, unappreciative, Pisces, Jesus man") who find himself on an ineluctable path to a self-crucifixion. Fourth, as in the "Heart Shaped Box" storyboards in *Journals,* the narrator merges himself with his young daughter. Therein, the letter rehearses the recurring Cobainian theme of a male subject who fears being cursed and, therefore, destined to turn into his morally bankrupt, abusive father: "I can't stand the thought of Frances becoming the miserable, self-destructive, death rocker that I've become." Finally, in the concluding paragraph of the letter, again, as throughout Cobain's other creative writings, the narrator presents his abject body as the physiological manifestation of his psychical agony and emotional pain. Also as in his lyrics and journals, the narrator sees his body as the very cause of his psychical and emotional distress: "Thank you from the pit of my burning, nauseous stomach," he writes, "[but] I'm too much of an erratic, moody baby!"

Although, as I insist, readers do not have to "reality check" the contents of the letter in order to understand how it functions to represent masculinity as a melancholic performance, the letter contains the key to its own motivation and its meaning. "This note," Cobain writes, "should be pretty easy to understand." He is correct. The words written here are motivated by and they explicitly communicate the narrator's narcissism: "I must be one of those narcissists who only appreciate things when they're gone." During the public memorial for her husband, the crowd listened to a recording of Courtney Love reading portions of the letter. She reads the excerpts in a manner that reveals precisely how the letter must be *experienced* as well as interpreted by readers. Love does not camouflage her anger or her contempt. She insists on exposing these final written words, not as the plaintive discourse of an unbearably anguished idealist, but rather as the self-serving justification of an inveterate narcissist.

Before beginning to read the letter, Love exhorts the crowds that had assembled for the occasion to call her recently deceased husband an "asshole": "He's such an asshole. I want you all to say 'asshole' really loud." Next, after reading the portion of the letter where Cobain complains about the burden of being a rock star, Love tearfully responds, "Well, Kurt, so fucking what—then don't be a rock star, you asshole." Then, responding to his assertion that "The worst crime I could think of would be to rip people off by faking it, pretending as if I'm having 100% fun," Loves retorts, "Well Kurt, the worst crime *I* can think of is for you to just continue being a rock star when you fucking hate it, just fucking stop" (Love).

Love's exegesis demonstrates that one must in fact read the suicide letter in the same manner that the twentieth-century poet W. H. Auden reads Goethe's arguably autofictional novel:

Werther [the character] can still fascinate us. . . . To us [the novel] reads not as a tragic love story, but as a masterly and devastating portrait of a complete egoist, a spoiled brat, incapable of love because he cares for nobody and nothing but himself and having his way at whatever cost to others [,] . . . the egoist who imagines himself to be a passionate lover. (xi; cited also by Radden)

In the end, the letter is composed ostensibly in order to confirm the narrator's commitment to authenticity and to his music community ("punk courses 101"). It is also written, seemingly, to reconfirm his exceptional sensitivity ("I simply love people too much"). All these traits will lead to his extraordinary self-sacrifice. But in spite of the narrator's self-serving posturing in presenting himself as thoughtful, loving, overly sensitive, generous, and ethical, Love deftly reads between the lines of the body of the letter and its postscript in order to underscore his utter self-absorption. She refuses to accept this prologue, and the future-perfect performance that it announces, as the ultimate gesture of love and sacrifice for fans and family.

"I HATE MYSELF AND WANT TO DIE": THE IMAGE OF DEATH AS THE ULTIMATE SITE OF DESIRE IN THE COBAINIAN TEXT

Notwithstanding my reading of the content and the objective of Cobain's suicide letter on one level as transparent, my reading of certain of his other texts—like the song "Endless, Nameless" and like the journal entry "A Leonard Cohen Afterworld"—proves to be analogous to Kristeva's reading of Nerval's poetry and correspondence. Kristeva points out that Nerval's use of the metaphor of the "black Sun" for melancholy is brilliant, ingenious. The poet writes, "My only star is dead, and my constellated lute / Takes on the black Sun of Melancholia." This metaphor "admirably evokes the blinding intensity of an affect, [an emotional state], eluding conscious elaboration, a powerful attraction . . . more intense than any word or idea." Kristeva goes on to specify that "The narcissistic ambivalence of the melancholic affect alone finds, in order to represent itself, *the image of death as the ultimate site of desire*" (Kristeva, "On the Melancholic Imaginary," 10, emphasis added).

When one takes Cobain's creative writings as a whole and as texts that represent specifically a performance of grief for a lost, perfect future, "black Sun" also aptly suggests the inconceivable bleakness of the dominant psychical and emotional state that his texts evoke. The metaphor also suggests how melancholy structures thinking and writing, a mode of expression characterized by an uncanny use of symbols, wordplay, and by the conjoining of antithetical ideas and images, such as an astral body that is both blindingly luminous and disquietingly lightless.

Among all the evocations of discursive suicide in Cobain's writings, "Endless, Nameless" may represent the sole text in which the narrator—after insinuating, or forthrightly proclaiming, the pleasure brought on by the act of dying itself—begins to recount the aftermath of his much desired death: "Silence, Here I am.... I have died.... Death with violence / Excitement right here." The narrator in this song emerges as a melancholic subject precisely as psychoanalytic theory defines him, as someone whose loss is only imaginary. Or if his loss is real, either he misidentifies it or he is unconscious of it. The narrator of the song does not reveal what he has lost or its significance to him. On this topic, the text remains circumspect at best and utterly silent at worst. The song is equally circumspect concerning the identity of the narrator's executioner. But the narrator's death is represented as punishment for an unspecified sin and crime: "Go to Hell / Here I am.... Go to jail / In back of that crime." As I have concluded, however, from an analysis in chapters 3 and 4 of the theme of self-destruction throughout Cobain's writings, the reader is left to surmise that the narrator himself is, simultaneously, executioner, the executed criminal-sinner, and a witness to his own murder.

Thus, Cobain attempts to come to grips with melancholic pain in the same way as Nerval, according to Kristeva's analysis of Nerval's collective works. The grunge musician finds the same responses to gloom as the nineteenth-century poet. He, too, resorts to creative writing that includes some texts that are purely imaginary (poetry) and others that are ostensibly autobiographical (letters/journals). In addition, Cobain and Nerval create works of literature in similar ways and, it would seem, for similar reasons. Both write prose that functions to evoke rather than to elaborate what they are experiencing. In addition, both men resort to writing a specific kind of verse that is entrancing but that often displays an opacity that is daunting for readers to comprehend.

The two writers also create verse that Kristeva describes, in Nerval's case,

as an "anti-depressant." Writing in general, and writing verse specifically, constitutes an antidepressant, according to Kristeva. Writing poetry in particular counteracts or rechannels depression in the sense that the genre's literary mechanisms and techniques—metaphor, metonymy, rhyme, alliteration,
rhythm, etc.—successfully convert the effects of melancholy. These mechanisms and techniques transform melancholy into the indirect and at times
seemingly inscrutable and disorienting pattern of the sounds of poetry and
poetic prose. It is by necessity, therefore, that melancholic poetics are circular
and repetitive: They reveal a struggle to give form to a fluid, virtually formless
mental and emotional state.

In a manner similar to Kristeva, French creative writer, cultural critic, and
philosopher Hélène Cixous also sees possible clinical value in the "work" of
literature for assisting patients confronting loss. In *Coming to Writing*, Cixous
is influenced by Freud's essay "Creative Writers and Day-Dreaming," as I have
characterized it in chapter 2. She proposes that writing and dreaming go a long
way in assisting us as we experience and attempt to understand loss. Through
writing and dreaming, it is possible, Cixous theorizes, that we may effectively
begin to come to terms with impossible loss. We may confront despair in a
manner that is not suicidal but that affirms life itself. In this way, writing and
dreaming reconfirm "the immensely creative work of living" (Polatinsky, 5).[12]

Cobain's lyrics and journals, even more so than Nerval's poetry and letters,
make evident that, compared to the expression or the representation of ideas,
the expression of affects is not as economical. In other words, as Kristeva also
makes clear, a mental or emotional state is not sutured to language in the same
way as is an idea. It is for this reason that one cannot say that Cobain's lyrics,
or the narrative fragments in his journals, indicate that he understands his
melancholy. In attempting to give, as best he can, verbal expression to an affect
like melancholy, Cobain is not signaling that he is fully conscious of it. But the
act of verbalization at least does cause the affect to have a dual function. In the
first instance, his melancholy structures language in a unique way so that a
recognizable Cobainian *style* or voice emerges; and in the second instance, his
melancholy produces a distinctive Cobainian *thematic structure*.

Cobain's style, as I have shown, can be shorthanded simply as "postmodern." It is fragmentary, elliptical, multivocal, and prone to collage. Cobain's
themes, as also evident in the representation of a masochistic persona, em-

phasize writing as confessional, the acknowledgment of a psychical vulnerability and a corporeal debility: "I've crawled off to die like a cat under a house after he's been hit" (135). Thus the themes in Cobain's writings also function as allocutions, in the jurisprudential sense of the term. They disclose illicit actions and moral shortcomings: "I'll take as many chemicals as I can" (134). The subject allocutes with the expectation that he will receive his just punishment: "Give me what I deserve" (130), he cries out plaintively.

Notwithstanding the function of creative writing, Cobain, like Nerval, seems to intuit the limitations of this remedial activity, the production of the symbol, the creation of the literary text. The tonic of creativity proves to be perishable, ephemeral. The message that recurs in Cobain's most starkly melancholy texts is the same one that readers discern from Nerval's lamenting texts: Death provides the only route imaginable to permanent relief and unremitting happiness.

It is because the melancholic persona Cobain embraces is irretrievably despondent that he is forever anticipating a future-perfect existence. Even at the moment that Kristeva describes as "symbolic abdication," when Cobain's alter ego is reduced to the babblings and nonsense of a madman, he still phantasizes a future bliss. Discursive suicide in Cobain's lyrics and journals, as exposed earlier in this study and in the suicide letter in this chapter, represents death as a future-perfect moment, whatever the actual tense in which these texts are composed. The suicide letter, for example, shifts between the present and past tenses, even as the text serves ultimately as the overture to an imminent, vulnerary performance.

All of Cobain's melancholy texts, however, even when written in the past tense or when presenting the phantasy of an indefectible future, evoke at the same time a present, ongoing experience rather than a past memory. In the suicide letter, for example, although the first sentence in the second paragraph refers to Freddie Mercury of the rock group Queen in the past tense, the narrator himself remains intractably burrowed in the present. "[W]hen we're back stage and the lights go out and the manic roar of the crowds begins," he writes, "it doesn't affect me in the way in which it did for Freddie Mercury, who seemed to love, relish in the love and adoration from the crowd which is something I totally admire and envy." It is this temporal reality that makes disaggregating person, persona, and character in the Cobainian text challenging and frequently inconsequential for understanding the structure, content, and possible meaning of Cobain's writings. As I have affirmed from the very beginning of this study, whether one reads Cobain's lyrics and journals as autobiography, as autobiographical fiction, or as pure fiction, his texts remain implacably within the realm of phantasy.

Kristeva reads Nerval's at times opaque verse, like the enigmatic poem *"El Desdichado,"* in a way that suggests how readers can best approach Cobain's creative writings.[13] She demonstrates that we do not need to understand all the references in this poem from French legend or from Greek and Roman antiquity in order to be "seized by the phonic and rhythmic coherence of this text" ("On the Melancholic Imaginary," 10). Put another way, readers do not have to be able to explicate the inexplicability of phantasy or to reconcile the irreconcilable illogic of madness in order to be moved by the verse. In a similar manner, I conclude that readers of Cobain's lyrics, in a song such as "I Hate Myself," do not need to be able to solve the poem's enigma. They need not be able to identify any referent outside of the text in order to be transported by the song's melancholy. Readers can experience the depth of the narrator's disconsolation simply as a result of the song's rhythmic coherence:

[Verse 2]
Broken heart and broken bones
. . .
[Chorus]
End it someday
What's that sound? (repeated four times)

In fact, some of Cobain's lyrics prove, as does Nerval's poetry, that the melancholic subject, like the poet, is a true "historian, not so much of his real history as of the symbolic events that have led his *body* to signification, or indeed, that threaten to overwhelm his consciousness" with madness (Kristeva, "On the Melancholic Imaginary," 11, emphasis added). Each of these writers composes autobiographical fiction, and the texts he pens come to constitute in effect his "real" life. Cobain, like Nerval, attains in his writings a remarkable degree of insight, even if neither writer succeeds in becoming fully aware of the nature or scope of his melancholy, and even if neither succeeds in elaborating it.

For both writers, their psychical, if not to say their "psychotic," conflicts position them so that they manifest a special relation to and skill with language itself. It is because of their relation to language that creative writing can possibly function for them as an antidote to depression. As I have demonstrated in part II of this study, the pleasure in the Cobainian text does derive partially from the reader's perception, if not appreciation, of the writer's beguiling manipulation of language. Cobain's ease with language, including his ability to exploit the sounds and meanings of words, produces texts that are seductive yet sometimes unsettling. In addition, the writing subject's own joy is manifest in the gleefulness expressed in the wordplay and, especially, in the perplexing juxtaposition of words and sounds, such as when the lyricist adjoins "mulatto," "albino," "libido," and "mosquito" in "Smells Like Teen Spirit."

In sum, Cobain's texts, overall, reaffirm that the "melancholic imaginary," to insist on the elegant simplicity of Kristeva's expression, can lead to uncannily creative productions. Poetry and poetic prose can mobilize despair, even if they do not, like psychoanalytic therapy, offer a way of truly transcending despondency, of living beyond it. But precisely because creative productions nonetheless do offer a way to receive despair and to allow it to assume a shape, if not a precise and singular meaning, literary texts like those written by Cobain might have a real-world, positive function to fulfill. In other words, as Kristeva—in her role as a trained psychoanalyst—confirms about the value of discourses on melancholy, an examination of Cobain's aesthetic strategies do more than simply provide access to an experience of melancholy. They do more than provide a way for the reader to enjoy his writings. A literary analysis of his lyrics and journal entries could also provide, for the percipient clinician, a portal to therapeutic intervention. Therefore, whereas Robert Burton insists in *The Anatomy of Melancholy* that writing about melancholy can have meaning, I argue that if one uses Cobain's texts as evidence, *reading* about melancholy can also be remedial.

When one examines Cobain's creative writings, specifically as evocations and representations of melancholy, his texts compel us to repose, along with David Farrell Krell and other philosophers, a determinative, two-pronged question: Is melancholy—understood as a condition tied to an experience of profound loss—simply an emotion, an affect? Or, by contrast, is melancholy a process, an event to be narrated? Put differently, is this type of mourning a fatality, like a guitarist born with a physical challenge such as idiopathic sco-liosis? Or, on the contrary, is this type of mourning the result of a specific life trajectory, like the experiences of a frequent and overly enthusiastic stage diver, concert brawler, and moshpit dancer who develops chronic traumatic enceph-alopathy (CTE)?

In sometimes confusing but always clever ways, Cobain's writings repre-sent melancholy as both a fatality, a congenital trait, and as the result of specific life choices. The persona he takes on, for example, proudly proclaims idiopathic scoliosis as his very own cross to bear. And Cobain attributes the symptoms of brain degeneration that characterize CTE not only to the "stump-dumb Joe," the "plankton," and the "white trash" that he vilifies in his journals, liner notes, and lyrics. He also puts forth these symptoms—which include "impulse con-trol problems, aggression, depression, and paranoia" (McKee)—as the defining characteristics of the very persona he adopts and carefully cultivates in his written texts. Therefore, certain of Cobain's texts assist us in thinking through some complex questions concerning the origins and the nature of melancholy and the ultimate fate of its victims, questions with which theorists and clini-cians continue to grapple. His creative writings also illuminate another ques-tion that continues to be debated within psychoanalytic theory concerning the reason why mourning sometimes fails. A nuanced reading of Cobain's lyrics and journal fragments allows readers to observe the work of mourning in prog-ress, a labor that sometimes fails because of the very nature and scope of the loss and a subject's inability to come to terms with it.

Cobain's creative texts prove nonetheless that mourning can spark the imagination in specific ways. They prove that a "creative engagement with suf-fering . . . transforms pain into a lived enrichment of the individual's human sta-tus" (Polatinsky, 224). It is this kind of creative engagement with suffering that characterizes, to varying degrees, the persona in which Cobain is so utterly in-vested. Because when he is singing, strumming, dreaming, drawing, or writing through the pain, then rather than avoiding excruciation, he is embracing it as a means to self-knowledge and to a self-transformation. During these moments of creativity, instead of self-destructing, he succeeds in taking on the psychical and physical pain in order to reaffirm living. During especially vulnerable mo-ments, however, discursive suicide emerges as the creative solution to unen-durable suffering. The persona Cobain takes on—the alter ego with which the historical Kurt Cobain seems to merge himself inextricably—confirms during these moments of unremitting despair that he is, ultimately and inexorably, seduced by the image of death as *the* ultimate site of desire. Cobain's lyrics and journal entries, in this sense, operate to confirm the ineffable pleasures that one's own demise promises.

NOTES

INTRODUCTION

1. Throughout this book, I use the "ph" spelling of phantasy to underscore the specific meaning that Melanie Klein (as well as other scholars and practitioners who base their work on her theories) gives to the term. For Kleinians, unconscious phantasy plays a pivotal role in the structuring and the content of psychic life. My use of "phantasy" constitutes what Sánchez-Pardo in *Cultures of the Death Drive* refers to as a "graphic maneuver" (10), but that I characterize as an "orthographic strategy" designed to reinforce Klein's concept. At the same time, this strategy disrupts the everyday meaning of "fantasy," which can designate simply a daydream. As I explore in detail in my analysis of Cobain's creative writings in chapters 3 and 4, I want to draw particular attention to the fact that Klein's elaboration of the concept establishes a connection between phantasy, the mitigation of anxiety, and experiences of the male body.

2. The Lexington series "seeks not only to demonstrate the influence of Romantic literature on rock ... but [it argues] that rock itself is a late twentieth-century expression of Romanticism—an extension, continuation, partner, or doppelgänger of this eighteenth- and nineteenth-century phenomenon" (Rovira, "Theorizing Rock," 2). All the volumes in the series contain essays that draw from earlier works like Robert Pattison's *The Triumph of Vulgarity: Rock Music in the Mirror of Romanticism*. Although I am more interested in Cobain's relation to the French Romantics, I find several of the essays in *Post-Punk, Goth, and Metal as Dark Romanticism*, edited by Rovira, to be particularly relevant to my reading of Cobainian grunge, as I define it as a literary genre that has both Romantic and Gothic undertones.

3. See Chris McDonald's "Exploring Modal Subversion in Alternative Rock."

4. Barthes distinguishes between voice and language. In the strictest sense, "the grain of the voice" refers to how the human body inflects the singing voice. It refers to the body's capacity to communicate in a way that does not depend on language or the rules of a semiotic system. As I shall explore in chapter 4, Cobain can be said to write, and to write with, the male body.

5. There are other cogent arguments about the limitations of examining music as text and about the shortcomings of some literary analyses of lyrics, such as McClarey and Walser's "Start Making Sense." In spite of the limitations, these kinds of textual analyses do make significant contributions to scholarship in popular music and culture. In addition, Simon Warner in *Text and Drugs and Rock 'N' Roll* and Richard Goldstein in *The Poetry of Rock*, among other writers,

have demonstrated that there is a rich tradition of provocative and persuasive literary analyses of rock lyrics.

6. As Strong also confirms, grunge is not unique in this respect. She draws from the work of scholars like Tony Kirschner, who theorize how listeners understand and experience music genres.

CHAPTER ONE

1. This debate resembles a similar one undertaken by some historians and enthusiasts of rock who attempt to identify the earliest rock song written, recorded, and distributed.

2. I use "scene" and "subculture" in a way that indicates the overlapping of the meanings of the two terms. The hallmark of a scene, when I use the term to reference Cobain's music production, is the person-to-person and, quite frequently, the body-to-body contact that takes place during live performances. I use "subculture" in a manner similar to Ryan Moore, whose work I draw upon substantially in this chapter. If a scene is characterized by localized contact, a subculture, as Moore specifies, transcends the local and emerges as the result of the ways in which various scenes connect and communicate, increasingly in the twenty-first century, via social as well as traditional media.

3. I am inspired here by Peter Van der Merwe's account of the history of popular music in *The Origins of Popular Style* and by Robert Walser's critique of this account in "Review of *Origins of Popular Style*."

4. One can debate whether or not there is a "Seattle-ness" to the music Cobain produced. Specific geographical locations have long been associated with a particular sound: Detroit or Nashville, for example. With Seattle, as with other locales, two processes were taking place. On the one hand, musicians, audiences, owners of venues, and tastemakers in the region came to think about and communicate a sense of identity for the music they were making and listening to. On the other hand, the local record industry, and eventually the national and international industries as well, promoted the Seattle sound as a major component of their marketing strategies.

5. For a succinct account of the notion of "authenticity" in rock music, see Joe Connell's "The Problem of Authenticity." And for an analysis of the notion of authenticity in Cobain specifically, see Wood's "Pained Expression." Making a distinction between music as art and creativity and music as commerce was nothing new. As early as the 1950s, David Riesman in "Listening to Popular Music" was distinguishing between the majority of listeners, whom he characterized as displaying undiscriminating tastes, and a small minority of listeners, whom he deemed to be more discerning. Riesman's distinction was retheorized in the 1960s as a generational divide, with youth being the minority that, beyond music, inspired a subcultural mode that applied to aesthetics more generally and to politics and attitudes toward aspects of contemporary life, like sex and consumerism.

6. Grossman, in "Identity Crisis," provides a summary account of the bands and songs that characterize the relationships and the transitions between rock, punk, and grunge.

7. "While some punks critiqued the macho culture of misogyny and violence, they sometimes repeated these tendencies" (Grossman, 25). One can see, however, the masculinist orientation

of the counteraesthetic that U.S. punk proposed in the way that Lester Bangs—one of the rock journalists in the early 1970s who helped to articulate the political and aesthetic essence of punk—"praised the Stooges' manic singer Iggy Pop for his confrontational antics. [Pop's persona and performance style] seemed to embody all the *male* adolescent angst that Bangs thought fundamental" to authentic rock music (R. Moore, 45, emphasis added). Notwithstanding generalizations of this type, there was a great diversity among the various local U.S. punk scenes in terms of attitudes and actions concerning gender and sexuality, evident in lyrics as well as in stage performances (Gunckel).

8. See, for example, Henry Rollins's (Black Flag) tour diaries as excerpted in *The Portable Henry Rollins*. Among the critics who inquire about the relation between hardcore and violence, see Bannister's *White Boys, White Noise* and R. Moore's *Sells Like Teen Spirit*.

9. The confusion of hard rock with heavy metal is understandable since heavy metal does derive some of its signature elements from hard rock. Jon Pareles, writing in the *New York Times* in 1988, proposes that "In the taxonomy of popular music, heavy metal is a major subspecies of hard rock—the breed with less syncopation, less blues, more showmanship and more brute force" ("Heavy Metal, Weighty Words"). If heavy metal and hard rock share certain sonic and performative elements, it is in distancing itself from its blues roots that heavy metal distinguishes itself from hard rock, which, on the contrary, adheres to and exploits its blues antecedents. Some commentators like Everett True argue that listeners' perception of what constitute metal and hard rock has changed over the years since Nirvana. In particular, True writes, listeners' perception of metal has become more "extreme" such that Led Zeppelin, once put unquestionably into the metal category, is now thought of as hard rock (116).

10. See, for example, "Maligning the Music: Metal Detractors" in Weinstein. It was in large measure against the overproduced and "inauthentic" rock music of the 1970s exemplified by heavy metal that punk rock established itself.

11. Even though metal appeals especially to certain white teen boys and young men, as the music evolved in the 1980s, one can see why it might appeal to the persona Cobain was taking on. Metal's fan base became older and perhaps less working-class; and the genre attracted more young women, in part, because of glam metal. In North America, two subgenres of metal came to dominate the overall scene during the '80s. Thrash metal, a subgenre undergirded by experiences of anger and alienation, inflected heavy metal in a specific way. By contrast, glam metal (or hair metal), constituted a subgenre epitomized by bands as diverse as Mötley Crüe, Quiet Riot, Bon Jovi, and Guns N' Roses. For an account of these subgenres, in addition to Walser, see Philip Auslander's *Performing Glam Rock* and Stephen Davis's *Watch You Bleed*.

12. See Ed Power's account of Queensrÿche, the progressive metal band from Bellevue, Washington. Cobain samples one of the group's songs on the "Montage of Heck" cassette he recorded before the release of *Bleach*.

13. K Records was cofounded, owned, and operated in Olympia by musician (Beat Happening) and songwriter Calvin Johnson on the model of SST and other independent labels. The label has promoted and greatly influenced the anticorporate, underground subculture.

14. The Seattle bands in general were certainly influenced, directly or indirectly, by the Washington D.C. band Fugazi (1987–2003). In the way that Fugazi broke away from the sonic

and lyrical restraints of hardcore, they provided an example of a different kind of music that was appealing to many listeners who were becoming displeased with the limitations of hardcore performance and less tolerant of its macho posturing.

15. Riot Grrrl gradually became a social movement whose philosophy and practice were designed to raise the consciousness and facilitate the self-expression of young women. Participants advertised and promoted the music in DIY zines, on radio shows, and in the production and distribution of records. "Riot grrrl bands performed music that was much like that of original punk and hardcore; [it was] urgent and visceral, [yet it challenged] masculinist notions of expertise while unleashing intense emotions and physical sensations" (R. Moore, 127–29). For more on the essence and the evolution of the riot grrrl movement, see Chelsea Starr's *Because, Riot Grrrl* and Marisa Meltzer's *Girl Power.*

16. Strong has written convincingly about the interrelations between grunge and Generation X. See also Furek's "The Death Proclamation of Generation X." For Cobain's relationship to the subgroup, see Pecora and Mazzarella's "Kurt Cobain." For details on the politics of grunge, see Shevory's "Bleach Resistance." For an assessment of how grunge's ethics are grafted onto performances of hegemonic masculinities, see Bannister's *White Boys, White Noise* and Kitts, Tolinski, and Steinblatt, *Nirvana.*

17. There are several detailed accounts of the creation and the success of Sup Pop Records. See Thurston Moore's *Grunge* and Justin Henderson's *Seattle Grunge.*

18. Some critics do not consider all of Weezer's music to be emo, even if it has been important for the development of the subgenre. For the history of emo, see Andy Greenwald's *Nothing Feels Good* and Matt Diehl's *My So-Called Punk.*

19. Among the dozens of emo social media sites, one finds emopuddle.com, clubemo.com, emowire.com, emopassions.com, and realemos.com. For the names of emo bands, lead singers, the titles and dates of songs and albums, see Träger's "Emocosms" and Ryalls's *Emo Angst.* For gay men in emo, see Peters's "Emo Gay Boys."

20. *Screaming Life* was printed without page numbers.

21. "In an intense night of songwriting and jamming, one of [Pearl Jam's] members—it has never been stated which one—gave so much effort and feeling that he ejaculated into his pants. The ejaculate is sometimes referred to as pearls and since it burst forth while in a jam session … they just had to use it" ("Band Name Origins").

22. I do not enter into the recent polemic surrounding the origin and the meaning of "white trash." In chapter 4, though, I do explore briefly how and why Cobain uses the term in his journals but not in his lyrics.

23. It is not surprising that a grunge "look" would be adopted by national fashion houses and would appear on runways. This look included wool caps covering unwashed, unkempt hair, flannel shirts, and Doc Martin boots. Nor is it surprising that national magazines (*Details, Spin, Parade*) would enhance the myth further by writing about grunge as a "lifestyle." For an entertaining account of grunge's influence on fashion, see Fp Julia's "The History of Grunge."

24. For the prominence of heroin in the Seattle grunge scene, see, Tim Jonze's "Mike Starr and the Deadliest Musical Genre"; and for the post-Nirvana era, see Peggy Anderson's "Tragedy Strikes Grunge Scene Again."

CHAPTER TWO

1. Because Cobain's creative writings are structured around representations of a masochistic phantasy, these texts must be read within the Beat tradition of representing white masculinity. That his lyrics and journals enter into a dialogue with the writings and biographies of the Beats is not surprising. Over the years, popular music has turned to various writers and literary traditions for inspiration. However, "the Beat Generation has provided . . . the most fertile and frequent literary nourishment for rock musicians" (Warner, 21). It is easy to see the overarching reasons for this particular inspiration for rockers in general and for Cobain specifically. The Beat aesthetic, which subscribes to the personal, confessional narrative and poem, has coincided with rock's own aesthetic since the earliest development of the genre from the 1960s to today (see Coupe's *Beat Sound*). It is via rock's Beat inspirations that the genre has an evident connection to Romantic traditions. Cobain's journals, for example, reveal a particular fascination with the works and the very person of William Burroughs, with whom he collaborated on a 1993 project ("The 'Priest' They Called Him").

2. In *The Pleasure in the Text,* Barthes puts forth an interesting, subtle argument. He makes a distinction between what has been translated into English as readerly texts (*"lisible"*) and writerly texts (*"scriptible"*). The former are conventional texts. The pleasure the reader experiences from engaging with a readerly text is that of a passive consumption. This kind of text does not challenge the reader's subjectivity. By contrast, a writerly text can lead to an even more intense pleasure (*"jouissance"*). This kind of text challenges the reader's sense of self; it perturbs the reader's consciousness. The reader actively engages with the text instead of merely consuming it passively. These are the kinds of texts, as I suggest in the introduction, that can function as a palliative for the depressed fan or reader.

3. At any particular moment, there are scores of Facebook groups devoted to Cobain and Nirvana. Between July 2016 and February 2017, the following three groups seem to have been among the most active: "Kurt Cobain and Nirvana" (fifty thousand members); "Kurt Cobain Forever" (twenty-five thousand members); "Original Nirvana Fans" (forty thousand members).

4. At the same time, and although I do not enter into the details of this debate, Cobain's *real* body, like the human body in general, can be and has been a blank canvas onto which journalists and fans have inscribed their own expectations and desires. Strong and Bickerdike touch on this topic, but it is especially on social media that we see the extent to which fans project their phantasies onto images of Cobain's body.

5. When I indicate that the male body is central to the Cobainian creative project, I hasten to underscore also that I am not conceiving of the body as a fixed materiality, but rather as contingent and pliable.

6. In classical psychoanalysis, a hysterical symptom erupts as the result of a patient's conflicted, unconscious (sexual) phantasy. Hysterics (like Freud's patient Dora) can identify as male or female. Like the dreamer, the hysteric plays all the roles in the story (dream, phantasy) being told (P. Adams).

7. Ute Berns has written tellingly on what critics within that field of literary analysis known as narratology have termed "performativity." Narratology constitutes the branch of literary criticism that examines how writers structure narratives and how the literary devices they use

function. In narratology, Berns writes, "the concept of performativity has been most productive in as far as it draws attention to the different [ways narratives can imitate a performance]. This [imitation] encompasses narratives that are corporeally enacted as well as narratives that attempt to evoke or transform—in written, visual or acoustic presentations—the material qualities or dramatic immediacy of performances" (94).

8. In making these distinctions between character, real person, and persona, I draw in particular from Simon Frith's *Performing Rites*, David Graver's "The Actor's Body," and Philip Auslander's *Performing Glam Rock*.

9. "'Creative Writers and Day-Dreaming' explores the origins of daydreaming and its relationship to the play of children; it is Freud's most straightforward exploration of the creative process" (Person, ix).

10. See the journal *Auto/Fiction* and the site autofiction.org.

11. As for the spelling of his first name, Charles Cross speculates that Cobain probably adopted it because he admired the music of a metal band from Aberdeen, Metal Church, whose lead singer was Kurdt Vanderhoff (*Here We Are Now*, 186). Stephen Tow in *The Strangest Tribe*, however, summarizes what others have written concerning the origin of this spelling, tracing it to an inadvertent error on a C/Z Records compilation titled *Teriyaki Asthma*. The record includes Cobain's song "Mexican Seafood," which, like *Bleach*, was released in 1989. The graphic artists preparing the cover simply did not know how Cobain spelled his name; and when they were unable to reach him to confirm, they went with "Kurdt Kobain" because they were pressed for time. They made the decision partly in ignorance but also partly in fun. After seeing it, writes Tow, "Kurt thought it was a pretty funny way to misspell it . . . so from that point on, he went way out of his way to misspell his [own] name" (189).

CHAPTER THREE

1. Jessica Wood provides a summary of all the descriptions of Cobain's voice published prior to 2012. For Nirvana's sound, in addition to works by Crisafulli, Gaar, and Soulsby, see True's *Nirvana*, Azerrad's *Come As You Are*, and McDonald's "Exploring Modal Subversion."

2. True and Crisafulli provide at the end of their studies a concise chronology of Nirvana's entire repertoire.

3. Lyrics to certain songs were published in 2004 in *Nirvana: The Lyrics*. No transcriber or editor is indicated for these versions of Cobain's songs. There are dozens of sites that include Cobain's lyrics, such as SongLyrics.com, AZLyrics.com, MetroLyrics.com, GeniusLyrics.com, and LyricsMode.com. In my own work, however, I have found the lyrics posted on the *Nirvana Fan Club* site to be especially helpful. I am also indebted to musician-poet (and my friend) Gregory Toth for transcribing and verifying the lyrics to the songs examined in this chapter.

4. This version can also be found at http://pigeonsandplanes.com/music/2015/08/listen-to -17-pre-nirvana-demos-from-kurt-cobains-fecal-matter-band.

5. Stipes's composing and performance style can be compared to Cobain's. Stipes has characterized some of his early lyrics as "nonsense," and listeners consider some of his songs to be indecipherable. In addition, like Cobain, Stipes too mumbles and wails while singing, as evident on the 1983 album *Murmur*. As for Morrissey, he can be compared to Cobain in terms of themes.

Many of his lyrics, like Cobain's, represent loss, doom, and pain. In addition, Morrissey also possesses a pessimistic view of cultural institutions like schools and churches, and he incorporates violence and even references to suicide in his lyrics (for example, in the song "There Is a Light That Never Goes Out"). In fact, as alternative music emerged in the 1980s, across the board, "the predominant emotional tone was pessimistic, marked by an overall sense of loss—of innocence, of love and (arguably) of traditional masculine power" (Bannister, 133). Morrissey's "I'm Not a Man" constitutes a précis of this emotional tone. In this song, the narrator enumerates all the ways, both significant and insignificant, in which he is not a "man," from the way he walks and sits to his refusal to "destroy this planet."

6. See, in particular, Humphrey, Tow, R. Moore, Bannister, and Azerrad.

7. Readers cannot take as necessarily accurate or insightful what Cobain has said about how he writes, the subjects he writes about, or the relation between the lyrics and the music in his songs. But what he has said during interviews and written in his journals, even if disingenuous, alerts us to the social and cultural interests and the aesthetic sensibilities of the persona he was at times unwittingly projecting.

8. Soulsby neglects to specify, however, that these listeners are overwhelmingly white, ostensibly straight, young men. This missing analysis leads him to a slight misreading of the importance of the male body in Cobain lyrics. He also dismisses Cobain's journals as devoid of interest for admirers of Cobain's music. I take up the topic of the relationship between Cobain's lyrics and his journals in the next chapter.

9. As Soulsby points out ("Analysing Nirvana's Songs"), Cobain was not the first musician to use the word "incesticide." New York–based Australian musician and songwriter James George Thirlwell employs it in a song included in a compilation disk released in November 1992. Cobain's album was released in December of the same year.

10. "As part of the infamous 'swimming test,' women accused of being witches were dragged to the nearest body of water, stripped to their undergarments, bound and then tossed in to see if they would sink or float. Since witches were believed to have spurned the sacrament of baptism, it was thought that the water would reject their [bodies] and prevent them from submerging" (Andrews). Another reference is made to this practice in "Serve the Servants" in the line "If she floats then she is not a witch like we thought."

11. As masochists, narrators and characters are dominated. They are captured, abused, or neglected by various other characters such as romantic partners, friends, and persons of authority (parent, judge, school or medical officials). They present themselves in various ways as "negative creeps" who deserve and who are willing to be punished for their actual transgressions or simply for their natural inclination toward malfeasance. The narrator in "Insurance," for example, is on trial and is poised to be justly punished and imprisoned. In addition, "Paper Cuts" and "Sappy" both enact some form of restraint, capture, or imprisonment.

12. Cross writes that Cobain "loved porcelain doll heads; and he frequently repainted them or added touches like human hair or teeth" (*Unseen,* 94). On occasion, he also hanged, burned, bashed—or mutilated in other ways—some of the dolls he collected.

13. I read "Been a Son" contrary to a popular interpretation of the song in which, according to Crisafulli, for example, "a put-upon daughter's worth goes so unnoticed that she might as well

have died at birth if she wasn't going to be born with a penis" (115). Therefore, I do not read the song as a commentary on those cultures that privilege the birth of boys. Contrary to many online commentators, I see no textual evidence that would authorize reading "Been a Son" *narrowly* as a commentary on Donald Cobain's attitude toward his daughter Kimberly. The details in this song, like in others, resist being read *simply* as comments on specific people and events in Cobain's life.

14. Amniotic fluid can be yellow or pinkish (Reece); its presence in this song ties it to the Cobain theme of cleansing, as I examine it below, because the fluid is reported to smell like bleach or the commercial cleansing powder Comet (see the essay "What To Expect" [whattoexpect.com]).

15. The inspiration for "Paper Cuts," according to some commentators, was the situation of a young child whom Cobain either knew or simply knew of. Crisafulli writes, "The kid had come from a home in Aberdeen where the abusive parents had kept several children constantly locked in a single room . . . the only concession to hygiene was a pile of newspapers that the kids were expected to use as their toilet" (38). I continue to argue, however, that these types of real-world details do not facilitate an understanding of how this song works as an individual text or how it functions as part of Cobain's overall lyrical works.

16. In addition to Cobain (vocals and guitar), Fecal Matter in 1985–86 included, at various times, Dale Crover (bass guitar and drums), Greg Hokanson (drums), Buzz Osborne (bass guitar), and Mike Dillard (drums). Cobain had also been a member of other earlier bands, some very briefly, including The Stiff Woodies, The Sellouts, Skid Row, and Ed, Ted, and Fred.

17. A named female character also appears in the Fecal Matter song "Buffy's Pregnant."

18. According to Nicolson in "New Music Express" and Soulsby writing in his blog "Nirvana Legacy," the song very likely has its origins in real events. Relying on accounts by biographers, and Charles Cross in particular, Nicolson indicates that Cobain's maternal uncle (Patrick Fradenburg) had accused his own maternal uncle of raping him when he was a child. Both Nicolson and Soulsby state that Fradenburg had been secretly gay, moved to San Francisco, and subsequently became infected with HIV.

19. I return to this theme of the absence of the penis as an organ of pleasure and as an emblem of power and authority in part III of this book.

20. The penis is mentioned in a line in "Buffy's Pregnant" as an utterance by the high-school jock character: "Boy how I'd like to do her" / "like to jump her bones" / "slip her the hard beef injection."

21. For a succinct history of the different recordings of "Spank Thru," including the different drummers and the different group names under which it was recorded, see Crisafulli (212–14).

22. I explore in chapter 4 how representations of male penetration in Cobain's journals functions to tell us something significant about masculine identity, the male body, and experiences of power and pleasure.

23. As with representations of the penis in Cobain's writings, I return to this notion of gender and sexual fluidity in part III.

24. I transcribe "Token Eastern Song" from the *With the Lights Out* CD. The song has been referred to as "Born in a Junkyard" and "Happy Hour." Cobain changed the lyrics during live performances (nirvanalive.com).

25. Cobain seems to have considered "I Hate Myself and Want to Die" as a joke title and a throwaway song, one that he "could write in his sleep," as he confesses to one interviewer (Mallon). Originally bandied about as the title for *In Utero*, the song was released on the compilation *The Beavis and Butt-Head Experience*. As Tom Mallon writes, "the band buried the lurching piece of infectious sludge-pop because they (rightly) feared that no one would get its black humor. '[It was] nothing more than a joke,' Cobain told *Rolling Stone* in late 1993. 'We knew people wouldn't get it; they'd take it too seriously. It was totally satirical, making fun of ourselves'" ("No Apologies").

26. In addition to the images posted at "livenirvana.com/art/drawings," others can be found at several sites, including "needsomefun.net/Kurt-cobain-own-drawings-and-paintings."

27. According to Charles Cross in *Cobain Unseen*, Cobain took pride in stealing crucifixes to create multidimensional art pieces and to decorate his home.

CHAPTER FOUR

1. I initially proposed the thesis for the first section of this chapter in a 2013 essay in volume 1 of the *European Journal of American Culture* titled "A Pool of Razor Blades and Sperm: A Phantasy of White Heterosexual Masculinity in Kurt Cobain's *Journals*." Portions of that essay are reproduced here with the permission of Intellect Limited through PLSclear. Presently, I develop more comprehensively how gender, sexuality, and race interrelate in Cobain's personal writings. I target explicitly his representation of whiteness and his misrepresentation of blackness. In this chapter, I use "*Journals*," capitalized and italicized, to refer to the published versions of Cobain's notebooks. I use either "journals" or "notebooks" to refer to all of his personal writings that are known to exist. Except for family members, to my knowledge, only biographer Charles Cross and filmmaker Brett Morgan, who directed *Kurt Cobain: Montage of Heck* (2015), have had access to all the materials from Cobain's personal archives.

2. The essay by Chapman and Rutherford represents one of the earliest efforts to examine and to critique the myths surrounding masculinity and men's real and symbolic power. For an analysis of the so-called crisis of white masculinity and its relation to how femininity and blackness are represented in American culture, see Brenton Malin's *American Masculinity*.

3. In examining the structure and content of *Journals*, I draw from the extensive scholarship on autobiography, autofiction, and on journal and memoir writing. In particular, studies by Braud, Hubier, and Mazlish have shaped my reading of *Journals* as the construction of a gendered and racialized persona.

4. There are too many sites devoted to Cobain to list here; the most accessed, as of January 2018, seems to have been "cobain.com." And, as indicated earlier, there are several dozen Facebook groups.

5. I draw from scholars who theorize that cultural productions, like poetry and music, are always the result of more than the individual artist alone; they are always collective practices. See H. Becker's "Art as Collective Action" and R. Peterson's "The Production of Culture."

6. When I cite an entry from *Journals*, I indicate only during the first citation the spelling, grammatical, or syntactical errors in that passage. I also insert within brackets appropriate punc-

tuation, but only when necessary to eliminate confusion and to indicate how I am interpreting a particular fragment. In every instance, I include the crossed-out text while also specifying which parts of an entry are written between the lines or in the margins.

7. In my examination of gender, self-knowledge, and power in Cobain's writings, I do not draw explicitly from Foucault. I recognize, however, that many of my observations concerning the status of the white male body in *Journals* can be read in light of Foucault's seminal work. Cortney Alexander demonstrates, by way of Judith Butler's thesis in *Gender Trouble*, how Foucault's theories of subjectivity, power, and knowledge can help to illuminate how Cobain represents gender in his creative texts.

8. Klein writes three essays in particular that discuss the relation between phantasy and creativity: "Our Adult World and Its Roots in Infancy," "Infant Anxiety Situations Reflected in a Work of Art," and "Some Reflections on the Oresteia." But the most comprehensive accounting of Kleinian aesthetics, including the relationship between unconscious phantasy and gender identity, has not been undertaken by Klein herself but by other analysts and theorists, in particular Hanna Segal and Nicky Glover, who interpret and build on Klein's work.

9. As suggested in the introduction, I am using "lean on" in the Freudian sense of *Anlehnung* and in the common sense of "depends on" and "to be modeled on."

10. To add to the uncanny disorientation that *Journals* as a whole engenders for readers, the image of the chef is a slight variation of another image, which I do not reproduce, that Cobain titles "Hairspray Queen," presented as the representation of a "male rock monster" (3).

11. I have already broached in chapter 2 the significance of the psychoanalytic notion of hysteria for my reading of Cobain. Penley and Willis follow Freud in designating a symptom as hysterical when it emerges because of a person's simultaneous masculine and feminine unconscious, sexual phantasy (xviii).

12. Goober Pyle and Gomer Pyle are characters on *The Andy Griffith Show* that aired on American television from 1960 to 1968. In a subsequent entry, as I reveal below, Cobain plays on the word "pyle" when his first-person narrator once again describes his own penetration. And, as the entry indicates, Gary Coleman is the actor who played a character named Arnold on the series *Different Strokes* (1978–1986); the actor Emmanuel Lewis played the title character on *Webster* (1983–1989). At the time, both Coleman and Lewis were the rare black teen actors who were leads in prime-time comedy shows aimed principally at white viewers. Telly Savalas appeared in the title role in the 1973–1978 series *Kojak*. Both the actor and the character are bald, dapper, and macho.

13. The text includes complete versions of the following songs: "Downer" (47); "Blew" (48); "Mr. Moustache" (49); "Floyd the Barber" (50); "Paper Cuts" (51); "Hairspray Queen" (53); "Mexican Seafood" (54); "Pen Cap Chew" (57); "Aerozepplin" (58); "Aneurysm" (97); "Sappy" (98); "Verse Chorus Verse" (99, 153, 154); "Dive" (101); "Primary" (101); "I Think I'm Dumb" (119, 203); "I Started It First" (130); "Smells Like Teen Spirit" (146, 151 155); "Lithium" (150); "In Bloom" (152); "On a Plain" (157); "Frances Farmer" (197); "Heart Shaped Box" (198); "Four Month Media Blackout" ["Radio Friendly Unit Shifter"] (210, 211); "I Like Girls" ["All Apologies"] (224); "Travelin' White Trash Couple" ["Swap Meet"] (258); and "Curmudgeon" (274).

14. In Cross's biography as well as in Dave Thompson's, Wendy Cobain suffered abuse at the hands of a boyfriend after she separated from Cobain's father.

15. This is not a radical statement. The assertion that black artists must conform to a white standard to become popular is a familiar one within the music press as well as within popular music scholarship. This notion can be traced back to the 1930s and Theodor Adorno's theories on jazz. Simon Frith makes a nuanced version of this argument in his discussion of race and the corporate control of music distribution in *Performing Rites*. Nelson George also makes a compelling version of this argument *The Death of Rhythm & Blues*.

16. This entry reveals Cobain's extraordinary sense of detail. The stargazer lily, for example, is not just any flower. Its usually pleasant perfume affects a minority of people in a negative way. For these people the flower's odor is foul and causes difficulty in breathing, headaches, nausea, and vomiting, all recurring symptoms, to some degree, of the persona Cobain continually takes on.

17. On some recordings released during the 1980s and 1990s by Folkways Recordings and by the Library of Congress, the musician's name is rendered as "Leadbelly." The performer himself wrote his stage name as two words. "Lead Belly" is now the current practice. Cobain uses both forms in his notebooks.

18. Lead Belly functions in *Journals* much like the "Magical Negro" in certain cultural representations of African Americans. Scholars have analyzed this trope especially in cinematic representations. Magical Negro cinema puts forth films that showcase "lower-class, uneducated, and magical Black characters who transform . . . broken white characters into competent people" (Hughey, 543). Some of these films have been celebrated as politically progressive. Others have been condemned as damaging and regressive because they resort to stereotypes and play to racialized phantasies. See, for example, Zuleyka Zevallos's "Hollywood Racism."

19. See the biographies written by Wolfe and Lornell and by Garvin and Addeo. See also the online biographies at britannica.com/biography/Leadbelly, http://blackhistorynow.com/leadbelly/, and especially William Ruhlmann's biography posted at allmusic.com/artist/lead-belly-mn0000124390/biography.

20. One YouTube version of the MTV video, of which there are several, had been viewed over 86 million times as of May 2018. Many rock musicians have covered Lead Belly songs (The Beach Boys, Creedence Clearwater Revival, Led Zeppelin, etc.). One cannot know the details of Cobain's knowledge of and engagement with black cultural production in general and with the works of Lead Belly in particular. His comments about Lead Belly—when introducing "Where Did You Sleep Last Night?" ("my favorite performer") and during interviews (Hubbard, 13; Chiesa, 44)—confirm that he was attempting to enlighten his audiences by introducing them to an underappreciated American talent.

21. The very notion of "black" or "white" music is a complicated one; it continues to be part of an ongoing discussion among scholars. Negus aptly summarizes and contextualizes the early stages and the significance of this debate (*Popular Music Theory*, 99–107).

22. Besides compilations of "favorites," there are a few other lists in the text. They are of two types: either songs by other musicians Cobain has recorded or whose music he wants to record later (82, 89, 233, 248), or songs from set lists (69, 230).

23. Given Cobain's professed music aesthetics, performance style, and gender politics, instead of Lead Belly, a more apt model and idol for the persona he takes on might have been singer, songwriter, and guitarist Sister Rosetta Tharpe, "the Godmother of Rock." See the following: Stereo Williams's essay "The First Badass Female Guitarist: Meet Sister Rosetta Tharpe, the Godmother of Rock 'n' Roll"; Jonathan Graham's "Forgotten Guitar: Before Hendrix, Elvis and Chuck Berry, There was Sister Rosetta Tharpe"; and the PBS Black Cultural Connections podcast "The Godmother of Rock 'N' Roll."

24. Though not included on Cobain's lists, there are exceptions, of course, as seen in Afro-punk. In addition, punk evolved differently in the United States and in England. The Clash, for example, are an English punk band composed of white men "who explicitly acknowledged their affection for reggae and their sense of identification with [the genre's] overtly socio-political use by black people" (Negus, 108).

25. The "Scarecrow/Jesus" image also appears in the actual "Heart Shaped Box" video directed by Anton Corbijn and first released in 1993. This image is especially evocative. A thirty-something, anorexic-appearing actor with blue eyes and long blond hair hangs on the cross. He cannily resembles, simultaneously, an older-looking Kurt Cobain and a more emaciated-looking Jesus Christ.

26. See in particular Jack Hamilton's *Just Around Midnight*.

27. The first verse of Berry's song describes this performer. Berry writes in his autobiography that he changed "colored" to "country" in the fourth line in order to attenuate the racial implication of his lyrics (*Chuck Berry*, 157): "Deep down in Louisiana close to New Orleans / Way back up in the woods among the evergreens / There stood a log cabin made of earth and wood / Where lived a country [colored] boy named Johnny B. Goode / Who never ever learned to read or write so well / But he could play a guitar just like a-ringin' a bell."

28. Bannister and R. Moore follow in the tradition of other historians of rock who confirm Norman Mailer's intuition as expressed in "The White Negro" and Eric Lott's thesis as laid out in *Love and Theft* concerning the relationship between black cultural production and white masculine identity. From this perspective, the rock genre, overall, represents a dialectic of "love and theft" of black cultural capital of "hipness" and folk authenticity. Lott examines blackface minstrelsy as a sympathetic identification with and, simultaneously, a fear of and revulsion to black dialect, music, and dance. "This interplay between the desire for black male bodies and the mimicry and commercial exploitation of black music and style is ongoing in American popular culture; but it was particularly strong in the early days of rock 'n' roll and white appropriations of the blues" (R. Moore, 171).

29. I return briefly to this exception in the next chapter when I explore in detail how Cobain succeeds in creating a masochistic persona in his creative writings.

30. Doty's eye-opening collection of essays, titled *Making Things Perfectly Queer*, puts a queer spin on some familiar figures in popular culture such as the sitcom *Laverne and Shirley* and the entertainer Jack Benny. Doty does not argue that all these characters in mass-consumed films and television are queer, properly speaking. He writes, "Notorious for its ability to suggest things without saying them [explicitly], connotation has been the representational and inter-

pretive closet of mass culture queerness for far too long [. . .]; the concept of connotation allows straight culture to use queerness for pleasure and profit in mass culture without admitting to it" (xi–xii). Doty argues further "that queerness may be the most pervasive dynamic in mass culture, albeit in disguised form. [He concludes that] 'Only heterocentrist / homophobic cultural training prevents everyone from acknowledging this queerness'" (Hadleigh, 47, citing Doty). I return to the notion of a queer reading of so-called straight texts in chapter 5.

31. As I specify in part I, I am making a simple distinction between identity (a primary or fixed sense of who one is) and identification (an act or instance of identifying). Moreover, by refusing to take on a stereotyped blackness in his actual performances and, at the same time, by putting forth an explicitly antiracist position in his notebooks, Cobain separates himself from some other white musicians, like Elvis most notably, when they cover black music and lyrics (Coyle, 153). In terms of written texts that conflate autobiography and fiction and that describe the performances of black and white musicians, Cobain also distinguishes himself from Anthony Kiedis (of the group Red Hot Chili Peppers), for example, in the writing of *Scar Tissue,* his 2004 memoir. Cobain is different even though, like Elvis, Kiedis, and other musicians, he too uses black cultural productions in order to construct and to perform a specifically white masculine identity.

CHAPTER FIVE

1. For a comprehensive account of the psychoanalytic notion of perversion and its relation to neurosis, psychosis, and normative masculine gender and sexual identities, see Jonathan Dollimore's *Sexual Dissidence.* See also Dany Nobus and Lisa Downing's *Perversions.* In this chapter and the next, I continue to use the masculine pronoun "he" when referring to the subject within classic psychoanalytic theory in order to underscore the privileging of the male subject that the theory effectuates.

2. Discussions of masochism are also invariably politically charged. See Lynn Chancer's *Reconcilable Differences,* which provides an introduction to the politics of sadomasochism.

3. Although psychoanalytic theory argues that a profound sense of lack, alienation, and alterity are features common to all subjectivities, these features have been culturally attributed to the female/feminine subject. The normative male/masculine subject is predicated on a denial of these specific characteristics. "For Lacan, *alienation* [or a sense of lack, inadequacy] is not an accident that befalls the subject and [that] can be transcended, but an essential, constitutive feature of the subject. The subject is fundamentally split, *alienated* from himself, and there is no escape from this division, no possibility of 'wholeness or synthesis'" (nosubject.com/Alienation).

4. The *Standard Edition* of Freud's works in English confuses two terms that have different meanings in German, *Instinkt* ("instinct") and *Trieb* ("drive"). Writers often translate both terms as *instinct.* Because of the confusion, some English readers arrive at conclusions that do not comport precisely with Freud's thesis. For example, Freud indicates that the "death instinct" is a drive. But he specifies that a drive differs from an instinct because a drive is not essential for the continued existence of the organism. Most anglophone scholars use the term "death drive"; some writers, especially those who subscribe to Lacanian psychoanalysis, use the abbreviated "drive," as if Freud wrote about a single drive only. He posits in fact several drives.

5. I am using "agony" in the Greek/Latin root of *"agon,"* in order to designate a physical contest or struggle and an accompanying mental suffering, especially like that of Christ on the Mount of Olives.

6. On the psychoanalytic meaning of the penis/phallus distinction, as well as the philosophical and metaphorical implications of this distinction, see Robert Silhol's "On the Signification of the Phallus."

7. "Masculinity, Masochism, and the Crucifixion: The Male-Body-In-Pain as Redemptive Figure" is Brintnall's PhD dissertation that he reconceptualized, revised, and expanded in the book *Ecce Homo: The Male-Body-in-Pain as Redemptive Figure.* I find the earlier version of his thesis more pertinent for my reading of Cobain, however, because it presents a more compelling literary and cultural analysis.

8. Savran concludes that what was presented in the 1950s as nonhegemonic and a resisting mode of masculinity—as seen in the real life and in the fiction and poetry of the Beats—after that period established itself as more or less mainstream in the succeeding generation. One can trace the way in which the white male hipster, as epitomized by Norman Mailer's "White Negro," evolves into the 1960s countercultural masculinities, as exemplified by the resisting and irreverent hippie and by the white political radical, such as Tom Hayden. Although the new masculinities of the '50s and '60s were poised to resist and disrupt the conventional masculinity that characterized the post–World War II period, they became hegemonic because they came to reflect the reactions and the strategies of white men to regroup in light of the social and economic challenges they were facing. These challenges emerged, as Savran argues, in wake of the civil rights, women, and gay liberation movements.

9. In addition to taking a beating, an action film hero like Rocky or Rambo can be said to be feminized to the extent that his spectacular muscles are put on display as objects of desire. For example, in *First Blood* (1982), *Rambo: First Blood Part II* (1985), and *Rambo III* (1988), "the process of making Rambo a spectacle produces intriguing side effects. On the one hand, his enormous strength, self-confidence, and resilience clearly mark him as a phallic male. . . . On the other hand, his masculinity and muscles are so constantly and extravagantly on parade that he simultaneously undergoes what can be described only as a feminization. . . . Lacan observes that both 'virile display' and 'exaggeration of masculinity' appear as 'feminine'" (Savran, 199).

10. As Gilman suggests, one sees this kind of son's anxiety especially in Kafka's work: "One of the central anxieties in Kakfa's life and work . . . [is that] one is fated to become the father" (vii).

11. Elizabeth Grosz in *Volatile Bodies* and Josep Armengol in "Toward a History of the Male Body," among other scholars, have shown that a "natural body" has never existed but rather that all bodies are invariably formed within a specific cultural practice and at a specific historical moment. As I also indicate in chapter 2, a critical examination of Cobain's representations of the male body suggests just as much.

12. Cobain writes in the liner notes, "Last year, a girl was rapped by two wastes of sperm and eggs while they sang the lyrics to our song 'Polly.' I have a hard time carrying on knowing there are plankton like that in our audience. Sorry to be so anally P.C. but that's the way I feel. Love, Kurdt (the blond one).

13. Hervey and Higgins in *Thinking Translation* are not writing about Cobain or even about masculinity or gender identity at all but about the general concept and function of poetic expression.

14. Cobain performed "They Hung Him on the Cross" during live performances. The version of the song to which I refer is a 1989 demo by The Jury, Cobain's collaboration with members of Screaming Trees. The version can be found on YouTube.

15. Brintnall also writes about the tendency to reduce all that is important in patriarchal culture "to father and sons by circumscribing desire to male homoerotic negotiations and [by] aggrandizing male subjects as the ultimate object of virtually all desire" ("Masculinity, Masochism, and the Crucifixion," 52). Although Brintnall does not explicitly reference René Girard, his analysis is indebted to Girard's *Violence and the Sacred,* a book whose principal thesis is underpinned by the notion that all of hegemonic culture can be interpreted as negotiations of power and pleasure between men.

16. For comments on the *GQ* commemoration, consult the *US Weekly* article "Courtney Love Recalls Sex Life, Romance With Kurt Cobain: 'He's a Hard Act to Follow'" There are numerous online sites that discuss the *GQ* article specifically and Cobain's anatomy in general; these sites both predate and postdate the article. As of December 2015, here is the site with the most references and links to other sites; it gives a sense of the nature of the online discussions: bungledand thebotched.blogspot.com/2011/05/kurt-cobain-has-huge-penis.html. See also evilbeetgossip .com/2011/10/12/courtney-love-explains-the-romantic-beginnings-of-her-relationship-with -kurt-cobain. For the video purportedly showing Cobain exposing his penis, see youtube.com /watch?v=iooj_3A1iTM.

17. All the artwork attributed to Cobain can be found on line at "Live Nirvana Guide to Kurt Cobain's Art" (livenirvana.com/art/paintings.php).

18. The third use of the word "penis" is found in what appears to me to be a fragment from another video proposal. Cobain writes, "Add scene where I hand the guitar to the audience. I think its [*sic*] from Reading and the penis and flower petal; face in camera performance piece Kurdt does in Rio" (239). And I have already cited in chapter 4, the fourth occurrence of the word in one of the storyboards for "Heart Shaped Box" (256).

19. I am not the first to conflate resurrection and erection. In *The Sexuality of Christ,* art critic Leo Steinberg calls attention to Renaissance images of the adult Christ, either dead or dying on the cross, with an erection. He explains that the desire to show Christ's penis was an aesthetic choice guided by the artists' abiding religious principle. Christ's "manhood," as it were, emphasized precisely his humanity before his ascent into Heaven. At the same time, Christ with an erection is proof of his chastity. By way of numerous examples, Steinberg confirms that "during the late Middle Ages and the Renaissance, the word 'resurrection' . . . [was] used as a double-entendre, connoting both the divine event and the humble mortal fact of an erection" (Siegel, "Pope Francis and the Naked Christ").

20. In this respect, Cobain's ethics, if not his aesthetics, differ radically from those of two of his avowedly straight contemporaries in alternative music who also might appear to be embracing queer sexualities: Tesco Vee of the Meatmen (1981–1988) and Jimmy Flemion of the

Frogs (1980–1989). As Drew Daniel has demonstrated, these two front men, at various times in their lyrical production and their stage performances, should be considered "queer minstrels." These are straight performers who, for fun if not for profit, take on gay personas in their lyrics and performances. Tesco, for example, has appeared on stage in provocative attire, presenting his body as the object of male desire. But he gives a performance that is blatantly homophobic. He has also composed songs like "I'm Glad I'm Not a Girl" and "Lesbian Death Dirge" that are sexist and misogynistic, in spite of their contradictory lyrics that can also be read in places as sympathetic to women and feminism. One sees the same offensive queer minstrelsy in performances by the Frogs, who recorded a novelty album, *It's Only Right and Natural* (1989), containing songs that appear to be gay anthems. But the songs on this album, like "Been a Month Since I've Had a Man," are meant as a joke, since the members of the group are not queer. At the time, the Frogs were exposed by a reviewer in the fanzine *Homocore* as "Homophobes trying to pass as homos. Shit of the lowest order" (Daniel, 17).

21. For example, a 2015 special edition of the journal *Men and Masculinities* is devoted to the so-called queering of heteromasculinity and the theorizing of this identity as a site of social disruption and progressive change.

22. The plural nature of heterosexuality is also made evident in Chrys Ingraham's *Thinking Straight*. Since the 1990s, one of the most visible celebrities within the tradition of so-called queer straights is James Franco. In a chapbook of poems and observations titled *Straight James / Gay James* (2016), Franco creates a persona and explores the complexity and the fluidity of sexual and gender identity. He declares himself "gay in my art and straight in my life." Professing that he is gay "up to the point of intercourse," Franco inhabits a persona, then, that differs from the one Cobain constructs, since gay intercourse is not excluded from the persona Cobain inhabits. For a queer critique of Franco's posturing, one that could apply equally to Cobain, see Jameson Fitzpatrick's "A Queer Take on James Franco." See also Teo Bugbee's "How James Franco Exploits Queerness to Cover His Tracks."

23. I am thinking of queer theory as it first emerged within the writings of de Lauretis, Sedgwick, and Butler, who, from different theoretical perspectives, set out to identify and contest hegemonic and marginalized gender and sexual identities.

24. Thomas is referring to his own work in *Straight With a Twist*, and he is citing Annamarie Jagose's *Queer Theory* and Leo Bersani's *Homos*.

CHAPTER SIX

1. As indicated in the previous chapter, I purposefully retain the masculine pronouns and adjectives as found within classic psychoanalytic theory. Further, throughout this chapter, I use "melancholy" to refer to the principal affect I uncover within some of Cobain's writings. Although classic psychoanalytic theory, like many contemporary theorists, routinely uses "melancholia" when designating a pathological response to loss, I employ "melancholy" except when I am citing the works of others. As will become clear from my examination of Cobain's writings, I do not make a distinction between what some writers consider "normal" *melancholy*, understood as a transitory mood, and chronic and debilitating *melancholia*. It will also become clear that I use

"melancholy" as both a noun and as an adjective. I use it as a qualifier especially in the expression "melancholy text," which I often contrast with "masochist text."

2. See Tammy Clewell's reading of Freud and her analysis of Peter Sacks's study of the English elegy in "Mourning Beyond Melancholia" (48–50).

3. In describing the way Cobain's narrators and characters mourn the loss of the testerical mode and their blocked mourning of the loss of the phallic mode, I am, of course, structuring this difference around Freud's distinction between mourning and melancholy as two distinct ways of responding to loss. Freud theorizes that loss can be either structural, that is, social and universal, or it can be personal and historically contingent. In both instances, as I indicate, he distinguishes between "melancholia" and "mourning" by postulating the former as a pathological reaction to an imaginary loss.

4. In addition to Radden, there are other excellent accounts of the history and the theorizing of melancholy. See, for example, Raymond Klibansky, Erwin Panofsky, and Fritz Sayl's *Saturn and Melancholy* and Stanley Jackson's *Melancholy and Depression*.

5. The debate on the possible, so-called benefits of depression has re-emerged within recent scholarship such as Kay Jamison's "Manic-Depressive Illness and Creativity" and Charlotte Waddell's "Creativity and Mental Illness."

6. See Klein's "The Depressive State: Mourning and its Relation to Manic-Depressive States" (1940).

7. Since homosexuality exists within a culture that inflicts violence on nonconforming bodies and imposes guilt on insurgent subjects, Sánchez-Pardo reads Klein's "The Effects of Early Anxiety-Situations on the Sexual Development of the Boy" in a way that demonstrates how "homosexuality and melancholia appear to be inextricably linked in a heterocentric and heterosexist system of sexual difference" (112).

8. As I indicate at the beginning of this study, I define "subjectivity" as all the psychological and emotional experiences, including episodes of melancholy, which lead a person to a sense of self, an identity. I define "agency" as all the behaviors and actions that confirm one's identity for other people as well as for oneself.

9. Kristeva's personal reputation has recently been called into question as the result of allegations that she worked during the 1970s as "an agent of Communist Bulgaria's State Security services" (Wolin). She has vigorously denied these allegations, which have affected neither the validity nor the rigor of her theoretical works.

10. I pursue the parallels between Cobain and Nerval and the French Romantic tradition, as I also indicate in the introduction, because of my own training and research interests. Cobain's writings, however, also enter into dialogue not only with the German movement *Sturm und Drang* exemplified by *Werther*. His lyrics and journals also have a filiation with a long anglophone literary tradition that includes, in addition to English Romantic poetry, "confessional literature, novels of sensation, and Victorian autobiography" (Micale, 114). These genres are ones in which male authors often questioned traditional notions of gender, including how masculinity and femininity are manifest in the arts and sciences and in the way humans think, feel, and act.

11. This letter has become a part of the public record as the result of numerous of lawsuits filed after Cobain's death, including one by Courtney Love's former attorney (Rhonda Holmes) against Love herself. This particular suit is explained in "Celebrity Legacies: Kurt Cobain's Estate at the Heart of 20 Years of Fighting" (blog.trialandheirs.com/celebrities/kurt-cobain-sparked-creation-grundge-rock-estate-sparked-fights).

12. Related to this topic, research published by the National Institutes of Health indicates that Cobain's suicide evoked deep sorrow and sadness on the part of fans, but it did not produce the copycats that some professionals had expected. "The data obtained from the Seattle King County area suggest that the expected 'Werther effect' apparently did not occur" (Jobes and Berman, 260) for several reasons. These reasons include the nature of the media coverage of Cobain's suicide, the efforts of the region's crisis center and community outreach programs, and, I would add, the potential of Cobain's lyrics and journals to touch fans in a positive way.

13. The very title of Nerval's 1853 poem is enigmatic. The Spanish "El Desdichado" can be translated into English as "the despairing, disheartened, inconsolable one." Here is a translation of the first and third stanzas, both of which display the Cobainian aesthetics that I have been exploring:

I am the Dark One,—the Widower,—the one left disconsolate
The Aquitaine Prince whose Tower is destroyed:
My only star is dead,—and my constellated lute
Takes on the black Sun of Melancholia.

Am I Love or Phoebus?... Lusignan or Biron?
My forehead still retains the crimson color left by the Queen's kiss;
I dreamt of the empty Cave where the siren resides...

BIBLIOGRAPHY

Adams, Parveen. "Per Os(cillation)." In *Male Trouble,* edited by Constance Penley and Sharon Willis, 3–25. Minneapolis: University of Minnesota Press, 1992.

Adorno, Theodor W. "On Jazz." *Discourse* 1989 [1936]: 44–69.

Ahad, Badia Sahar. *Freud Upside Down: African American Literature and Psychoanalytic Culture.* Chicago: University of Illinois Press, 2010.

Alexander, Cortney. "'I'm not like them but I can pretend': A Feminist Analysis of Kurt Cobain's Gender Performance." PhD dissertation. De Paul University, 2009.

Alford, C. Fred. *Melanie Klein and Critical and Social Theory: An Account of Politics, Art, and Reason Based on Her Psychoanalytic Theory.* New Haven, CT: Yale University Press, 1989.

Allman, Kevin. "The Dark Side of Nirvana's Kurt Cobain." In *Cobain on Cobain: Interviews and Encounters,* edited by Nick Soulsby, 375–94. Chicago: Chicago Review Press, 2016.

Anastasi, Aaron P. "Adolescent Boys' Use of Emo Music as Their Healing Lament." *Journal of Religion and Health* 44, no. 3 (2005): 303–19.

Anderson, Peggy. "Tragedy Strikes Grunge Scene Again; Insiders Blame Heroin." *Moscow-Pulman Daily News,* June 17, 1994. http://news.google.com/newspapers ?nid=2026&dat=19940617&id Accessed December 10, 2014.

André, Jacques. "Immanent Masochism." *Journal of Psychoanalysis.* n.d. http://www .journal-psychoanalysis.eu/imanent-masochis. Accessed June 2015.

Andrews, Evan. "Seven Bizarre Witch Trial Tests." *History Lists,* March 18, 2014. http://www.history.com/news/history-lists/7-bizarre-witch-trial-tests. Accessed October 12, 2016.

Aristotle. "Problems II." In *The Gendering of Melancholy,* edited by Jennifer Radden, 57–60. New York: Oxford University Press, 2002.

Armengol, Josep M. "Toward a History of the Male Body in U.S. Literature and Culture." In *Embodying Masculinities: Towards a History of the Male Body in U.S. Culture and Literature,* edited by Josep M. Armengol, 1–13. New York: Peter Lang, 2013.

Aron, Lewis. "The Internalized Primal Scene." *Psychoanalytic Dialogues* 2 (1995): 195–237.

Auden, W. H. "Foreword." In J. W. von Goethe, *The Sorrows of Young Werther and Nouvella.* Translated by Elizabeth Mayer and Louise Bogan, i–xxii. New York: Modern Library, 1984.

Auslander, Philip. *Performing Glam Rock: Gender and Theatricality in Popular Music.* Ann Arbor: University of Michigan Press, 2006.

Azerrad, Michael. *Come As You Are: The Story of Nirvana.* New York: Doubleday, 1994.

——. *Our Band Could Be Your Life: Scenes From the American Indie Underground, 1981–1991.* New York: Little Brown, 2001.

"Band Name Origins—Am I Right." http://www.amiright.com/names/origins/p.shtml. Accessed August 1, 2016.

Bane, Michael. *White Boy Singin' the Blues: The Black Roots of White Rock.* New York: Da Capo Press, 1982.

Bannister, Matthew. *White Boys, White Noise: Masculinities and 1980s Indie Guitar Rock.* Burlington, VT: Ashgate, 2006.

Barthes, Roland. *Image, Music, Text.* New York: Hill and Wang, 1977.

Beasley, Chris. "Introduction." *Men and Masculinities* (June 2015): 135–39.

Becker, Howard. "Art as Collective Action." *American Sociological Review* 39 (1974): 767–76.

Becker, Ron. *Gay TV and Straight America.* New Brunswick, NJ: Rutgers University Press, 2006.

Beebe, Roger. "Mourning Becomes . . .? Kurt Cobain, Tupac Shakur and the Waning Effect." In *Rock Over the Edge: Transformations in Popular Music Culture,* edited by Roger Beebe, Denise Fulbrook, and Ben Saunders, 311–34. Durham, NC: Duke University Press, 2002.

Bennett, Stephen Earl, and Stephen Craig. *After the Boom: The Politics of Generation X.* Lanham, MD: Rowman & Littlefield, 1997.

Berns, Ute. "The Concept of Performativity in Narratology: Mapping a Field of Investigation." *European Journal of English Studies* (April 2009): 93–108.

Berry, Chuck. *Chuck Berry: The Autobiography.* New York: Random House, 1989.

Bersani, Leo. *The Freudian Body: Psychoanalysis and Art.* New York: Columbia University Press, 1986.

——. *Homos.* Cambridge, MA: Harvard University Press, 1995.

Bickerdike, Jennifer Otter. *Fandom, Image and Authenticity: Joy Devotion and the Second Lives of Kurt Cobain and Ian Curtis.* New York: Palgrave Macmillan, 2014.

Bieber, Irving. "Comments on 'The Depressed Masochist' by R. C. Friedman." *Journal of the American Academy of Psychoanalysis* (1991): 684–85.

Blanchot, Maurice. *The Gaze of Orpheus, and Other Literary Essays.* Translated by Lydia Davis. Barrytown, NY: Station Hill Press, 1981.

Bollas, Christopher. *The Shadow of the Object: Psychoanalysis of the Unthought Known.* London: Free Association Books, 1987.

Bordo, Susan. *The Male Body: A New Look at Men in Public and in Private.* New York: Farrar, Straus and Giroux, 2000.

Braud, Michel. *La forme des jours: Pour une critique du journal personnel.* Paris: Seuil, 2006.

Brintnall, Kent L. *Ecce Homo: The Male-Body-in-Pain as Redemptive Figure.* Chicago: University of Chicago Press, 2011.

———. *Masculinity, Masochism and the Crucifixion: The Male-Body-in-Pain as Redemptive Figure.* PhD dissertation, Emory University, 2007.

Bugbee, Teo. "How James Franco Exploits Queerness to Cover His Tracks." *Jezebel,* January 24, 2018. themuse.jezebel.com/how-james-franco-exploits-queerness -to-cover-his-tracks-1822345498. Accessed June 19, 2019.

Burroughs, William, and Kurt Cobain. "The 'Priest' They Called Him." Tim Kerr Records, 1993. CD.

Burton, Robert, Floyd Dell, and Paul Jordan-Smith. *The Anatomy of Melancholy.* New York: George H. Doran Co., 1927.

Butler, Judith. *Bodies That Matter: On the Discursive Limits of "Sex."* New York: Routledge, 1993.

———. *Gender Trouble: Feminism and the Subversion of Identity.* New York: Routledge, 1990.

———. "Melancholy Gender—Refused Identification." *Psychoanalytic Dialogues* (1995): 165–80.

Callies, Tania. "Culture populaire et construction de la realité sociale des adolescents: Étude du cas Kurt Cobain." Thesis, Université de Montréal, 1999.

Chancer, Lynn C. *Reconcilable Differences: Confronting Beauty, Pornography, and the Future of Feminism.* Los Angeles: University of California Press, 1998.

Chapman, Rowena, and Jonathan Rutherford. "The Forward March of Man Hated." In *Male Order: Unwrapping Masculinity,* edited by Rowena Chapman and Jonathan Rutherford, 3–20. London: Lawrence & Wishart, 1988.

Chiesa, Guido. "Two or Three Things I Know About Kurt Cobain." In *Cobain on Cobain: Interviews and Encounters,* edited by Nick Soulsby, 41–48. Chicago: Chicago Review Press, 2016.

Cixous, Hélèle. *Coming to Writing and Other Essays.* Translated by Sarah Cornell. Cambridge, MA: Harvard University Press, 1991.

Clewell, Tammy. "Mourning Beyond Melancholia: Freud's Psychoanalysis of Loss." *Journal of the American Psychoanalytic Association* 52, no. 1 (2004): 43–67.

Cobain, Kurt. "Incesticide Compilation Liner Notes." In *Cobain on Cobain: Interviews and Encounters,* edited by Nick Soulsby, 372–74. Chicago: Chicago Review Press, 2016.

———. *Le Journal de Kurt Cobain.* Translated by Laurence Romance. Paris: Oh! Editions, 2002.

———. *Journals.* New York: Riverhead Books, 2003.

Cohen, Cathy J. "Punks, Bulldaggers, and Welfare Queens: The Radical Potential of Queer Politics?" *GLQ* 3 (1997): 437–65.

Cohen, Jason, and Michael Krugman. *Generation Ecch! The Blacklash Starts Here.* New York: Fireside, 1994.

Connell, Joe. "The Problem of Authenticity in Male-Dominated Rock Music Journalism." *The Manchester Media Group,* n.d. mancunion.com/2015/11/09/problems-authenticity-male-dominated-rock-music-journalism. Accessed November 1, 2016.

Coupe, Laurence. *Beat Sound / Beat Vision: The Beat Spirit and Popular Song.* Manchester: Manchester University Press, 2012.

Coyle, Michael. "Hyjacked Hits and Antic Authenticity: Cover Songs, Race, and Postwar Marketing." In *Rock Over the Edge: Transformations in Popular Music Culture,* edited by Roger Beebe, Denise Fulbrook, and Ben Saunders, 133–57. Durham, NC: Duke University Press, 2002.

Crisafulli, Chuck. *Nirvana: Teen Spirit: The Story Behind Every Song.* New York: Thunder's Mouth Press, 2006.

Cross, Charles R. *Cobain Unseen.* New York: Little, Brown and Company, 2008.

———. *Heavier Than Heaven: A Biography of Kurt Cobain.* New York: Hyperion, 2001.

———. *Here We Are Now: The Lasting Impact of Kurt Cobain.* New York: Harper Collins, 2014.

Cross, Charles R. and Jim Berkenstadt. *Nevermind: Nirvana. Classic Rock Albums.* New York: Schirmer Books, 1998.

Crotty, Jim, and Michael Lane. "The Problem Is You're Now a Caricature." In *Cobain on Cobain: Interviews and Encounters,* edited by Nick Soulsby, 359–70. Chicago: Chicago Review Press, 2016.

Dahl, Dick. "Is It Only Rock 'N' Roll?" *Utne Reader,* May/June 1992, 42–43.

Daniel, Drew. "'Why Be Something That You're Not?': Punk Performance and the Epistemology of Queer Minstrelsy." *Social Text 116* 31, no. 3 (2013): 13–34.

Davis, Stephen. *Watch You Bleed: The Saga of Guns N' Roses.* New York: Gotham Books, 2008.

Deleuze, Gilles, and Leopold Sacher-Masoch. *Masochism: Coldness and Cruelty, Venus in Furs.* Translated by Jean McNeil. New York: Zone Books, 1989.

Diehl, Matt. *My So-Called Punk: Green Day, Fall Out Boy, The Distillers, Bad Religion—How Neo-Punk Stage-Dived into the Mainstream.* New York: St. Martin's Griffin, 2007.

Dollimore, Jonathan. *Sexual Dissidence: Augustine to Wilde, Freud to Foucault.* Oxford: Clarendon Press, 1991.

Doty, Alexander. *Making Things Perfectly Queer: Interpreting Mass Culture.* Minneapolis: University of Minnesota Press, 1993.

Doubrovsky, Serge. *Fils.* Paris: Gallimard, 1977.

Duncombe, Stephen, and Maxwell Tremblay. "White Riot?" In *White Riot: Punk Rock and the Politics of Race,* edited by Stephen Duncombe and Maxwell Tremblay, 1–17. New York: Verso, 2011.

Edelman, Lee. *No Future: Queer Theory and the Death Drive.* Durham, NC: Duke University Press, 2004.

Endino, Jack. *Jack Endino.* July 31, 2015. endino.com. Accessed December 16, 2016.

Epstein, Daniel. "Rolling Stone." *No Apologies: All 102 Nirvana Songs Ranked.* April 18, 2015. rollingstone.com/music/lists/no-apologies-all-102-nirvana-songs-ranked-20150408/spank-thru-20150408. Accessed April 14, 2016.

Fantina, Richard, ed. *Straight Writ Queer: Non-Normative Expressions of Heterosexuality in Literature.* Jefferson, NC: McFarland & Co, 2006.

Farndell, Arthur. *On the Nature of Love: Ficino on Plato's Symposium.* London: Shepheard-Walwyn, 2016.

Felluga, Dino Franco. "Introductory Guide to Critical Theory." *The Symbolic Order,* July 7, 2002. cla.purdue.edu/english/theory/psychoanalysis/definitions/symbolic order. Accessed December 28, 2017.

Finke, Michael C. "An Introduction." In *One Hundred Years of Masochism: Literary Texts, Social and Cultural Contexts,* edited by Michael Fink and Carl Niekerk, 1–13. Atlanta: Rodopi, 2000.

Fish, Duane. "Serving the Servants: An Analysis of the Music of Kurt Cobain." *Popular Music and Society* 19, no. 2 (1995): 87–102.

Fitzpatrick, Jameson. "A Queer Take on James Franco's 'Straight James / Gay James.'" *Lambda Literary,* January 16, 2016.

Freud, Sigmund. "Beyond the Pleasure Principle." In *The Standard Edition of the Complete Psychological Works of Sigmund Freud.* Translated by James Strachey. London: Hogarth Press, 1994. Vol. XVIII, 1953 [1920], 3.

——. *A Child Is Being Beaten: A Contribution to the Study of the Origin of Sexual Perversion.* In *The Standard Edition of the Complete Psychological Works of Sigmund Freud.* Translated by James Strachey. London: Hogarth Press, 1994. Vol. XVII, 1955 [1919], 179–204.

———. "Civilization and its Discontents." In *The Standard Edition of the Complete Psychological Works of Sigmund Freud.* Translated by James Strachey. London: Hogarth Press, 1994. Vol. XXI, 59, 1953 [1929, 1930].

———. "Creative Writers and Day-Dreaming." In *The Standard Edition of the Complete Psychological Works of Sigmund Freud.* Translated by James Strachey. London: Hogarth Press, 1994. Vol. XIX, 1953 [1907, 1908], 143.

———. "The Economic Problem of Masochism." In *The Standard Edition of the Complete Psychological Works of Sigmund Freud.* Translated by James Strachey. London: Hogarth Press, 1994. Vol. XIX, 1961 [1924], 159–70.

———. "Mourning and Melancholia." In *The Standard Edition of the Complete Psychological Works of Sigmund Freud.* Translated by James Strachey. London: Hogarth Press, 1994. Vol. XIV, 1953 [1917], 237–58.

———. "Three Essays on the Theory of Sexuality." In *The Standard Edition of the Complete Psychological Works of Sigmund Freud.* Translated by James Strachey. London: Hogarth Press, 1994. Vol. VII. 1953 [1905]. 130–243.

Frith, Simon. "The Good, the Bad, and the Indifferent: Defending Popular Culture from the Populists." *Diacritics* 21, no. 4 (1991): 102–15.

———. *Performing Rites: On the Value of Popular Music.* Cambridge, MA: Harvard University Press, 1996.

Frith, Simon, and Angela McRobbie. "Rock and Sexuality." *Screen Education* (1978): 3–19.

Furek, Maxim W. *The Death Proclamation of Generation X: A Self-Fulfilling Prophecy of Goth, Grunge, and Heroin.* New York: iUniverse, 2008.

Gaar, Gillian G. *Nirvana's in Utero (33 1/3).* New York: Continuum, 2006.

Garvin, Richard M., and Edmond Addeo. *The Midnight Special: The Legend of Leadbelly.* New York: Bernard Geis Associates, 1971.

Gasparini, Philippe. *Autofiction: Une aventure du language.* Paris: Éditions du Seuil, 2008.

George, Nelson. *The Death of Rhythm & Blues.* New York: Patheon, 1988.

Gerber, Justin. "Review: Nirvana—*In Utero* [20th Anniversary Edition]." *Consequences of Sound,* September 25, 2013. consequenceofsound.net/2013/09/album-review-nirvana-in-utero-20th-anniversary-edition. Accessed July 5, 2017.

Gillibert, Jean. *L'image réconciliée: L'homme de constitution.* Paris: Payot, 1979.

Gilman, Sander L. "Preface." In *One Hundred Years of Masochism: Literary Texts, Social and Cultural Contexts,* edited by Michael Finke and Carl Niekerk, i–x. Atlanta, GA: Rodopi, 2000.

Girard, René. *Violence and the Sacred.* Baltimore: Johns Hopkins University Press, 1977.

Giroux, Henry. *Channel Surfing: Race Talk and Destruction of Today's Youth.* New York: St. Martin Press, 1997.

Glick, Robert, and Donald Meyers. "Introduction." In *Masochism: Current Psychoanalytic Perspectives,* edited by Robert Glick and Donald Meyers, 1–15. Hillsdale, NY: Analytic Press, 1998.

Glover, Nicky. *Psychoanalytic Aesthetics: An Introduction to the British School.* London: Karnac, 2009.

Goethe, Johann Wolfgang von. *The Sorrows of Young Werther.* Translated by Burton Pike. New York: Modern Library, 2005.

Goodwyn, Tom. "Courtney Love: 'Kurt Cobain was well fucking hung.'" *New Music Express, May 26, 2011.* nme.com/news/music/nirvana-124-1286955. Accessed December 26, 2017.

Goldblatt, Mark J. "Suicide and Masochism: The Evolving Relationship Between Guilt, Suffering, Self-Attack and Suicide." *Psychoanalytic Psychotherapy* (2010): 93–100.

Goldstein, Richard. *The Poetry of Rock.* New York: Bantam, 1969.

Graham, Jonathan. "Forgotten Guitar: Before Hendrix, Elvis and Chuck Berry, There Was Sister Rosetta Tharpe." *Guitar World,* August 30, 2016. guitarworld.com /forgotten-guitar-hendrix-elvis-and-chuck-berry-there-was-sister-rosetta -tharpe/25851. Accessed November 23, 2016.

Graver, David. "The Actor's Body." In *Performance: Critical Concepts in Literary and Cultural Studies,* 2:157–74. London: Routledge, 2003.

Greenwald, Andy. *Nothing Feels Good: Punk Rock, Teenagers, and Emo.* New York: St. Martin's Griffin, 2003.

Grossman, Perry. "Identity Crisis: The Dialectics of Rock, Punk and Grunge." *Berkeley Journal of Sociology* 41 (1996–97): 19–40.

Grosz, Elizabeth. *Volatile Bodies: Toward a Corporeal Feminism.* Bloomington: Indiana University Press, 1994.

Gruzelier, Jonathan. "Moshpit Menace and Masculine Mayhem." In *Oh Boy! Masculinities and Popular Music,* edited by Freya Jarman-Ivens, 59–75. New York: Routledge, 2007.

"Guide to Kurt Cobain's Art." *Nirvana Live, 2015.* livenirvana.com/art. Accessed February 28, 2017.

Gunckel, Colin. "Defining Punk." *Journal of Popular Music Studies* 30, no. 1–2 (2018): 155–70.

Hadleigh, Boze. "Review of Making Things Perfectly Queer: Interpreting Mass Culture." *Film Quarterly* (Summer 1994): 46–47.

Halberstam, Judith. *In a Queer Time and Place: Transgender Bodies, Subcultural Lives.* New York: New York University Press, 2005.

Hall, Stuart. "Introduction." In *Representation: Cultural Representations and Signifying Practices,* edited by Stuart Hall, 1–11. London: Sage, 1997.

Hamilton, Jack. *Just Around Midnight: Rock and Roll and the Racial Imagination.* Cambridge, MA: Harvard University Press, 2016.

Hebdige, Dick. *Subculture: The Meaning of Style.* London: Methuen, 1979.

Henderson, Justin. *Seattle Grunge.* Berkeley, CA: Roaring Forties Press, 2010.

Hervey, Sandor, and Ian Higgins. *Thinking Translation, a Course in Translation Method: French to English.* New York: Routledge, 1992.

Heylin, Clinton. *From the Velvets to the Voidoids: A Pre-Punk History for a Post-Punk World.* New York: Penguin Books, 1993.

Hubbard, Hanmi. "It's the Classic Punk Rock Rags-to-Riches Story." In *Cobain on Cobain: Interviews and Encounters,* edited by Nick Soulsby, 8–38. Chicago: Chicago Review Press, 2016.

Hubier, Sébastien. *Littératures intimes: Les expressions du moi, de l'autobiographie à l'autofiction.* Paris: A. Colin, 2003.

Hughey, Matthew. "Cinematic Racism: White Redemption and Black Stereotypes in 'Magical Negro' Films." *Social Problems* 56 (2009): 543–77.

Humphrey, Clark. *Loser: The Real Seattle Music Story.* New York: Harry N. Abrams, 1999.

Huq, Rupa. *Beyond Subculture: Pop, Youth and Identity in a Postcolonial World.* New York: Routledge, 2006.

Ingraham, Chrys, ed. *Thinking Straight: The Power, the Promise, and the Paradox of Heterosexuality.* New York: Routledge, 2005.

Jackson, Stanley. *Melancholy and Depression: From Hippocratic Times to Modern Times.* New Haven, CT: Yale University Press, 1986.

Jagose, Annamarie. *Queer Theory: An Introduction.* New York: Oxford University Press, 1996.

Jamison, Kay Redfield. "Manic-Depressive Illness and Creativity." *Scientific American* (1997): 44–49.

Jobes, David, and Alan Berman. "The Kurt Cobain Suicide Crisis: Perspectives from Research, Public Health, and the News." *Suicide and Life-Threatening Behavior* (Fall 1996): 260–71.

Jonze, Tim. "Mike Starr and the Deadliest Musical Genre." *The Guardian,* March 9, 2001. www.thegardian.com/music/2011/mar/10. Accessed March 10, 2011.

Julia, Fp. "The History of Grunge." *BLDG/25,* September 9, 2103. freepeople.com/2013/09/history-grunge. Accessed December 5, 2016.

Kahn, Seth. "Kurt Cobain, Martyrdom and the Problem of Agency." *Studies in Popular Culture* 22, no. 3 (April 2000): 83–96.

Kavadlo, Jesse. "The Terms of the Contract: Rock and Roll and the Narrative of Self-Destruction in Don DeLillo, Neil Pollack, and Kurt Cobain." *Studies in Popular Culture* (2007): 87–104.

Keightley, Kier. "Reconsidering Rock." In *Cambridge Campanion to Pop and Rock,* edited by Simon Frith, Will Straw, and John Street, 109–42. Cambridge: Cambridge University Press, 2001.

Kelly, Christiana. "Kurt and Courtney Sitting in a Tree." *Sassy* (1992).

Kent, Nick. "Isn't There Somebody Out There?" *The Guardian,* November 29, 2002. theguardian.com/books/2002/nov/30/nirvana.music. Accessed March 8, 2014.

Kiedis, Anthony, and Larry Sloman. *Scar Tissue.* London: Little, Brown Book Group, 2004.

Kirschner, Tony. "The Lalapalooziation of American Youth." *Popular Music and Society* 18, no. 1 (1994): 69–89.

Kitts, Jeff, Brad Tolinski, and Harold Steinblatt. *Nirvana and the Grunge Revolution: The Seattle Sound: The Story of How Kurt Cobain and His Seattle Cohorts Changed the Face of Rock in the Nineties.* Milwaukee: Hal Leonard Corp., 1998.

Klein, Melanie. "The Depressive State: Mourning and its Relation to Manic-Depressive States." In Melanie Klein, *Love, Guilt and Reparation & Other Works 1921–1945,* 344–69. London: Virago, 1988.

——. "The Effects of Early Anxiety-Situations on the Sexual Development of the Boy." In Melanie Klein, *The Psycho-analysis of Children.* Translated by Alix Strachey, 240–78. New York: Delacorte Press, 1975.

——. "The Importance of Symbol-Formation in the Development of the Ego." In Melanie Klein, *Love, Guilt and Reparations & Other Works 1921–1945,* 219–32. London: Virago, 1988.

——. "Our Adult World and Its Roots in Infancy." In Melanie Klein, *Love, Guilt and Reparations & Other Works 1921–1945,* 247–63. London: Virago, 1988.

——. "Some Reflections on the Oresteia." In Melanie Klein, *Envy, Gratitude and Other Works 1946–1963,* 275–99. London: Virago, 1988.

Klibansky, Raymond, Erwin Panofsky, and Fritz Sayl. *Saturn and Melancholy: Studies in the History of Natural Philosophy, Religion and the Arts.* New York: Basic Books, 1964.

Krafft-Ebing, Richard von. *Psychopathia Sexualis.* London: Forgotten Books, 2015 [1886].

Krell, David Farrell. *The Purest of Bastards: Works of Mourning, Art, and Affirmation in the Thought of Jacques Derrida.* College Park: Pennsylvia State University Press, 2000.

Kristeva, Julia. *Black Sun: Depression and Melancholia.* Translated by Leon S. Roudiez. New York: Columbia University Press, 1989.

———. "On the Melancholic Imaginary." *New Formations* (1987): 5–18.

———. *Revolution in Poetic Language.* Translated by Margaret Waller. New York: Columbia University Press, 1984.

Kurt Cobain: Montage of Heck. Directed by Brett Morgan. 2015. Film.

Kusz, Kyle. "'I Want to Be the Minority': The Politics of Youthful White Masculinities in Sport and Popular Culture in 1990s America." *Journal of Sport and Social Issues* 25, no. 4 (2001): 390–416.

Lacan, Jacques. *Écrits.* Translated by Bruce Fink. New York: Norton, 2006.

Lane, Christopher. "The Psychoanalysis of Race: An Introduction." In *The Psychoanalysis of Race,* edited by Christopher Lane, 1–37. New York: Columbia University Press, 1998.

Lauretis, Teresa de. "Queer Theory: Lesbian and Gay Sexualities, An Introduction." *differences: A Journal of Feminist and Cultural Studies* (1991): iii–xi.

"Leadbelly." *BlackHistoryNow, June 2, 2011.* blackhistorynow.com/leadbelly. Accessed November 6, 2016.

"Leadbelly: American Music." *Encyclopedia Britannica, n.d.* britannica.com/biography/Leadbelly. Accessed November 6, 2016.

Leader, Darian. *The New Black: Mourning, Melancholia and Depression.* Minneapolis: Graywolf Press, 2018.

Lee, Joan Oluchi. "The Joy of the Castrated Boy." *Social Text 84–85* 23, no. 3–4 (2005): 35–56.

Lehman, Peter. *Running Scared: Masculinity and Representations of Male Bodies.* Detroit: Wayne State University Press, 2007.

Lejeune, Philippe. *Le pacte autobiographique.* Paris: Seuil, 1975.

Levine, Michael, and Justin Henderson. *Grunge.* New York: Abrams Image, 2009.

Loewenstein, Rudolph M. "A Contribution to the Psychoanalytic Theory of Masochism." *Journal of the American Psychoanalytic Association* 5, no. 2 (1957): 197–234.

Lott, Eric. *Love and Theft: Blackface Minstrelsy and the American Working Class.* New York: Oxford University Press, 1993.

Love, Courtney. "On the Suicide of Her Husband." *Gifts of Speech* (1994). gos.sbc.edu/1/love.html. Accessed August 6, 2016.

Macrorie, Ken. *Telling Writing.* Portsmouth, NH: Boynton/Cook Publishers, 1985.

Mailer, Norman. *The White Negro.* San Francisco: City Light Books, 1957.

Malin, Brenton J. *American Masculinity under Clinton: Popular Media and the Nineties "Crisis of Masculinity."* New York: Peter Lang, 2005.

Mallon, Tom. "Rolling Stone." *No Apologies: All 102 Nirvana Songs Ranked,* April 8, 2015. http://www.rollingstone.com/music/lists/no-apologies-all-102-nirvana-songs-ranked-20150408/i-hate-myself-and-want-to-die-20150408. Accessed March 23, 2017.

Marcus, Greil. "Artist of the Year: Kurt Cobain." *Rolling Stone,* May 13, 1999, 46–50.

——. "Comment on Mark Mazullo, 'The Man Whom the World Sold.'" *The Musical Quarterly* (2000): 750–53.

Marlan, Dawn. "Review: Prozac Nation." *Chicago Review* 42, no. 1 (1996): 93–102.

Marsh, Dave. *The Heart of Rock and Soul.* New York: Da Capo, 1999.

Mazlish, Bruce. "Autobiography and Psychoanalysis: Between Truth and Self-Deception." *Encounters* (n.d.): 28–37.

Mazullo, Mark. "The Man Whom the World Sold: Kurt Cobain, Rock's Progressive Esthetic, and the Challenges of Authenticity." *The Music Quarterly* (2000): 713–55.

McClarey, Susan, and Robert Walser. "Start Making Sense! Musicology Wrestles With Rock." In *On Record: Rock, Pop and the Written Word,* edited by Simon Frith and Andrew Goodwin. London: Routledge, 1990.

McDayter, Ghislaine. "Byron and Twentieth-Century Popular Culture." In *Palgrave Advances in Byron Studies,* edited by Jane Stabler, 130–44. Basingstoke: Palgrave Macmillan, 2007.

McDonald, Chris. "Exploring Modal Subversion in Alternative Rock." *Popular Music* 19, no. 3 (2000): 355–63.

McKee, Ann. "What Is CTE?" *Concussion Legacy Foundation,* n.d. concussionfoundation .org/CTE-resources/what-is-CTE. Accessed July 18, 2019.

Medovoi, Leerom. "Mapping the Rebel Image: Post Modernism and the Masculinist Politics of Rock in the U.S.A." *Cultural Critique* (1991–1992): 153–88.

Mehlman, Charles T. "Idiopathic Scoliosis." *Medscape,* January 29, 2016. emedicine. medscape.com/article/1265794-overview. Accessed October 1, 2017.

Meltzer, Marisa. *Girl Power: The Nineties Revolution in Music.* New York: Faber and Faber, 2010.

Micale, Mark. *Hysterical Men: The Hidden History of Male Nervous Illness.* Cambridge, MA: Harvard University Press, 2008.

Moore, Ryan. *Sells Like Teen Spirit: Music, Youth Culture, and Social Crisis.* New York: New York University Press, 2010.

Moore, Thurston. *Grunge.* New York: Harry A. Abrams, 2009.

Mullins, Stephen D., and Garth Mullins. "Most Things Piss Me Off, I Can't Help It." In *Cobain on Cobain: Interviews and Encounters,* edited by Nick Soulsby, 117–23. Chicago: Chicago Review Press, 2016.

Muños, José Esteban. "Gimme Gimme This . . . Gimme Gimme That: Annilation and Innovation in the Punk Rock Commons." *Social Text 16* 31, no. 3 (2013): 95–109.

Murray, Nick. "No Apologies: All 102 of Nirvana Songs Ranked." *Rolling Stone* (2015). rollingstone.com/music/lists/no-apologies-all-102-nirvana-songs-ranked-2015 0408/they-hung-him-on-a-cross-the-jury-20150408. Accessed August 28, 2016.

Musser, Amber Jamilla. "Masochism: A Queer Subjectivity?" *Rhizomes* (Fall 2005/ Spring 2006). rhizomes.net/issue11/musser.html. Accessed March 8, 2016.

———. *Sensational Flesh: Race, Power, and Masochism.* New York: New York University Press, 2014.

Muto, Jan. "He Was the Woman of His Dreams: Identity, Gender, and Kurt Cobain." *Popular Music and Society* (1995): 69–85.

M'Uzan, Michel de. "A Case of Masochistic Perversion and an Outline of a Theory." *International Journal of Psychoanalysis* 54, no. 4 (1973): 455–67.

Negus, Keith. *Popular Music Theory: An Introduction.* Middletown, CT: Wesleyan University Press, 1997.

Nerval, Gérard de. *Oeuvres Completes.* Vol. 1. Paris: H. Champion, 1926–32.

Nguyen, Mimi. "Its (Not) A White World: Looking for Race in Punk." In *White Riot: Punk Rock and the Politics of Race,* edited by Stephen Duncombe and Maxwell Tremblay, 257–28. New York: Verso, 2011.

Nicolson, Barry. "New Music Express." *Kurt Cobain's Fecal Matter,* n.d. nme.com /features/Kurt-Cobains-fecalmatter. Accessed August 21, 2016.

Niekerk, Carl. "Race and Gender in Multantuli's Max Havelaar and Love Letters." In *One Hundred Years of Masochism: Literary Texts, Social and Cultural Contexts,* edited by Michael Finke and Carl Kiekerk, 171–90. Atlanta: Rodopi, 2000.

"Nirvana Lyrics." *Nirvanaclub.com,* n.d.nirvanaclub.com. Accessed July 1, 2016.

"Nirvana." 2016. *Reddit,* June 25, 2017. reddit.com/r/Nirvana/comments/4°q1fi/do _you_think_kurt_cobain_was_attractive/#bottom-comments.

"Nirvana Lyrics." *AZLyrics.com,* n.d. azlyrics.com. Accessed June 10, 2016.

"Nirvana Lyrics." *GeniusLyrics,* n.d. geniuslyrics.com. Accessed June 10, 2016.

"Nirvana Lyrics." *LyricsMode.com, n.d.* lyricsmode.com. Accessed June 10, 2016.

"Nirvana Lyrics." *Nirvanaclub.com,* n.d. nirvanaclub.com. Accessed July 1, 2016.

"Nirvana Lyrics." *SongLyrics.com,* n.d. songlyrics.com. Accessed June 10, 2016.

Nobus, Dany, and Lisa Downing. *Perversions: Psychoanalytic Perspectives / Perspectives on Psychoanalysis.* New York: Karnac, 2006.

NPR. May 3, 2015. npr.org/2015/05/03/403568839/kurt-cobain-speaks-through-art -and-audio-diaries-in-montage-of-heck. Accessed January 12, 2016.

Nyong'o, Tavia. "Punk'd Theory." *Social Text 84–85* 23, no. 3–4 (2005): 19–34.

Pareles, Jon. "Heavy Metal, Weighty Words." *New York Times,* July 10, 1988. nytimes .com/1988/07/10/magazine/heavy-metal-weighty-words.HTML. Accessed November 7, 2016.

Pattison, Robert. *The Triumph of Vulgarity: Rock Music in the Mirror of Romanticism.* New York: Oxford University Press, 1987.

Pécker, Beatriz. "They're Just in Their Seats and It's Really Strange." In *Cobain on Cobain: Interviews and Encounters,* edited by Nick Soulsby, 298–301. Chicago: Chicago Review Press, 2016.

Pecora, Norma, and Sharon R. Mazzarella. "Kurt Cobain, Generation X, and the Press." *Popular Music and Society* (Summer 1995): 3–22.

Penley, Constance, and Sharon Willis. "Introduction." In *Male Trouble,* edited by Constance Penley and Sharon Willis, vii–xix. Minneapolis: University of Minnesota Press, 1993.

Person, Ethel Spector. "Preface." In *On Freud's "Creative Writers and Daydreaming,"* edited by A. Servulo et al., ix–xxi. New York: Karnac Books, 2013.

Peters, Brian M. "Emo Gay Boys and Subculture: Postpunk Queer Youth and (Re) Thinking Images of Masculinity." *Journal of LGBT Youth* (May 2010): 129–46.

Peterson, Charles, Michael Azerrad, and Bruce Pavitt. *Screaming Life: A Chronicle of the Seattle Music Scene.* New York: Harper Collins, 1995.

Peterson, Richard. "The Production of Culture: A Prolegomenon." In *The Production of Culture,* edited by Richard Peterson. Longon: Sage, 1976.

Pfeil, Fred. *White Guys: Studies in Postmodern Domination and Difference.* London: Verso, 1995.

Pickering, Mike. "The Past as Source of Social Aspiration: Popular Song and Social Change." In *Everyday Culture: Popular Songs and the Vernacular Milieu,* edited by Mike Pickering and Tony Green, 39–69. Philadelphia: Open University Press, 1987.

Pieterse, C. B. "A Case Study of Kurt Cobain." Dissertation, Nelson Mandela Metropolitan University Summerstrand, n.d.

Polatinsky, Stefan. *The Secret Life of Loss in the Work of Jacques Derrida and Hélène Cixous.* MA thesis, University of the Witwatersrand, 2010.

Power, Ed. "How Grunge and the Marketing Men Killed Queensrÿche." *Irish Examiner,* November 26, 2016. irishexaminer.com/lifestyle/artsfilmtv/how-grunge-and-the -marketing-men-killed-queensryche-432564.html. Accessed May 10, 2017.

Powers, Ann. "Queer in the Streets, Straight in the Sheets." *Utne Reader,* November/ December 1993, 74–80.

Quellette, Mark A. "'A Family Romance': Oedipal Melancholia and Masochism in The Good Soldier." n.d. academia.edu/1933188/_A_Family_Romance_Oedipal_ Melancholia_and_Masochism_in_The_Good_Soldier. Accessed January 14, 2015.

Radden, Jennifer. *The Nature of Melancholy: From Aristotle to Kristeva.* New York: Oxford University Press, 2002.

Ragland, Ellie. *Essays on the Pleasures of Death.* New York: Routledge, 1995.

Reece, Tamekia. "Pregnancy Discharge: Yeah, It's a Thing." *Fit Pregnancy and Baby,* n.d. fitpregnancy.com/pregnancy/pregnancy-health/whats-drip. Accessed September 28, 2016.

Reik, Theodor. *Masochism in Modern Man.* Translated by Margaret Beigel and Gertrude Kurth. New York: Farrar, Straus, 1949.

——. *Masochism in Sex and Society.* Translated by Margaret H. Beigel and Gertrude M Kurth. New York: Grove Press, Inc., 1962.

Riesman, David. "Listening to Popular Music." *American Quarterly* 2, no. 4 (Winter 1950): 359–71.

Robinson, Sally. *Marked Men: White Masculinity in Crisis.* New York: Columbia University Press, 2000.

Rollins, Henry. *The Portable Henry Rollins.* New York: Villard, 1997.

Rovira, James. "Introduction: Rock and Romanticism." In *Rock and Romanticism: Blake, Wordsworth, and Rock from Dylan to U2,* edited by James Rovira, vi–xxiv. Lanham, MD: Lexington Books, 2018.

——. "Introduction: Theorizing Rock / Historicizing Romanticism." In *Rock and Romanticism: Post-Punk, Goth, and Metal as Dark Romanticism,* edited by James Rovira, 1–25. New York: Palgrave Macmillan, 2018.

Ruhlmann, William. "Lead Belly." *All Music,* n.d. allmusic.com/artist/lead-belly -mn0000124390/biography. Accessed November 6, 2016.

Ryalls, Emily. "Emo Angst, Masochism, and Masculinity in Crisis." *Text and Performance Quarterly* 33, no. 2 (2013): 83–97.

Sacks, Peter M. *The English Elegy: Studies in the Genre from Spencer to Yeats.* Baltimore: Johns Hopkins University Press, 1985.

Saint-Aubin, Arthur Flannigan. "The Male Body and Literary Metaphors for Masculinity." In *Theorizing Masculinities,* edited by Harry Brod and Michael Kaufman, 239–58. Thousand Oaks, CA: Sage Publications, 1994.

——. "'A Pool of Razor Blades and Sperm': A Phantasy of White, Heterosexual Masculinity in Kurt Cobain's Journals." *European Journal of American Culture* 32, no. 1 (2013): 5–23.

——. "Testeria: The Dis-ease of Black Men in White, Supremacist, Patriarchal Culture." *Callaloo* 17, no. 4 (1994): 1054–88.

Sánchez-Pardo, Esther. *Cultures of the Death Drive: Melanie Klein and Modernist Melancholia.* Durham, NC: Duke University Press, 2003.

Savage, Jon. "Sounds Dirty: The Truth About Nirvana." In *The Cobain Dossier,* edited by Martin Clark and Paul Woods, 63–75. London: Plexus, 1999.

Savran, David. *Taking It Like a Man: White Masculinity, Masochism, and Contemporary American Culture.* Princeton, NJ: Princeton University Press, 1998.

Schehr, Lawrence. *The Shock of Men: Homosexual Hermeneutics in French Writing.* Stanford, CA: Stanford University Press, 1995.

Schiesari, Juliana. *The Gendering of Melancholy: Feminism, Psychoanalysis, and the Symbolics of Loss.* Ithaca, NY: Cornell University Press, 1992.

Schippers, Mimi. *Rockin' Out of the Box: Gender Maneuvering in Alternative Hard Rock.* New Brunswick, NJ: Rutgers University Press, 2002.

Schor, Naomi. *Bad Objects: Popular and Unpopular.* Durham, NC: Duke University Press, 1995.

Schroeder, Eric, and John Boe. "An Interview with Ken Macrorie: 'Arrangements for Truthtelling.'" *Writing on The Edge* 15 (2004): 4–17.

Sedgwick, Eve Kosofsky. *Between Men: English Literature and Male Homosocial Desire.* New York: Columbia University Press, 1985.

Segal, Hanna. *Melanie Klein.* New York: Viking, 1980.

Seshadri-Crooks, Kalpana. "The Comedy of Domination: Psychoanalysis and the Conceit of Whiteness." In *The Psychoanalysis of Race,* edited by Christopher Lane, 53–79. New York: Columbia University Press, 1998.

Shevory, Thomas. "Bleach Resistance: The Politics of Grunge." *Popular Music Society* (Summer 1995): 23–47.

Siegel, Lee. "Pope Francis and the Naked Christ." *The New Yorker,* December 17, 2013. newyorker.com/books/page-turner/pope-francis-and-the-naked-christ. Accessed July 14, 2017.

Silhol, Robert. "On the Signification of the Phallus." In *Literature and Psychology: Proceedings of the Eleventh International Conference on Literature and Psychology,* 79–83. Lisbon: Instituto Superior de Psicologia, 1995.

Silverman, Kaja. *The Acoustic Mirror: The Female Voice in Psychoanalysis and Cinema.* Bloomington: Indiana University Press, 1988.

———. *Male Subjectivity at the Margins.* New York: Routledge, 1992.

Sirc, Geoffrey. "Composition Eye / Orpheus's Gaze / Kurt Cobain's Journals." *Composition Studies* 33, no. 1 (2005): 11–30.

Soulsby, Nick. "Analysing Nirvana's Songs." Web blog post. n.d. nirvana-legacy.com /category/analysing-nirvana-songs. Accessed June 10, 2016.

———, ed. *Cobain on Cobain: Interviews and Encounters.* Chicago: Chicago Review Press, 2016.

———. *Dark Slivers: Seeing Nirvana in the Shards of Incesticide.* Kindle edition. Longon: Running Waters Productions, 2012.

Spiccia, Lucio. "Atomic." In *Cobain on Cobain: Interviews and Encounters,* edited by Nick Soulsby. Translated by Alessandra Meineri, 199–210. Chicago: Chicago Review Press, 2016.

Starr, Chelsea. "Because, Riot Grrrl: Social Movements, Art Worlds, and Style." PhD dissertation, University of Irvine, 1999.

Steinberg, Leo. *The Sexuality of Christ in Renaissance Art and in Oblivion.* Chicago: University of Chicago Press, 1983.

Straw, Will. "Systems of Articulation, Logics of Change: Communities and Scenes in Popular Music." *Cultural Studies* 5, no. 3 (1991): 368–88.

Strong, Catherine. *Grunge: Music and Memory.* Burlington, VT: Ashgate Publishing, 2011.

Suleiman, Susan Rubin. "Aragon's 'Le mentir-vrai': Reflections on Truth and Self-Knowledge in Autobiography." *Romantic Review* 92 (2001): 61–72.

Sutcliffe, Phil. "Back into the State of Mind I'm in Every Few Months." In *Cobain on Cobain: Interviews and Encounters,* edited by Nick Soulsby, 415–33. Chicago: Chicago Review Press, 2016.

Thanem, Torkild, and Louise Wallenberg. "Buggering Freud and Deleuze: Toward a Queer Theory of Masochism." *Journal of Aesthetics & Culture* (2010): 1–10.

"The Godmother of Rock & Roll: Sister Rosetta Tharpe." *PBS: Black Cultural Connections,* n.d. pbs.org/black-culture/shows/list/rock-and-roll-rosetta-tharpe. Accessed November 23, 2016.

Thomas, Calvin. "Foreword." In *Straight Writ Queer: Non-Normative Expressions of Heterosexuality in Literature,* edited by Richard Fantina, 1–6. Jefferson, NC: McFarland and Co., 2006.

——. "Reenfleshing the Bright Boys: Or, How Male Bodies Matter to Feminist Theory." In *Masculinity Studies and Feminist Theory: New Directions,* edited by Judith K. Gardiner, 60–89. New York: Columbia University Press, 2002.

——. *Straight With a Twist: Queer Theory and the Subject of Heterosexuality.* Champaign: University of Illinois Press, 2000.

Tobin, Robert. "Mosochism and Identity." In *One Hundred Years of Masochism: Literary Texts, Social and Cultural Contexts,* edited by Michael Finke and Carl Niekerk, 33–52. Atlanta, GA: Rodopi, 2000.

Tow, Stephen. "Interviewing the Thrown Ups' John Leighton Beezer." *The Strangest Tribe,* September 19, 2011. thestrangesttribebook.wordpress.com/2011/09/19 /interviewing-the-thrown-ups-john-leighton-beezer. Accessed December 5, 2016.

——. *The Strangest Tribe: How a Group of Seattle Rock Bands Invented Grunge.* Seattle: Sasquatch Books, 2011.

Träger, Eike. "Emocosms: Mind-Forg'd Realities in Emo(tional) Rock Music." In *Rock and Romanticism: Post-Punk, Goth, and Metal as Dark Romanticisms,* edited by James Rovira, 183–97. New York: Palgrave Macmillan, 2018.

True, Everett. *Nirvana: The Biography.* Cambridge, MA: Da Capo Press, 2007.

Van der Merwe, Peter. *The Origins of Popular Style: The Antecedents of Twentieth-Century Popular Music.* London: Oxford University Press, 1989.

Waddell, Charlotte. "Creavity and Mental Illnesss: Is There a Link?" *Canadian Journal of Psychiatry* (1998): 166–72.

Walker, Clinton. *Highway to Hell: The Life and Death of AC/DC Legend Bon Scott.* Portland, OR: Verse Chorus Press, 1994.

Walser, Robert. "Review of 'Origins of Popular Style' by Peter Van der Merwe." *Journal of Musicological Research* 12, no. 1/2 (1992): 123–32.

———. *Running with The Devil: Power, Gender, and Madness in Heavy Metal.* Middletown, CT: Wesleyan University Press, 1993.

Warner, Simon. *Text and Drugs and Rock 'N' Roll: The Beats and Rock Culture.* London: Bloomsbury Publishing, Inc., 2013.

Weinstein, Deena. *Heavy Metal: The Music and Its Culture.* New York: Da Capo Press, 2000.

"What To Expect." *So What Exactly Does Amniotic Fluid Look Like,* n.d. whattoexpect .com/forums/june-2010-babies/topic/so-what-exactly-does-amniotic-fluid-look -like.html. Accessed September 27, 2016.

White, Miles. *From Jim Crow to Jay-Z: Race, Rap, and the Performance of Masculinity.* Champaign: University of Illinois Press, 2011.

Williams, Stereo. "The First Badass Female Guitarist: Meet Sister Rosetta Tharpe, the Godmother of Rock 'n' Roll." *Guitar World,* May 28, 2016. thedailybeast.com/articles /2016/05/28/the-first-badass-female-guitarist-meet-sister-rosetta-tharpe-the -godmother-of-rock-n-roll.html. Accessed November 23, 2016.

Wolfe, Charles K., and Kip Lornell. *The Life and Legend of Leadbelly.* New York: Harper Collins, 1992.

Wolin, Richard. "Was a Renowned Literary Theorist Also a Spy? The Strange Case of Julia Kristeva." *The Chronicle of Higher Education,* June 20, 2018. chronicle.com /article/Was-a-Renowned-Literary/243719. Accessed June 13, 2019.

Wood, Jessica L. "Pained Expression: Metaphors of Sickness and Signs of 'Authenticity' in Kurt Cobain's Journals." *Popular Music* (October 2011): 331–49.

Wurtzel, Elizabeth. *Prozac Nation: A Memoir.* New York: Riverhead Books, 1994.

Yudice, George. "What's a Straight White Man to Do?" In *Constructing Masculinity,* edited by Maurice Berger, Brian Wallis, and Simon Watson, 267–83. New York: Routledge, 1995.

Zanes, Warren. "A Fan's Notes: Identification, Desire, and the Haunted Sound Barrier." In *Rock Over the Edge: Transformations in Popular Music Culture,* edited by Roger Beebe, Denise Fulbrook, and Ben Saunders, 291–310. Durham, NC: Duke University Press, 2002.

Zaplana, Esther. "Breaking the Mold: Male Rock Performance, Glam, and the (Re) Imagining of the Male Body in the 1960s and 1970s." In *Embodying Masculinities: Towards a History of the Male Body in U.S. Culture and Literature,* edited by Josep M. Armengol, 63–82. New York: Peter Lang, 2013.

Zevallos, Zuleyka. "Hollywood Racism: The Magical Negro Trope." *Other Sociologist,* January 24, 2012. othersociologist.com/2012/01/24/hollywood-racism. Accessed May 16, 2016. 1.

INDEX

185–86; and masculine subjectivity, 9; moral masochism, 177; and power, 170, 173; relation to masculine modes of existing, 173; relation to masculinity, 186–87. *See also* masochism, history of

masochism, history of, 172–75; retheorizing of, 172–73; and the relationship to masculinity, 186–87; and the role of women in masochistic desire, 175–76

masturbation, 102–5

Mathis, Johnny, 156

McCartney, Paul, 77

Meat Puppets, 29

Medovoi, Leerom, 61

melancholy/melancholia, 18, 209–15, 219–22; connection between melancholy as psychiatric suffering and corporeal scarring, 221–22; as a fixed disposition, 211–12; as inextricably linked with masochism, 171, 207–9; making melancholy masculine and gay, 222–25; social implication of, 212–13

"Melancholy Gender" (Butler), 222

Mercury, Freddie, 237

Metallica, 28

"Mexican Seafood" (Cobain), 88, 174

Mocale, Mark, 141

"Milk It" (Cobain), 82, 90–92, 93; and KC's feminization of the body and psyche of the male character in, 91–92; a signature KC song, 90–91

"mindless adolescence," 34

Minutemen, 20, 29

Misery (King), 187

Moore, Ryan, 20, 25–26, 42, 53, 155, 244n2, 254n28

Morrissey, 77

Morrison, Jim, 185

moshpit(s), 27

Motörhead, 28

"Mourning and Melancholia" (Freud), 211

Mr. Epps and the Calculations, 32

"Mr. Moustache" (Cobain), 85, 86, 94, 181; comic of, 182–83, 189

"Mrs. Butterworth" (Cobain), 112, 113–14, 115, 118

Mudhoney, 18–19, 29

Muños, José, 47, 60

music: black music, 154, 155, 255n31; black or white music, 253n21; exploitation of black music, 160, 254m28; as text, 243–44n5

Musser, Amber Jamilla, 169

My Chemical Romance, 35

Naked Lunch (Burroughs), 158

narratology, 247–48n7

natural bodies, 256n11

Nature of Melancholy, The (Radden), 219

"Negative Creep" (Cobain), 111, 179

Negus, Keith, 17, 19, 43

Nerval, Gérard de, 10, 226, 234, 235–36, 238; parallels with KC, 259n10

Nevermind (Nirvana), 4, 15, 16, 29, 76, 85, 196; method used in the writing of, 78–79

Nguyen, Mimi, 23

Nirvana, 4, 55; and the cover and modification of "Love Buzz," 55–56, 57; as describing a "world of youthful alienation," 34; destruction of its instruments by the members of, 31; as the epitome of Seattle grunge, 19; genesis of, 103; performance of at the Roseland Ballroom, 27

Nirvana: The Lyrics, 248n3

Norris, Jim, 40

Novoselic, Krist, 103, 154

NWA, 153

Nyng'o, Tavia, 47

Olympia, Washington, showcasing of women performers in, 30

"On a Plain" (Cobain), 81

One Flew Over the Cuckoo's Nest (Kesey), 184

On the Road (Kerouac), 184

Osborne, Buzz, 77, 157

Seattle, 244n4; male bonding and homoeroticism as part of the Seattle underground, 37–38; mix of heavy metal and punk subcultures in, 28–29

Sedgwick, Eve Kosofsky, 204

Seeger, Pete, 154

"Self-Defeating Personality Disorder," 169

Sells Like Teen Spirit (Moore), 53

Seshadri-Crooks, Kalpana, 47, 162, 165

Seven Year Bitch, 40

sexism, 31

Sex Pistols, 15

Sexual Dissidence (Dollimore), 255n1

Shakur, Tupac, 53

Shiesari, Juliana, 213, 218

Shocking Blue, 55

Silverman, Kaja, 173, 180, 186–88, 194, 208

Slayer, 28

"Sliver" (Cobain), 80

"Smells Like Nirvana" (Yankovic), 74

"Smells Like Teen Spirit" (Cobain), 64, 75, 86, 89, 112, 139; significance of the first line of, 113; video of, 126

Sorrows of Young Werther, The (Goethe), 224

Soul Asylum, 22

Soulsby, Nick, 55, 56, 62, 68, 73, 74, 75, 80; on KC's lyrics, 84, 93–94, 249n8; negative critical reaction to KC's *Journals,* 122

"Spank Thru" (Fecal Matter), 82, 95–96, 102–5, 106, 107, 118, 196, 216; different versions of, 103; KC's attachment to phallic potential in, 218; the penis as the main character in, 102–3; role of in the genesis of Nirvana, 103

Spice-Box of the Earth, The (Cohen), 185

Springsteen, Bruce, 67

Squid Row, 33

SST Records, 30

Stalcy, Lane, 40

Starr, Mike, 40

"Stay Away" (Cobain), 89–90

Stiff Woodies, The, 38

Stipe, Michael, 77, 248–49n5

Stooges, The, 32

Straight Writ Queer: Non-Normative Expressions of Heterosexuality in Literature (Fantina), 203

Strong, Catherine, 3, 51–52

Styx, 21

subculture, 242n2; punk subculture, 28–29

Sub Pop Records, 18–19, 30, 38–40; identity of, 33–34

Subterranean Pop, 33

"Suicide and Masochism" (Goldblatt), 200–201

Suleiman, Susan, 64

Surrealists, 21

Sutcliffe, Phil, 78

"Swap Meet" (Cobain), 83, 148–49, 152

Taking It Like a Man: White Masculinity, Masochism, and Contemporary American Culture (Savran), 9, 46, 183

testeria/testerical mode, 58, 102, 215, 259n3; theorizing of, 58

"Testeria: The Dis-ease of Black Men in White Supremacist, Patriarchal Culture" (Saint-Aubin), 58

Tharpe, Rosetta, 166, 254n23

"They Hung Him on a Cross" (Lead Belly), 118, 154, 193, 257n14

Thirlwell, James George, 249n9

Thomas, Calvin, 59

Thompson, Hunter S., 184

thrash metal, 28

Three Essays on the Theory of Sexuality (Freud), 173

Thrown Ups, 40–41

TKO, 29

"Touch Me I'm Sick" (Squid Row), 33

Tow, Stephen, 40–41

Träger, Eike, 35

"Travelin' White Trash Couple" (from KC's *Journals*), 166

True, Everett, 30, 210, 245n9

www.ingramcontent.com/pod-product-compliance
Lightning Source LLC
Chambersburg PA
CBHW030922150426

42812CB00046B/492